The Politics and Plays
of Bernard Shaw

Sculpture of Bernard Shaw by Sir Joseph Epstein, 1934 (Dan H. Laurence/Shaw Collection, Archival and Special Collections, University of Guelph Library).

The Politics and Plays of Bernard Shaw

by JUDITH EVANS

McFarland & Company, Inc., Publishers

Jefferson, North Carolina, and London

Library of Congress Cataloguing-in-Publication Data

Evans, Judith, 1916–
    The politics and plays of Bernard Shaw / by Judith Evans.
        p.   cm.
    Includes bibliography and index.

    ISBN 0-7864-1323-9 (softcover : 50# alkaline paper) ∞

    1. Shaw, Bernard, 1856–1950—Political and social views.
2. Politics and literature—Great Britain—History—19th century.
3. Politics and literature—Great Britain—History—20th century.
4. Political plays, English—History and cricitism.   I. Title.

    PR5368.P6 E93 2002
    822'.912—dc21
                                                2002009000

British Library cataloguing data are available

Cover photograph ©2002 Art Today. Background ©2002 PhotoDisc

Manufactured in the United States of America

*McFarland & Company, Inc., Publishers
    Box 611, Jefferson, North Carolina 28640
    www.mcfarlandpub.com*

Acknowledgments

My two main sources of information about Bernard Shaw, his thinking, and his plays have been the four volumes of his letters published by Max Reinhardt and edited by Dan H. Laurence, and the Bodley Head edition of his plays, published in seven volumes under the editorial supervision of Dan H. Laurence. I acknowledge Mr. Laurence's permission to quote from these works and I extend my thanks for this permission and for the personal help that he has given me.

In looking for Shaw's early expression of his political thinking, one turns inevitably to the publications of the Fabian Society, namely the Fabian Tracts and the Fabian Essays. Shaw was himself a leading Fabian and a major contributor to their writings. Permission to quote from these has been granted by the Fabian Society and is much appreciated.

There is, of course, a great wealth of Shaw literature, and for general information one turns to the Society of Authors acting on behalf of the Shaw Estate. They have given permission for quotations from Shaw to be used, and their assistance is valued.

There is a famous bust of Shaw by Epstein which is currently housed in the Library of the University of Guelph, Ontario. The library has generously donated a photograph of this bust and given permission for it to be used as an illustration for this book.

Early encouragement can be of great importance to an author, especially when it continues. Such encouragement was given by Professor R. F. Dietrich of the University of Florida. The time has come to say "Thank you."

Finally I come home to Warwickshire and express my special thanks for and appreciation of the work undertaken by the late Helen Banks of Wolverton, Stratford-on-Avon, in preparing the manuscript for publication. This was no easy task and I am greatly indebted to her. Noel Banks, also of Wolverton, has undertaken two tasks: reading the proofs and preparing the index. His help has been greatly appreciated.

Contents

PART IV. A Reluctant Icon (1940–1950)

Preface

Do politics and the playhouse go together? For Bernard Shaw they most certainly did. As a playwright with a message he saw the theatre as the ideal medium for conveying his view of life, which was essentially socialistic. Also, to Shaw the theatre was ideally a latter-day temple of the arts functioning within the community.

But Shaw was, of course, multi-voiced not only as regards the characters he created within the theatre but also in his own persona as public speaker, essayist, tract writer and author of works on political economy. Much of the thinking that is expressed in his non-dramatic works is also contained in his plays. This is one of Shaw's distinguishing features.

A special point should also be made about the nature of Shaw's socialism and his philosophy in general: it was not static. He recognized social changes and the way they were expressed in manners and relationships, and presented these to his audiences throughout his long years of playwriting.

The purpose of this work is to offer a readily accessible means of looking at the nature and the progression of Shaw's thinking. All the plays in the major canon are reviewed, and, except for brief plays and playlets (which are grouped), are presented in sequential order. Cheek-by-jowl with the plays are reviews of a selection of non-dramatic works.

Shaw's life as a writer can be seen as consisting of four phases, and the book is structured accordingly, with a brief introduction and concluding summary for each phase.

PART I

POLITICS AND THE PLAYHOUSE (1876–1911)

1

Shaw Joins
the London Intelligentsia

When, in 1876, twenty-year-old Bernard Shaw arrived in London to join his mother and sister, he came to a city that was vibrant with intellectual life. Its many societies—literary, political, and philosophical—were supported by the intelligentsia; they offered a new way of life to Shaw.

There was at that time a great awareness of London as the capital of a thriving empire of great significance in the world: it was indeed something of a magnet. One of Shaw's contemporaries described it in these terms: "The brain of the Empire, where reside the leaders in politics and in commerce, in literature, in journalism and in art, and which consequently attracts the young men who aspire to be the next generation of leaders".[1] Shaw was to become one of these leaders; but he was a leader with a difference.

Mrs. Shaw and her daughter were pursuing musical careers but Shaw was destined to make his way in other circles. "Behold me, then," he wrote many years later, "in London in an impossible position. I was a foreigner—an Irishman—the most foreign of all foreigners when he has not gone through the British university mill."[2]

So what sort of a foreigner was this Irishman when he first came to London? His father belonged to the Irish landed gentry, but as a younger son he was without an inheritance and was something of a ne'er-do-well. Shaw coined the word "downstart" to describe himself and others who had slipped down from the social class into which they were born. The impression is that Shaw was brought up in a culture that was extremely conscious of social position. Religion also had, according to Shaw, very important social connotations. To be a Catholic was to be a social outcast. Shaw's extreme and lasting sensitivity in this area is illustrated by his attitude to his attendance at the Central Model Boys' School in Dublin. Ostensibly a nondenominational establishment, it was in fact, according to Shaw, Roman Catholic. He was so ashamed of having attended this school that he kept it a secret for eighty years.[3]

This perception of cultural barriers was not on Shaw's side alone. Sydney Olivier, one of his early associates, writes in the following terms about the close and enduring friendship that existed among Sidney Webb, Shaw, and himself: "But Webb and I were university graduates, I from Oxford, and we often judged Shaw's education and his appreciation of academically and socially established humanities to be sadly defective ... and his controversial arguments often cheap and uncritical: an attitude of priggish superiority which he no doubt fully appreciated."[4] Indeed Shaw did. He was to show this in a tribute he paid to Webb: "The difference between Shaw with Webb's brains, knowledge, and official experience and Shaw by himself was enormous.... I was often in the centre of the stage whilst he was invisible in the prompter's box."[5] It was also to show, with some bitterness, during the years of World War I, and it may be that the debonair persona that Shaw first adopted in his early London days had something to do with his consciousness that he was "different."

In fact, at this time Shaw extended his education considerably, for he took advantage of the facilities offered by that great institution, the library of the British Museum. It was here that Shaw studied Karl Marx and it was here that this "most foreign of all foreigners" met many famous authors, including his fellow countryman, the poet W. B. Yeats; George Gissing, the novelist who wrote realistically about the lives of the poor; and, most significantly, William Archer, critic, journalist, author, and translator of the plays of Henrik Ibsen. Archer was to play an important part in Shaw's life, for he was instrumental in finding him work as a critic, and it was with Archer as his co-author that Shaw began his first play, which eventually appeared as *Widowers' Houses*.

It was through his work as a critic that Shaw was to become well known in London. Earlier, he had with great determination set aside his shyness and joined a number of the various societies which were a feature of the corporate life of London's intelligentsia: the Zetetical, the Shelley, the New Shakespeare, the Bedford (a debating society), and most significantly, the Fabian Society. He tuned in to the "spirit of the age."

2

Shaw Joins
the Fabian Society

Probably the most momentous experience in Shaw's early years in London came when he joined the Fabian Society, for it was a meeting of kindred spirits with a common aim. The Fabians' declared purpose, around the time that the society was founded, was that of "reconstructing society ... in such manner as to secure the general welfare and happiness."[1] It was a society of socialists, aiming at "the reorganisation of Society by the emancipation of Land and Industrial Capital from individual and class ownership, and the vesting of them in the community for the general benefit."[2] They had a famous motto, "Educate, Agitate, Organise," which marked them as propagandists and indicated what the nature of their propaganda was to be. (It is thought that the word "agitate" is used in the sense of "revolve mentally, discuss, debate.") Theirs was to be a new kind of socialism, spread by evolution rather than revolution. There was a confidence among its members, who were mostly of the middle-class intelligentsia, that their concept of socialism was of the spirit of the age.

In the Fabian Society Shaw found a sense of purpose and fellowship. He was their great articulator from the time he joined in 1884 until his resignation from the Fabian Executive in 1911. He himself recorded the significance of his first attendance at a Fabian meeting, for he added a note to the minutes, saying that the occasion was "made memorable by the first appearance of Bernard Shaw."[3] Certainly Shaw very quickly made his presence felt. The Society had been founded in January 1884. Shaw attended his first meeting on May 16, was elected to membership on September 5, and joined the Executive on January 2, 1885. Later in the month he spoke as a Fabian at an Industrial Remuneration Conference held in the Prince's Hall, Piccadilly, where a future Prime Minister, A. J. Balfour, was also a speaker. The subjects he addressed—landlords, burglars, and

capitalists—were to be fleshed out in his plays, indicating that his political speeches and his drama had a common purpose.

Shaw persuaded Sidney Webb, whom he had met at the Zetetical
Society, to join the Fabians. Later Sydney Olivier, a colleague of Webb's
at the Colonial Office, was to become a member. These three, together
with Graham Wallas, sociologist and, later, lecturer at the London School
of Economics, became known as the "Big Four" of the early Fabian Executive. All became famous in their particular spheres. They were to enjoy
a lasting friendship and a unity of purpose; however, the closest bonding
was between Webb and Shaw, and they had the greatest early significance
in the Fabian Society. Here is what Olivier had to say about the Fabians:

> The only assortment of young middle-class men who were at that
> time thinking intelligently, in England, about social and eco-
> nomic conditions, gravitated into close contact with one another,
> like kindred particles in a fluid, and consolidated into an associ-
> ation out of whose propaganda, later, originated the British Par-
> liamentary Socialist Labour Party.[4]

Two of these propagandists, Webb and Olivier, were to become members of future Labour Governments, but the Society's principal spokesperson and the editor of its pamphlets, Shaw, was to tread a different
path and find fame as a playwright-philosopher and a sage.

Olivier refers only to men, but there were a number of distinguished
Fabian women. Among them was Beatrice Webb, wife of Sidney Webb
and joint author with him of several works on aspects of political economy. The Webbs, together with Shaw, were founders of the London
School of Economics. Beatrice Webb was anxious to make contact with
any millionaire who would be interested in funding this project. Charlotte Payne-Townshend, a wealthy woman of socialistic tendencies, was
persuaded to subscribe to the LSE. She was invited to join the Webbs,
Wallas, and Shaw on holiday. Beatrice thought that Charlotte "would do
very well for Graham Wallas," but in the event it was Shaw whom she
married. Beatrice recorded in her diary: "They have been scouring the
country together and sitting up late at night!"[5]

Shaw valued his Fabian experience, seeing it as of great significance
to his playwright's role. He tells how, soon after he joined the Fabians,
he was "able to write with a Fabian purview and knowledge which made
my feuilletons and other literary performances quite unlike anything that
the ordinary literary hermit-crab could produce.... He had in the Fabian
Politbureau an incomparable critical threshing machine for his ideas."[6]

Shaw is very generous to his fellow Fabians here. Did his original perception of being an outsider make him particularly grateful that he was gathered so warmly into the Fabian fold? The "Fabian purview and knowledge," as expressed corporately in *Fabian Essays in Socialism*, is reviewed in the next chapter.

3

Fabian Essays in Socialism: Shaw as Editor and Essayist

Fabian Essays in Socialism was a definitive work which brought a new vision of socialism to the world, suggesting how this socialism could be achieved without violence and by constitutional means. The first edition of the *Essays*, published in December 1889, sold out within a month. By the end of the following year some 27,000 copies had been sold. The concept of English socialism (or Fabian socialism) was to spread to mainland Europe and to Australia and New Zealand.

Within the Society the authors of the Essays, of whom there were seven, became known as "the Essayists"; the Fabian Society continues to use the format of the essay for some of its major publications. The editor of *Fabian Essays in Socialist Thought* (1984) declares that the first essays brought the Fabians "intellectual primacy among British socialist groups."[1]

What was it about the original Essays that made them so special, aside from the fact that Shaw was the author of two of them and also the editor?

I would suggest that a major factor was the imponderable "spirit of the age," the feeling that there was a resurgence of social consciousness waiting to supersede some evil and outmoded aspects of capitalism. The "wicked half century," as Shaw called the latter half of the nineteenth century, was on its way out.

In fact several of the Essayists record their consciousness of the spirit of the age, or *zeitgeist*. Webb, talking about the irresistible sweep of social tendencies, says "'The Zeitgeist' is potent."[2] Another Essayist, Hubert Bland, notes "the trend of things to Socialism,"[3] while Wallas defines the *zeitgeist* and describes its function: "Even the Time Spirit itself is only the sum of individual strivings and aspirations, and ... again and again in history changes which might have been delayed for centuries or might never have come at all, have been brought about by the persistent preaching of some new and higher life, the offspring not of circumstance but of hope."[4] There is also a great consciousness that when society has reached a stage where humankind has become interdependent, living in huge agglomerations, it must have the capability of going forward together. The socialist principles to which they aspire are seen as timeless.

The matter of style is of prime importance. To read the Essays is to realize that other Fabians besides Shaw were masters of the English language (though Shaw was, of course, the editor). One thinks particularly of Olivier, whose dignity of thought is matched by the dignity of his language.

There are reasons aplenty to account for the great and lasting impact of the Essays. Yet they began modestly enough as a course of lectures to be given in London and the provinces; they can, says Shaw, be taken "as a sample of the propaganda carried on by volunteer lecturers in the workmen's clubs and political associations of London."[5]

The book consists of three sections, The Basis of Socialism (four essays), The Organization of Society (two essays) and The Transition to Social Democracy (two essays). The essays in the first section, by Shaw, Webb, Clarke, and Olivier, define and describe the Fabian vision of a future society.

Shaw writes on the economic basis of socialism. His subject is a reminder to the present-day reader that his prime interest in socialism was derived from the aspects of political economy and corporate morality. When in later life he became disillusioned with political democracy, this did not mean that he had surrendered his socialism. As for the essay, it is among Shaw's finest work. It is given to few authors to write about economics with such superb clarity. The opening, which spans time and space, is sheer poetry:

> All economic analyses begin with the cultivation of the earth. To the mind's eye of the astronomer the earth is a ball spinning in space without ulterior motives. To the bodily eye of the primitive cultivator it is a vast green plain, from which, by sticking a spade into it, wheat and other edible matters can be made to spring.[6]

Shaw brilliantly defines socialism:

> Since inequality is bitter to all except the highest, and miserably lonely for him, men come greatly to desire that these capricious

gifts of Nature might be intercepted by some agency having the
power and the goodwill to distribute them justly according to the
labor done by each in the collective search for them. This desire
is Socialism.[7]

The reader is taken on a journey from the time humans first tilled the
soil and there was land in plenty to a time when, as the population increased,
land became scarce and there was a superfluity of labor. In England, after
the Industrial Revolution, an excess of labor over demand brought about a
situation where wages fell below the level of subsistence. It then became a
matter of morality to ensure that wealth was more evenly distributed.

As an economist and a socialist, Shaw does not blame the individual holder of wealth for these inequities but rather the current social system. He tended to hold this view throughout his life. Although as a
dramatist he found it necessary to personalize capitalism, such personal-
izations are often offstage characters.

Shaw's style of writing was subject to a change. Toward the end of
the essay, when the author's passion is aroused by the inequities of society, the clarity of the prose diminishes. This was characteristic of his later
writings as well.

Both Webb and Olivier, who write respectively on the historic and
moral bases of socialism, have a vision which centers on man-in-society.
While they look to the future with a degree of glad optimism, they also
express a consciousness—which gives a warning to their readers—of the
frailties of the evolutionary process. Webb writes: "Without the continuance and sound health of the social organism, no man can now live or
thrive; and its persistence is accordingly his paramount end." He also
asserts: "We now know that in natural selection at the stage of development where the existence of civilised mankind is at stake, the units selected
from are not individuals, but societies."[8]

Olivier writes in a similar vein when he presents the following dictum: "When a society perishes, as societies organically weak among
stronger competitors have done and will do, the individual perishes with
it, or is forced backwards with impaired freedom until a fresh social inte-
gration renews and extends his powers of self-development."[9] In Webb
and Olivier we have two future political leaders with declared standards
of social morality.

An erudite essay by William Clarke, third in numerical order
(Olivier's is fourth), looks at the industrial basis of socialism and traces
the growth of industry and capitalism from the twelfth century onward.
He focuses attention on industrialization during the nineteenth century,

taking the Lancashire cotton industry as an example. He has some prophetic words to say about unemployment which were to resonate in Shaw's play, *On the Rocks*, and continue to resonate to this day: "The 'unemployed' question is the sphinx which will devour us if we cannot answer her riddle."[10]

The emergence of a new kind of capitalist is noted. He is a member of a Joint Stock Company, or *Compagnie Anonyme*. "Through this new capitalist agency a person in England can hold stock in an enterprise at the Antipodes which he has never visited and never intends to visit, and which, therefore, he cannot 'superintend' in any way."[11] (Hector Malone of *Man and Superman* will be recognized as this sort of capitalist.)

The fifth essayist is Annie Besant, member of the Fabian Executive, leader of the Match Girls' strike, famous as a public orator, and a close friend of Bernard Shaw. Her skills in oratory spill over into her essay: its subject is "Industry under Socialism."

Annie Besant applies to her subject the Fabian concept of gradualism. Declaring that she is not a utopian, she describes her role as being constructive rather than creative. She is "only trying to work out changes practicable among men and women as we know them."[12] This she does in a comprehensive way. The problem of unemployment and its solution are central to her theme and her attitude is positive. Organizing the unemployed for productive industry is seen as "wise"; opening relief works is seen as "unwise." The author goes on to name three bodies which could take on responsibility for offering work to the unemployed: the County Councils, who could establish farms to provide work for the rural unemployed; the Municipalities, who could socialize local industries and launch housing projects; and the State, to which would fall the task of "taking over the great centralised industries, centralised for us by capitalists, who thus unconsciously pave the way for their own supersession."[13]

Although Annie Besant declares at the beginning that she is not a utopian, in her conclusion—and in the long term—her sights are set on Utopia. Her peroration runs as follows: "Under healthier and happier conditions, Humanity will rise to heights undreamed of now; and the most exquisite Utopias, as sung by the poet and idealist, shall, to our children, seem but dim and broken lights compared with their perfect day."[14]

"The Outlook" (for the transition to social democracy) is the title of the last essay in order of publication. Its author is Hubert Bland, the Society's Treasurer, who was to resign in 1911 because of ill health. Bland lays stress on the cyclical nature of history. "The world moves from system, through disorder, back again to system."[15] He argues that over the years the differences between the Tories on the political Right and the Liberals on the Left have virtually disappeared. He gives the credit to the spirit of the age, or in his parlance, the "great blind evolutionary forces [which] are the dynamic of the social revolution."[16] There is mention also of a change in attitude, "largely instinctive and wholly self preservative,"[17] of working people towards the State: once it was feared as an enemy, now it is regarded as a potential savior.

Like the other Essayists, Bland shows discernment. "It must not be forgotten," he warns, "that although Socialism involves State control, State control does not imply Socialism."[18]

"Transition" (to Social Democracy) is the title of Shaw's second essay, which precedes Bland's in published order. Much of its interest lies in the essayist's style and the persona that is projected. For this is Shaw's classic persona, which was to become, to a great extent, more famous than Shaw himself. The Preface tells how the Essays began life as lectures given to workingmen's clubs and political associations. This one had its origins in an address to the Economic Section of the British Association at Bath. The style is adjusted to suit the audience.

The speaker/essayist delivers his subject at breakneck speed, giving an account of the economic history of England from the Middle Ages to the present time, flinging out useful facts, witticisms, criticisms, and precepts on the way. It is pointed out that existing legislation has already taken the State some distance along the way towards socialism. Projections are given as to how the municipalization of certain industries will be ongoing and will lead to further socialization.

Shaw's mode of address is sophisticated, extrovert, sparkling, adapted to his perception of his audience, in sharp contrast to the objective clarity and quiet certitude of his first essay: a dramatist in embryo.

The Essay's ending epitomizes the subtle way in which Shaw adapted his subject matter to his erudite audience. He manages to convey a veiled threat in an utterly urbane way:

> The Socialists need not be ashamed of beginning as they did by proposing militant organization of the working classes and general insurrection. The proposal proved impracticable; and it has now been abandoned—not without some outspoken regrets—by English Socialists. But it still remains as the only finally possible alternative to the Social Democratic programme which I have sketched today.[19]

The Fabian Essays brought a message to the world. The Fabian Essayists were a nest of philosophers from which Shaw, the playwright-philosopher, took wing.

The Fabian Tracts: Shaw as Tract Writer and Editor

The Fabian Tracts are a continuing feature of the Society: the series began in the year of its foundation and continues to the present day. Shaw was both editor and contributor. By the time he resigned from the Fabian Executive in 1911 he had written fourteen tracts himself and had worked with Webb on a series about municipal government. Webb was an expert in this field and an important figure in the newly formed London County Council. Shaw himself served from 1897 to 1903 first as a member of the St. Pancras Vestry and then on the St. Pancras Council, which succeeded the Vestry. As editor and author Shaw made an enormous contribution to the Fabian Society, establishing a high standard of literary skills, articulating the Society's corporate thinking and making his individual contribution as a writer. In these capacities he spread the Fabian word.

In contrast with the Essays, which are concerned with the broad sweep of socialism, the tracts are concerned, in the main, with current issues. For posterity, they are in their entirety a record of social history. For the editor they provided an informed account of news and views. As a dramatist Shaw was able to present these issues on the stage, giving them a universality that does not belong to the tracts.

Shaw's first tract, "A Manifesto" (FT No. 2), was read at a Fabian meeting on September 19, 1884, just two weeks after he had been elected to membership: it was duly published. Each of the eighteen propositions that it contained were discussed and adopted separately by the Fabians. One or two of them were to remain central to Shaw's thinking for a very long time. A statement about the bringing up of children is one of many that have the typical Shaw touch; perhaps it is surprising that the meeting concurred with it:

That the State should compete with private individuals—especially with parents—in providing happy homes for children, so that every child may have a refuge from the tyranny or neglect of its natural custodians.[1]

The proposition that he makes about women in a neatly turned phrase has more of a Fabian flavor about it: "That Men no longer need special political privileges to protect them against Women, and that the sexes should henceforth enjoy equal political rights."[2] (It was to be some years before Shaw, in his highly political play, *The Apple Cart*, was able to celebrate the first woman to hold the rank of Cabinet Minister.)

The very titles of some of Shaw's early tracts indicate that he was immersed in Fabian politics. There were, for example, "The True Radical Programme" (FT No. 6, 1887), "Fabian Election Manifesto" (FT No. 40, 1892) and, most famously, "A Plan of Campaign for Labour" (FT No. 49, 1894).

Although the last of these is attributed to Shaw, it was, in fact, a (further) example of Shaw and Webb working together. It was to be a landmark in Fabian history, for, at a time when there were only two political parties with the capability of forming a government, it began the shaping of the Labour Party. The authors proposed, as an immediate objective, that there should be fifty Labour candidates in the forthcoming general election. Edward Pease says of this tract: "Thousands of working-class politicians read and remembered it, and it cannot be doubted that the 'Plan of Campaign for Labour,' as it was called, did much to prepare the ground for the Labour Party which was founded so easily and flourished so vigorously in the first years of the twentieth century."[3]

One important pamphlet that Shaw wrote for the Fabian Society is not included in the numbered tracts. It is entitled "Fabianism and the Empire: A Manifesto." Written at the time of the South African (Boer) war, it marks the Fabian Society's acknowledgement of the inevitability of imperialism and its hope that, although in its origins imperialism was driven by capitalism, in due course empires could be modified to become federations of socialistic states. The writing of this pamphlet, and persuading members to accept it, marked a high point in Shaw's dialectic skills, for the Society was deeply riven in its views on the South African war. But the success was not achieved without a struggle, and in the meantime some distinguished members were lost, including Ramsay MacDonald, who was to become the first Labour Prime Minister.

By the time Shaw wrote this pamphlet he was already the author of three major plays about empire. The last of these had a great deal to say about the seedier side of imperial power.

5

Shaw and the Theatre

At the same time that a new kind of socialism was being introduced by the Fabian Society, a new kind of drama was making its way onto the English stage. This New Drama, or Higher Drama as it was also called, was in contradistinction to the sort of play being produced by the commercially driven theatre of London's West End, which tended to portray fictional aspects of life rather than its realities, and was centered on action rather than discussion. The New Drama owed its inspiration largely to the Norwegian playwright, Henrik Ibsen, and, in England, to his translator, William Archer, whom, it will be recalled, Shaw had met in the library of the British Museum.

The New Drama had a number of Fabian supporters. Shaw writes of attending a performance of Ibsen's *Hedda Gabler* "with a large and intelligent contingent of Fabians."[1] Two members of the Fabian Executive, Charles Charrington and Harley Granville Barker, both confrères of Shaw, were to become famous men of the theatre.

Several bodies and associations which were concerned with the New Drama came into being; they included the Independent Theatre (Le Théatre Libre), the Afternoon Theatre, and the Stage Society. Shaw, who was a great joiner, was associated with several of these groups and was a member of the committee of the Stage Society. He also entered the theatre by another door as a critic, thanks to William Archer's influence. First he became a critic of art, then of music, and finally, from 1895 to 1898, of drama. It was during this period that Shaw—and his persona—became well known to the public at large. The *Sunday World* observed in 1891: "Everybody in London knows Shaw, Fabian Socialist, art and musical critic, vegetarian, ascetic, humourist, artist to the tips of his fingers, man of the people to the tips of his boots. The most original and inspiring of men—fiercely uncompromising, full of ideas, irrepressibly brilliant—an Irishman."[2]

As drama critic for the *Saturday Review* Shaw offered a great deal to the theatregoer, presenting an alternative, and very new, approach to the drama. He was also the subject of a great deal of opprobrium, not least because he inserted a considerable amount of socialism into his critiques. Frank Harris, Shaw's debonair editor, who was to become one of his biographers, gives both sides of the story: "At first he [Shaw] was strenuously objected to by many of my readers, who wrote begging me to cancel their subscriptions or at least to cease from befouling their houses with 'Shaw's socialistic rant and theatric twaddle.'"[3] He then goes on to show how Shaw captured the interest of young theatregoers by quoting Clement Scott of the *Daily Telegraph*: "Life was not worth living without it [the *Saturday Review*]; it gave us the latest news from the front. And we craned our necks nightly over the gallery rails to see Shaw our champion take his seat among the well-groomed critics in their 'glad rags.'"[4]

It was because of his activism in the theatre that Shaw completed his first play, which he had started in collaboration with William Archer and then laid aside. He recalls the circumstances: "An Anglo-Dutch Ibsen enthusiast (Grein) started a coterie theatre called The Independent Theatre, and after a success-of-scandal with Ibsen, committed himself to the statement that there are in England hundreds of dramatic masterpieces unacted by the commercial theatres."[5]

Shaw decided to produce one of these masterpieces by completing the play that he had begun with Archer: he called it *Widowers' Houses*. The play was duly produced by Grein, but he could only afford to present two performances.

Shaw then wrote a number of plays in quick succession while he was working as a critic. When the time came for him to leave the *Saturday Review*, he described in modest terms how his role as a critic had been helpful to him as a dramatist. He told the editor: "You not only made me known in the theatre, but forced me to think out its problems, and so helped me to success."[6] By then Shaw had written eight plays. Why did Shaw remain so long as a critic after he became a playwright? And what made him, in the end, give it up? The answers to both these questions are related to money, but there were other reasons as well.

Shaw's early plays were not popular with the critics; they did not command large audiences; sometimes they had extremely short runs, or there was difficulty in finding a producer. Even the directors of coterie theatres had to be concerned about financial viability. Although Shaw modified his style and subject matter to some extent, he refused to depart from his high calling as a playwright. On May 7, 1897, he wrote to Golding Bright as follows: "In the present condition of the theatre it is evident that a dramatist like Ibsen, who absolutely disregards the conditions which managers are subject to, and throws himself on the reading public, is taking the only course in which any serious advance is possible, expecially *[sic]* if his dramas demand much technical skill from the actors. So I have made up my mind to put my plays into print and trouble the theatre no further with them. The present proposal is to issue two volumes entitled 'Plays, Pleasant and Unpleasant.'"[7]

Nevertheless, there came a time when Shaw's income from his plays was such that he no longer needed to earn money as a critic. The turning point was *The Devil's Disciple*, which was first produced in America, and was a tremendous success there. He told Frank Harris that this play brought him more money than he could spend. There was a second reason, which Shaw described as follows: "I found the pump tiring me, and the water lower in the well."[8] His editor put it more bluntly: he said that Shaw was written out as a critic.

There were to be some golden years ahead for Shaw in the theatre in Germany as well as America. But it was not until the beginning of the twentieth century that he came into his own in England and found a theatre for his plays. This came about when Shaw's kindred spirit and fellow Fabian, Granville Barker, together with J. E. Vedrenne, took over the management of the Court Theatre in 1904 and made a feature of Shaw's plays. Artistic success came to Shaw and to the project. Frank Harris describes its significance to Shaw: "At the beginning of the Court Theatre campaign, Shaw was ranked in the theatrical world as an unprofitable outsider of the coterie theatres. At the end he was venerated as the most important British dramatist."[9] Hesketh Pearson, actor, author, contemporary of Shaw, and one of his biographers, writes of the Court's significance to English drama. The Vedrenne-Barker management was "without question the most noteworthy episode in English theatrical history since Shakespeare and Burbage ran the Globe on Bankside."[10]

6

A New Theory of Drama and a New Philosophy: *Major Critical Essays* and the Preface to *Three Plays by Brieux*

In *Fabian Essays in Socialism* Shaw and his fellow authors gave the world a new vision of socialism. In *Major Critical Essays* Shaw articulates a new concept of the drama, and also a new philosophy. (Shaw's Preface to *Three Plays by Brieux* is included in this chapter because the author here expands his focus and sees Brieux as extending further the scope of the New Drama.)

It is significant that the first of the critical essays began life, in the traditional Fabian manner, as one of a series of lectures on the subject of "Socialism in Contemporary Literature." It was given to a Fabian audience on July 18, 1890. This serves as a reminder that for some socialists—and more especially Shaw—socialism and literature were intertwined.

This first essay, "The Quintessence of Ibsenism," looks at the changed perception of the function of drama which followed the presentation of Ibsen's plays, in translation, on the English stage. They brought a new realism to the theatre and required a new sort of comprehension from the audience.

The second essay, "The Perfect Wagnerite: A Commentary on the Nieblungs' Ring" (1898), relates to a new kind of format, the music drama, which Wagner intended should supersede the opera, and be more meaningful. The tetralogy of which "The Ring" consists presents an allegory, which contains a philosophy that was to be of great and lasting significance to Shaw. His essay gives his interpretation of that allegory.

The concluding essay, "The Sanity of Art," which was first published some years before "The Perfect Wagnerite," is in some ways a companion piece to the later work but is of less interest.

"THE QUINTESSENCE OF IBSENISM" (1891)

"The Quintessence" introduces a new dramatic mode, the discussion play, in which discussion takes precedence over action and may also bring a play to its conclusion. The conventionally structured plot, with its alternatives of the happy or the tragic ending, is rejected. Ibsen's *A Doll's House* is cited as introducing this new mode. Shaw sees the moment when the heroine says to her husband, "We must sit down and discuss all this that has been happening between us" as a turning point in the history of the theatre: "It was by this new technical feature, this addition of a new movement, as musicians would say, to the dramatic form, that *A Doll's House* conquered Europe and founded a new school of dramatic art."[1] Plays structured in this way were to become known as plays of debate.

What sort of subjects were discussed in these debates? They were often matters of controversy, in Shaw's case as well as Ibsen's. As an introduction to Ibsen's topics, Shaw classifies his characters into three categories: the idealist, the realist, and the Philistine. The idealist is usually the villain of the piece, for he subscribes to a code of conduct to which he is either unable or unwilling to conform. Sooner or later circumstances arise which reveal him as a hypocrite; often he belongs to a hypocritical society. The realist sees himself and society as they really are: he follows the call of his inner self and goes forward to the truth. The easy-going Philistines make up the majority of the population.

It is seen as part of the playwright's function to tear down the barriers of hypocrisy: the unmentionable becomes mentionable. Perhaps the most famous example in Ibsen's case is *Ghosts*, in which a sexually transmitted disease is passed from the father, via his unsuspecting wife, to his son. The play ends with the son's agony and imminent deterioration through disease. In another of Ibsen's plays, corporate hypocrisy is exposed when it is revealed that the dignitaries of a town have kept silent about the fact that famous baths, which attract many visitors, are contaminated with sewage. Public knowledge of this would affect the town's prosperity and their own. In *A Doll's House* the matter for debate is the falsity of a relationship between a husband and wife. He treats her as a childlike creature and she responds in a childlike way until the moment of truth arrives and the famous debate ensues.

The three themes that Shaw presents here are of particular significance to a socialistic playwright: public health, public morality, and the nature of relationships within the family, which is the basic unit of society.

The concluding argument of the essay is that there should be a theatre devoted to Ibsen's works, on the grounds that his doctrine cannot be driven home if the plays are presented in the haphazard order of the commercial theatre.

Ibsen died in 1906. There were to be two further editions of "The Quintessence" (1913 and 1922) after his death with additional material included.

PREFACE TO *THREE PLAYS BY BRIEUX* (1909)

In acclaiming Eugène Brieux as the greatest French dramatist since Molière and naming him the heir to Ibsen, Shaw lays down some ground rules about the drama, as followed by Brieux, which he also followed himself. Not surprisingly, they each invoked the same sort of comment from the critics. Shaw's early plays were described as "not plays," while for the French, according to Shaw, Brieux's plays were not "du théâtre."

This criticism arose because of the nature of the plays' constructs, and it is in this respect that Shaw sees Brieux as being more advanced than Ibsen. Typically the Ibsen play ends in catastrophe or "tragedy." But this does not accord with present-day life, where the tragedy may lie, not in death, but in the continuance of life. When the playwright ceases to use these conventions, and takes "slices of life" for his material, the play concludes when the audience has seen enough to draw a moral from it, and so the playgoer becomes morally involved. The nub of Shaw's dramatic purpose is as follows: "You come away with a very disquieting sense that you are involved in the affair, and must find the way out of it for yourself and everybody else if civilization is to be tolerable to your sense of honor."[2]

A second and more sensational attribute of Brieux's writing emphatically marks him out as Ibsen's heir: that is, his fearless selection of topics. Ibsen writes about sexually transmitted diseases. So does Brieux in *Les Avariés* which contains a scene with a hospital setting. Brieux also writes about the use of contraceptives. *Les Trois Filles de Monsieur Dupont* considers the effect that the use of contraceptives may have on the family, on sexual relationships, and on the status of men and women. While Shaw also broached this topic, he confined it to the Preface of his play *Getting Married.*

Shaw observes that when a playwright takes on his supreme function as the Interpreter of Life, the trivializing critic, who seeks to apply his formula of "the well-made play," becomes an impertinence.

Brieux is included in a list of writers whom Shaw sees as having stripped off the masks of the nineteenth century and "revealed it as, on the whole, perhaps the most villainous page of recorded human history"[3]: Marx, Zola, Ibsen, Strindberg, Turgenev, and Tolstoy are named. Perhaps Shaw should be added to the list.

"THE PERFECT WAGNERITE: A COMMENTARY ON THE NIEBLUNGS' RING" (1898)

There is a sense in which "The Quintessence" and "The Perfect Wagnerite" complement each other.

As writers Shaw and Wagner had some common ground. Wagner had a socialistic background and was a political writer. He had been involved in the German revolution of 1848–49 and it was his intention in devising the new music-drama form to offer a more accessible and more meaningful art form than the conventional, elitist genre of the opera. And he not only shared Shaw's idea that a great dramatist should have a theatre dedicated to his works, he also established such a one in the new Festpielhaus at Bayreuth. It was here that "The Ring" had its first complete performance in 1876. In due course Shaw was to visit Bayreuth.

Although his music drama is based on Norse and German mythology, Wagner conceived of the hero, Siegfried, as a new type of man belonging to a new age, a post-revolutionary world. It is this aspect of the work that Shaw siezes upon, telling his readers: "It could not have been written before the second half of the nineteenth century, because it deals with events which were only then consummating themselves."[4] Indeed he sees "The Ring" as very much a slice-of-life drama, of the sort to which both Ibsen and he himself were dedicated: "Unless the spectator recognizes in it an image of the life he is himself fighting his way through, it must needs appear to him a monstrous development of the Christmas pantomimes."[5]

The principal task that Shaw sets himself in the essay is the interpretation of the allegorical matter that "The Ring" contains. That part of the allegory which relates to nineteenth-century capitalism offers no problem of interpretation. Alberic, the dwarf, is seen as representing that capitalism. Those who slave for Alberic, Shaw comments, "never see him, any more than the victims of our "dangerous trades" ever see the shareholders whose power is nevertheless everywhere."[6] Alberic the Dwarf often hovers in the wings of Shaw's plays.

The allegory that concerns Siegfried, the man of the present age, is the one about which Shaw and Wagner do not at all points agree. It relates to the philosophies of two famous German thinkers, Arthur Schopenhauer (1788–1860) and Friedrich Nietzsche (1844–1900). Both of these philosophers were personally known to Wagner.

Schopenhauer's philosophy was based on the will, "the-thing-in-itself," as he called it. The will is seen as the essence of all things, unfathomable, unchangeable, beyond space and time. It is present in all organic forms of matter, ascending to its highest form in the rationally guided actions of man. Shaw follows Schopenhauer to this point in his philosophy and sees Siegfried as an embodiment of the will. He looks on him as a latter-day Protestant who puts his trust in the will of his humanity rather than in the will of God as understood by earlier Protestants. He is described as a "type of the healthy man raised to perfect confidence in his own impulses by an intense and joyous vitality."[7] Thus is the will of God secularized.

But one lone person inspired by the will, or even a number of them, is insufficient to renew society. At this stage Shaw launches his concept of the need to breed a better race, to which he speaks on many future occasions, and more especially in his play, *Man and Superman*. He declares: "No serious progress will be made until we address ourselves earnestly and scientifically to the task of producing trustworthy human material for society.... It is necessary to breed a race of men in whom life-giving impulses predominate, before the new Protestantism becomes politically practicable."[8]

Shaw makes his own authoritative statement as to what our understanding of "The Ring" should be:

> The only faith which any reasonable disciple can gain from The Ring is not in love, but in life itself as a tireless power which is continually driving onward and upward ... growing from within, by its own inexplicable energy, into ever higher and higher forms of organization, the strengths and the needs of which are continually superseding the institutions which were made to fit our former requirements.[9]

"THE SANITY OF ART: AN EXPOSURE OF THE CURRENT NONSENSE ABOUT ARTISTS BEING DEGENERATE" (1895)

This last of the essays began life as an open letter (of considerable length) addressed to a Mr. Benjamin Tucker. Mr. Tucker had asked Shaw to write an article for the paper of which he was editor, the American magazine *Liberty*. The article was to be a commentary on a book by Dr. Max Nordau, *Entartung* (1892–93), the English translation of which had recently been published under the title *Degeneration*.

Nordau appears to have denunciated as degenerate vast numbers of those presently associated with the arts and literature, including the authors featured in Shaw's two previous essays, Ibsen and Wagner. It goes without saying that Shaw's experience as a critic of music and the arts well qualified him to reply.

But this is much more than a "reply" essay. It contains the essence of Shaw's thinking about creative evolution without any of the entanglements of allegory, and it presents a superman who is disassociated from Siegfried. In the Preface (which was written later than the essay, in 1907) a warning description of the Superman is given:

> He is undoubtedly going to empty a good deal of respectable moral-
> ity out like so much dirty water, and replace it by new and strange
> customs, shedding old obligations and accepting new and heavier
> ones. Every step of his progress must horrify conventional people.[10]

The moral and social progress of the human being in society is described: "The moral evolution of the social individual is from submission and obedience as economizers of effort and responsibility, and safeguards against panic and incontinence, to wilfulness and self-assertion made safe by reason and self-control."[11]

Shaw pays tribute to the contribution that the artist makes to society. He distinguishes between the great artist and the worthy artist. The latter enriches our lives by producing art forms that heighten the senses and ennoble the faculties into pleasurable activity. But the great artist is on a different plane: "By supplying works of a higher beauty and a higher interest than have yet been perceived, [he] succeeds after a brief struggle with its strangeness, in adding this fresh extension of sense to the heritage of the race."[12] Unusually for Shaw, he makes reference to those artists who are false to their calling: "The artist can be a prostitute, a pander and a flatterer."[13]

Shaw stays faithful to his Fabian belief that it is the duty of the State to offer access to the visual and the performing arts to society as a whole. He also argues, not for the first time, that art has by now won the privileges once accorded to religion. That is why "London shopkeepers who would fiercely resent a compulsory church rate ... tamely allow the London County Council to spend their money on bands, on municipal art inspectors and on plaster casts from the antique."[14] Since he also says that these London shopkeepers "do not know 'Yankee Doodle' from 'Luther's hymn,'" this seems more of a plug for an enlightened London County Council than praise for the average Londoner.

Ibsen, Wagner, Brieux, and Shaw: these were four great Europeans who brought great changes to the drama, altering its style and its content, bringing it nearer to the realities of life, and offering or inviting comment on those realities. It became Shaw's task to define and elucidate these contributions and to discern a unity of purpose. In doing this he enriches the reader's understanding of his own plays.

Plays Unpleasant

WIDOWERS' HOUSES (1892)

When Shaw wrote his first play on the subject of landlordism, he went to the core of Fabian socialism, for the question as to who should own the land was a fundamental issue, and the abuse of such ownership could be seen all around in the slums of the capital city. "The earth is the Lord's but the rent thereof is the landlord's" was a sardonic phrase in use at that time.

It was also a subject which had been explored in some depth, and as far as London was concerned there was a wealth of published information about it. Sidney Webb had written two tracts, "Facts for Socialists" (1887) and "Facts for Londoners" (1889), which embraced this issue. Charles Booth, the famous sociologist, had published *The Labour and Life of the People* (1889) which was to be the first installment of his monumental work, *The Life and Labour of the People of London*. Shaw himself had written on the subject of landlordism—though with special reference to the country landlord—in a Fabian tract entitled "To Provident Landlords and Capitalists: A Suggestion and a Warning" (1885).

And landlordism was a subject that was being explored not only by socialists and sociologists. There had been a Royal Commission on the subject, and the local government bodies known as Vestries had been given new powers to deal with landlords, as is mentioned in the play.

In writing *Widowers' Houses* Shaw brings a totally new approach, and a missionary zeal, to the drama. He translates to the stage, not the high-sounding principles of the social reformer, nor the emotions, sorrows, and degradations of those whose lives are blighted by a social evil, nor the remorse of those who have lived on ill-gotten gains and now see the light, but the hard, cold facts of the existing situation, and how it is possible for it to be improved if society uses its duly elected corporate bodies to achieve a corporate goal, whereby the exploitation of the tenant becomes either impossible or impractical.

This is a play designed to arouse the public conscience rather than the private emotions. We see neither the ground landlord, who lives else-where in London, nor the slums and their pitiful inhabitants. But Shaw does not stint his audience of facts or of the sources from which they emanate. There are references to a Parliamentary Blue Book, to the Royal Commission on Housing, and to the powers vested in local government with regard to housing. Nor does he mince his words, either in the Pref-ace or in the play.

In the Preface, Shaw is forthright about where the responsibility lies; it is with "the whole body of citizens,"[1] who must see that the slums are replaced with decent dwellings. In the play, he shows how collectivism has already begun to work. "Theres no doubt," says the rent collector, Lickcheese, "that the Vestries has legal powers to play old Harry with slum properties, and spoil the house-knacking game if they please."[2]

There is another element in the play besides landlordism. This chiefly concerns Blanche, who is the first of many New Women that Shaw was to present on the stage. Blanche, unlike the traditional heroine, is vio-lent. When she loses her temper with her maid—it is so much easier to lose one's temper with a dependent—she seizes her by the hair and throat. Disruption between Blanche and Trench brings a tense moment when she stands in his way: "She is provocative, taunting, half defying, half inviting him to advance, in a flush of undisguised animal excitement." The text says: "It suddenly flashes on him that all this ferocity is erotic: that she is making love to him."[3] He responds in kind.

Theatregoers are to become accustomed not only to this New Woman but to a new kind of courtship. Of this there are to be examples in Shaw's next play, *The Philanderer*.

Widowers' Houses was first produced by the Independent Theatre at the Royalty Theatre on December 9, 1892.

THE PHILANDERER (1893)

Widowers' Houses presents a society in which wealth is based on the exploitation of others, and where the forces of social change are moving towards a betterment of the situation. In *The Philanderer* an inward-look-ing, self-regarding social group is presented. Here the social-change ele-ment relates to new codes of manners and behavior, especially between the sexes. In the Preface the author describes this behavior as "unpleasant":

he says that it arises from outmoded marriage laws, but this is not self-evident.

Central to the play is the Ibsen Club, in the sheltered environment of which a new code of conduct can be acted out without incurring opprobrium. The traditional London club, the refuge of the well-to-do man who seeks to escape from domesticity and femininity, is turned inside out, for this club is open to both sexes, and the "manly man," together with the "womanly woman" is excluded. The use of clubland and the many inversions of its customs, such as the young Sylvia Craven's wish to be addressed as "Craven, old boy" make good theatre. The club also stands as a metaphor for the sheltered environment in which the Ibsenite woman, also known as the New Woman, and her corollary, the Ibsenite man, act out their new patterns of behavior. It is significant that the aforementioned Sylvia, when in the club, wears a Norfolk jacket and breeches, but has a detachable skirt ready to hand, presumably for when she emerges into the outer world.

One wonders why Shaw makes so much use of Ibsen's name in the play. Is he using it purely as a metaphor for social change? Are the three Ibsenite women of the play truly representative of New Women in real life? At a time when women were making their mark in the world and addressing themselves to social problems (as was, for example, Beatrice Webb of the Fabian Society), the women of the play are all shown as being dependent on their fathers, even though one of them is a widow. As we see them moving between home and club, there is something pathetic about their introspection and their lack of contact with the world outside. One father has actually joined the Ibsen club in order to extend his protection of his offspring beyond the home. Their show of independence, and the new, less feminine, code of manners that they adopt, seem quite superficial.

Nevertheless, each of the three women represents some aspect of the New Woman.

Grace, the widow, who is in love with Charteris, the philanderer of the title, has learned to look with dispassionate eyes at the institution of marriage. She makes this anti-romantic pronouncement: "I'm an advanced woman. I'm what my father calls the New Woman.... That is why I will never marry a man I love too much.... I should be utterly in his power. That's what the New Woman is like. Isn't she right, Mr. Philosopher?"[4]

Julia Craven, who, far from rejecting the philandering philosopher, actively pursues him, represents the more flawed New Woman. In behavior she follows fashion, rather than philosophy. When previous conventional restrictions on behavior are removed as far as Ibsenites are concerned, she finds it difficult to contain the passion of her emotions.

When Charteris, for his own preservation, engineers a match for Julia and she realizes what he has done, her first response comes in physical terms: "In a paroxysm half of rage, half of tenderness, she shakes him, growling over him like a tigress over her cub."[5] In earlier days, if the conventions had not kept this physical passion under control in real life, it would certainly have been kept off the stage.

The young Sybil Craven, sister of Julia, is as yet untouched by sexual love, but she has an important contribution to make concerning the attitude of Ibsenite men towards women: it is of the essence of Ibsenism. She tells Charteris: "You talk to them [i.e., women] just as you do to me or any other fellow. Thats the secret of your success. You cant think how sick they get of being treated with the respect due to their sex."[6]

Nor does Charteris, who is introduced as "the famous Ibsenite philosopher," adopt a traditional mode of address when he talks about individual women to their parents. He tells Grace's father that his other daughter, Sylvia, wishes to marry him, and he gives a similar message, on the same occasion, to Craven about his daughter, Julia. The destruction of falsities and reticences when speaking to and about women is, perhaps, the most Ibsenite feature of the play.

Charteris is, of course, the key figure, often speaking, the reader may suppose, with the authorial voice. Shaw did, in fact, declare that this character was based on himself, especially as regards Charteris's passionate relationship with Julia. He told Frank Harris: "I escaped seduction until I was twenty-nine.... If you want to know what it was like, read the *The Philanderer*, and cast her [Jenny Patterson] for the part of Julia, and me for that of Charteris. I was, in fact, a born philanderer."[7] This gives a special poignancy to Charteris's comment to Grace: "The struggle between the Philosopher and the Man is fearful, Grace. But the Philosopher says you are right."[8]

The Philanderer is a difficult play to read, partly because of the Ibsen element, and partly because of Shaw's own ambiguity about it. At the time when Shaw wrote *The Philanderer*, several of Ibsen's plays were available in translation and had been presented on the English stage. Some of them had been reviled by the critics. Shaw himself, as he had shown in "The Quintessence," was in tune with Ibsen's thinking, and had helped spread the Ibsenite word. Yet in the play Ibsen is, as it seems, trivialized, vulgarized, and sensationalized. Changes in manners are, for the most part, flaunted rather than substantiated. Is this how Shaw saw the English reaction to Ibsen?

Shaw's own later attitude to the play raises further problems. In June 1896 he told Golding Bright: "In 'The Philanderer' you had the fashionable cult of Ibsenism and New Womanism on a real basis of clandestine sensuality."[9] Later in the year he wrote to Ellen Terry: "I cannot make up my mind about 'The Philanderer.' Sometimes I loathe it, and let all my friends persuade me ... that it is vulgar, dull, & worthless. Sometimes I think that it is worth playing."[10]

There was a long delay between the writing of the play and its appearance on the stage. It was first presented at the Cripplegate Institute in London by an amateur group, the New Stage Club. The first professional performance was at the Royal Court Theatre, London, on February 5, 1907.

MRS WARREN'S PROFESSION (1893)

The last of the "unpleasant plays" is undoubtedly the most challenging, for in taking Mrs. Warren's profession as a metaphor for a prostituted society, Shaw roundly condemns that society as one where the rich and seemingly respectable prey upon the poor and underprivileged. It is an exemplification of the first maxim that Shaw wrote on behalf of the Fabian Society: "That under existing circumstances wealth cannot be enjoyed without dishonor or foregone without misery."[11]

Widowers' Houses had broken new ground in entering the sociological arena. *Mrs Warren's Profession* continued to do this, but in a much more sensational way. Typically in the past, if an ex-prostitute were presented on stage, she was shown as a tragic and repentant figure, hoping to shield her innocent daughter from knowledge of her blameful past. Here we have the respectable Mrs. Warren, the ex-prostitute, living on the income derived from a chain of Brussels brothels (euphemistically known as hotels) of which she is part owner, and holding her own in society. She lives, with other members of the cast, in a sort of enclosed garden, distanced from the source of her income and other unpleasantnesses of life.

When Mrs. Warren's past is revealed and she talks to her daughter, Vivie, she tells about the economics of the situation, and how respectable society derives its income—but usually does not earn it—from the poor and the exploited.

Speaking from an environment that includes her own country cottage and the nearby rectory garden, she tells Vivie, who is newly graduated from university:

> You think that people are what they pretend to be: that the way
> you were taught at school and college to think right and proper
> is the way things really are. But it's not: it's all only a pretence,
> to keep the cowardly slavish common run of people quiet ... the
> big people, the clever people, the managing people, all know it.
> They do as I do, and think what I think.[12]

The cowardly slavish common run of people: it was among these
that Mrs. Warren had her origins, and it was from these that she made
her escape. Her half sisters, being less personable, were less fortunate: they
were not eligible for prostitution. One of them worked in a white lead
factory, a notoriously dangerous occupation. The other married a poorly
paid Government labourer and struggled to raise a family on his wages
until he took to drink.

Sir George Crofts, formerly one of Mrs. Warren's clients and now
her partner in the chain of hotels, also sees fit to open Vivie's eyes. He
tells Vivie: "I hope you dont think I dirty my own hands with the work."[13]
He has no intention of giving up his share in the brothels and is scan-
dalized when Vivie suggests this. "Wind up a business thats paying 35
per cent in the worst years! Not likely!"[14]

There is further enlightenment for Vivie, who won a scholarship to
Cambridge which was funded by Sir George's brother, a Member of Parliament. Stung by Vivie's holier-than-thou attitude, Sir George tells her
about the source of his brother's income and its link with prostitution.
"He gets his 22 per cent out of a factory with 600 girls in it, and not one
of them getting wages enough to live on. How d'ye suppose they manage when they have no family to fall back on? Ask your mother."[15]

"Decent society" is fleshed out by two more characters. Since Shaw
was no lover of the established church, it is not surprising that he chose
the village rector, the Reverend Samuel Gardner, for one of these parts.
(It was, of course, widely held that the younger sons of the gentry took
holy orders, without having any special vocation, in the expectation that
they would be offered a suitable living by the patron within whose gift it
lay.) This particular rector exemplifies hypocrisy and worldliness. He has
been a previous client of Mrs. Warren. His present scale of values is indicated when he speaks to his son about making a suitable marriage. Frank
claims that his father had told him that, "Since I had neither brains nor
money, I'd better turn my good looks to account by marrying somebody
with both." The father tells the son, "I was not thinking of money, sir. I
was speaking of higher things. Social position, for instance."[16]

Frank Gardner, the rector's son, is rather more than a character on which to hang the courtship of Vivie and the possibility of an incestuous marriage. He is the male counterpart of Mrs. Warren, who sees marriage to Vivie as a means of gaining access to a continuing life of idleness supported by money derived from prostitution. His negative way of life is symbolized by his ever-present gun.

Sir George also wishes to marry Vivie, and the shadow of incest, as one of the possible results of prostitution, hangs like a cloud over the play.

There is one more character who belongs in this collection of exotics, and means to stay in it. He is the "art for art's sake" man, who often makes his appearance in Shaw's plays and in his other writings. In this case he is Praed, who stands condemned for detaching himself from the realities of life. His moment of condemnation comes when he tells Vivie about the joys of foreign travel: "You would be charmed with the gaiety, the vivacity, the happy air of Brussels."[17] Vivie thinks of her mother's chain of brothels based in Brussels and is horrified. Hypocritical society pretends not to know, the "art for art's sake" man prefers not to know.

What about Vivie herself, the author's latest New Woman, university educated, of independent mind, shocked at the evils of society newly revealed to her (and based on Beatrice Webb)? Vivie leaves the enclosed garden, rejects her mother, and finds employment in the chambers of a woman friend in the city. From this vantage point she utters what might well be regarded as the key passage of the play:

> I am sure that if I had the courage I should spend the rest of my life in telling everybody.... The two infamous words that describe what my mother is are ringing in my ears and struggling on my tongue; but I cant utter them: the shame of them is too horrible for me.[18]

And Shaw himself was to be deprived of the opportunity of "telling everybody" through the medium of the stage for a very long time. The play fell afoul of the Censor and was not given a public performance in England until July 27, 1925, when it was presented at the Prince of Wales Theatre, Birmingham. It was first shown in America in 1902.

8

Plays Pleasant

ARMS AND THE MAN (1894)

A romanticized Bulgaria, a dashing cavalry officer, a heroine who dreams of romance and is surprised by a fleeing soldier seeking refuge in her bedroom: can these all be part of a play by Bernard Shaw? And was it really begun in the year that gave birth to that most realistic of plays, *Mrs Warren's Profession*? The answer is, of course, yes; and here we meet a seemingly different Shaw, witty, tongue-in-cheek, comedic, who offers a play which is to please the audience, become immediately successful, and later become endlessly popular in the musical comedy version, *The Chocolate Soldier*.

Here we have romantic attitudes towards love and war being ridiculed and eventually debunked by a down-to-earth Swiss mercenary who understands that modern wars are won by logistics and not by single cavalry charges. But then, as the play demonstrates, these Bulgarians are rather naive people, are they not, trying to ape the manners of more civilized people? The audience is given a very pleasant sense of superiority.

However, Shaw is saying rather more than that to those who choose to notice, and especially to those belonging to a particular coterie of the political Left. Some of this is said in a straightforward manner by the servant girl, Louka, who, unlike most of the others in the cast, is not a character culled from musical comedy. The cavalry officer, Sergius, courts the heroine, his intended bride, in romantic style, but thinks it appropriate to have a more earthy relationship with the servant girl. Louka, in one sentence, punctures Sergius's pretensions: "Did you," she asks him, "find in the [cavalry] charge that the men whose fathers are poor like mine were any less brave than the men who are rich like you?"[1] And again: "I have to get your room ready for you: to sweep and dust, to fetch and carry. How could that degrade me if it did not degrade you to have it done for you?"[2]

34

But the essence of the play lies in its allegory, by means of which, (like Wagner in "The Ring") the author offers a further, deeper meaning to his fellow Fabians and others of the political Left. In this allegory Sergius is not just an idealist in the abstract; he represents Robert Cunningham Graham, MP, of the Scottish gentry, member of the Social Democratic Federation, who joined in a demonstration on behalf of the unemployed. On a day which was to become known as Bloody Sunday (November 13, 1887) he, with one other person, broke through a police cordon in Trafalgar Square and was imprisoned for six weeks as a consequence. A colorful character, he did, when a Member of Parliament, utter the phrase which belongs to Sergius in the play: "I never apologize!"[3]

Sergius represents the idealistic, impractical kind of socialism, while Bluntschli, the Swiss mercenary, stands for socialism of the Fabian kind, realistic and pragmatic, as represented by Sidney Webb, on whom the character is based. The Bluntschli family chain of Swiss hotels, which is mentioned towards the end of the play, is a metaphor for the Webbs" concept of the "housekeeping State" which Sidney and Beatrice Webb envisaged as emerging from socialism: they published a book which bore this title.

The socialist politics of the play were for the few rather than the many, but the ridiculing of false values associated with the current ethos is available to all.

Arms and the Man was produced at the Avenue Theatre, London, on April 21, 1894. It was the first of Shaw's plays to be produced in America. The date was September 17, 1894. Shaw had now overcome the difficulty about having his plays produced, but he was to encounter a new problem. The wit and laughter of his new style of play began to fill the theatres, but the audiences—and the critics—tended to ignore the true meaning of the play. This misunderstanding of his playwright's purpose was frustrating to Shaw. The frustration was to continue for a very long time.

CANDIDA: A MYSTERY (1894)

It was back to England with a vengeance in *Candida*: here the play is set in a specific area of unfashionable London and the action takes place in the home of a specific kind of Fabian, namely, a Christian socialist who is a clergyman.

The Reverend James Mavor Morell reads all the right books, as his bookshelves indicate: *Fabian Essays*, Henry George's *Progress and Poverty* (an early influence in Shaw's life), William Morris's *A Dream of John Ball*, and Marx's *Capital*, which, it will be remembered, Shaw had studied in the library of the British Museum. Morell also belongs to the right organizations, the Guild of St. Matthew and the Christian Social Union for example. His diary is peppered with meetings of various left-wing bodies: the Hoxton Freedom Group, the Independent Labour Party, Tower Hamlets Radical Club, the Social Democratic Federation, and so on. We learn that he has used his influence for practical good. He shamed the Guardians of the local workhouse out of accepting the lowest tender because the employer concerned (Morell's father-in-law) paid "starvation wages."

Morell has also taken under his wing and into his home an idealistic young man, a poet in embryo, by the name of Marchbanks. It is from a conversation with this young man that we first get a glimpse of Morell's less confident other self lying beneath what Shaw describes in the Preface as his "clear, bold, sure, sensible, benevolent, salutarily shortsighted Christian Socialist idealism."[4] For it is the function of Marchbanks to express his own spirituality and to lend a listening ear to others. Morell tells Marchbanks:

> You will be one of the makers of the Kingdom of Heaven on earth; and—who knows?—you may be a master builder where I am only a humble journeyman.... I well know that it is in the poet that the holy spirit of man—the god within him—is most godlike. It should make you tremble to think of that—to think that the heavy burthen and great gift of a poet may be laid upon you.[5]

It is possible that in this passage Shaw is expressing unsatisfied spiritual yearnings of his own. Alternatively it may be one of the sources of a speculation sometimes made that Marchbanks is based on William Morris, whose idealism Shaw admired but did not share.

Given the ambience of the play, and the general tenor of the first three acts, one may well wonder why the title role is that of Morell's wife, Candida, rather than Morell himself, and why the play is sub-titled "A Mystery." One turns to the Preface (written much later than the play, in 1898) in which medievalism, the place of the Church in the Middle Ages, and what the author sees as a current religious revival, are all tenuously linked together: it seems to be suggested that Candida is a latter-day Madonna. In the play Candida appears as the Mother-Woman and in that capacity dominates the last act, in which there is a marked change of temperature. Finally, she assumes the function of Nora in Ibsen's

A Doll's House, and introduces, briefly, an English version of an Ibsen-style debate.

Candida, as a mother figure, does not exercise the maternal function over her children—no play by Shaw has young children in it—but over her husband and the boy poet, her would-be lover, and there is something maudlin about her relationship with the two men.

This may be partly due to the fact that Shaw's skill as a wordsmith seems to fail him when his characters talk about their emotions. For example, Morell surely fails to strike the right note when he kneels beside Candida's chair and tells her: "What I am you have made me with the labor of your hands and the love of your heart. You are my wife, my mother, my sisters: you are the sum of all loving care to me."[6]

More importantly, and more disturbingly, there is an undertone of eroticism between the Mother-Woman and the boy poet in their conversation at the beginning of Act III. Marchbanks is discovered reading poetry to Candida while she holds a brass poker, presumably a phallic symbol, upright in her hand. Marchbanks seems to be implying this obliquely when he compares the poker with the drawn sword that the mediaeval knight used to place between himself and his lady in circumstances where they were forced to share a bed. He says: "It [the poker] looked as if it were a weapon. If I were a hero of old I should have laid my drawn sword between us. If Morell had come in he would have thought you had taken up the poker because there was no sword between us."[7] One feels here that Marchbanks, like Morell before him, is using the wrong imagery, and has chosen the wrong language: it exudes a sense of unease. Michael Holroyd, Shaw's latter-day biographer, is perceptive about the situation: "The affinity between them is that of mother and son, and the weapon that guards them from Hell is the taboo of incest."[8]

It is at this point that the two parts of the play, one concerning Morell, and one concerning Marchbanks, coalesce and there is a hint of the sort of allegory that *Arms and the Man* contains. The result is that the pragmatic Christian socialist is left in possession, and the idealist is dispossessed.

Is this really intended as a "mystery" in the medieval tradition? Or is the mystery wholly contained in the author's observation—which is available only to the reader: "They do not know the secret in the poet's heart?"[9]

There are also the Ibsen connotations. When Candida has made her choice in favor of Morell, whom she sees as the weaker of the two men, she paraphrases Nora's famous words, saying: "Let us sit and talk comfortably over it like three friends."[10] Unlike Nora, Candida has no need to leave home: she has established herself as the dominant partner, and has joined the ranks of Shaw's New Women.

Perhaps not everyone would agree with Shaw's description of Morell (in a letter to Charles Charrington) as: "really nothing but Helmer [husband of Nora] getting fair play."[11]

Candida was first performed at Her Majesty's Theatre, Aberdeen, on July 30, 1897. It was presented by the Stage Society at the Strand Theatre, London on July 1, 1900.

YOU NEVER CAN TELL (1895–96)

This play is middle-class to the core. It presents typifying characters, shows the difference between generations, points out significant social changes and offers role models to the young, especially as regards relationships with parents and procedures relating to mating and marriage.

Early in the play there is a brilliant dialogue between yesterday's New Woman, newly arrived in England, and her old friend, Finch M'Comus, who puts her—and the audience—in the picture. Her views regarding a woman's right to enter the universities and the professions, and to be enfranchised, and the married woman's right to own property are now widely accepted. If Mrs. Clandon's daughter were to share her mother's former views they would not be a bar to her marrying the Archbishop of Canterbury. As for socialism, M'Comus tells her, it is now the received doctrine of the young. In fact Mrs. Clandon is not a socialist and claims that she can prove it to be a fallacy. She has her reply: "It is by proving that, Mrs. Clandon, that I have lost all my young disciples."[12]

If by any chance the audience is feeling complacent about their own modernity, that complacency is about to be shattered. One hears the authorial voice behind M'Comus's next comment: "There is only one place in all England where your opinions would still pass as advanced ... the theatre."[13]

The play has another marker of social change. The Clandons are staying at a seaside hotel (now a popular venue as a result of improved travel facilities). The son of the waiter is "at the bar." No, this does not mean, as the guests conjecture, that he is a potman: he has climbed the ladder of education now available to those with ability (thanks largely, in London, to the influence of Sidney Webb) and is a barrister.

The Clandon family have had a very unfortunate past with which they are about to be reconciled. Mrs. Clandon may have been a modernist, but her husband, from whom she is now separated, was a tyrant of the most brutal kind. By a coincidence—which in terms of the New Drama is the dramatist's meaningful rearrangement of the facts of life—the husband, Fergus Crampton, turns up at the Clandons' hotel. He wishes to be reconciled with his wife and offspring so that he may resume his parental role. It is here that a demonstration is given of the way in which education has the ability to break down class barriers, for Mr. Bohun, QC, son of the waiter, is called upon to mediate and achieve a reconciliation. He tells the father of his changed position vis-à-vis his children. "The strength of their position lies in their being very agreeable people personally. The strength of your position lies in your income."[14]

The barrister is right: the father's money is the deciding factor. Previously the son, Philip, has railed against the prospect of acquiring a father again after they have enjoyed "the unspeakable peace and freedom of being orphans."[15] (What was it Shaw said in Fabian Tract No. 2 about the need for every child to have a "refuge from the tyranny or neglect of its natural custodians"[16]?) When Philip hears about the money, however, he changes his mind and it appears that they arrive at a pragmatic solution: the passion and misery of former years are wiped away.

Meanwhile, the story of the two young lovers, Gloria Clandon, daughter of the wealthy father, and Valentine, the impoverished dentist, proceeds. Theirs is a new style of courtship, not subject to the conventional niceties of the past. Parental consent is not an issue. Nor is Gloria content to remain passive like the conventional heroine of former days. But the defining moment of the play comes when the Life Force (though the term is not used in the text) first makes its presence felt on the Shavian stage. The two young people become conscious of a magnetic power outside themselves moving them toward one another. They call it "Nature"; others were to call it "sex appeal."

Later, in *Man and Superman*, "Nature" becomes the "Life Force" and we learn that it is motivated towards the breeding of a better race. Here, Valentine and Gloria are left in happy innocence, a latter-day Adam and Eve.

But when Valentine is not listening to the voice of Nature he becomes rather more sophisticated. He tells his future mother-in-law of his modernity in what he calls "the duel of sex": "I learnt how to circumvent the Women's Rights woman before I was twenty-three: it's all been found out long ago. You see, my methods are thoroughly modern."[17] He has not, however, learnt to circumvent Nature.

Much of the energy of the play comes from the young Clandon twins, Dolly and Phil, who bring to their observations the freshness of youth and that special frankness that sometimes exists within a family group.

They, more than anyone else, demonstrate a change in manners and behavior towards greater informality. But there is a fragility about their vitality, and they, more than anyone else in the play, remain fixed in their period.

This last of the "pleasant plays" most fully realizes Shaw's intention of combining his playwright's purpose with marketability. It was first produced by the Stage Society at the Royalty Theatre on November 24, 1899.

9

Plays About Empire:
Three Plays for Puritans
and *The Admirable Bashville*

Early in the 1890s imperialism was very definitely "in the air": ideas about Britain's imperial role and the destiny of the British as an imperial race were pervasive. The dynamic of this imperialism was well expressed by two of its ardent and eminent supporters, one a politician, the other an art critic and writer. Joseph Chamberlain, who became Colonial Secretary in 1895, told the House of Commons in 1893: "I and those who agree with me believe in the expansion of the Empire and we are not ashamed to confess that we have that feeling, and we are not at all troubled by accusations of Jingoism."[1] It was his view that the British were "the greatest governing race the world has ever seen."[2] John Ruskin, in his inaugural address as Professor of Fine Arts at Oxford in 1869 told his audience: "This is what England must either do or perish; she must found colonies as fast and as far as she is able, formed of her most energetic and worthiest men."[3]

Such was the impassioned nature of imperialism: and the very word "Jingoism," whose use was revived at that time, gives the flavor of the opposition to it.

Shaw, whose mission as a playwright was to express and interpret the spirit of the age, now centered his plays on imperialism. But whereas Shaw regarded the socialist State as society's ultimate attainment, he also regarded imperialism, pragmatically, as a possible means to that end.

In his plays about empire, which were published as *Three Plays for Puritans*, Shaw offers some lessons of history to a jingoistic generation. But the most pertinent lesson, surely, is contained in *The Admirable Bashville*.

THE DEVIL'S DISCIPLE (1896)

The Devil's Disciple is about the will as a driving force towards nation-hood, a force to which, when the time is ripe, imperialism must give way. The action takes place in 1777, the year which followed the Declaration of Independence by the thirteen American colonies. The play is Shaw's first excursion into melodrama, and in this play he uses the traditional excitements of that genre: the arrest of the wrong man in a case of mistaken identity; the hero's self-sacrificing acceptance of that mistake, even at the foot of the gallows; the dramatic ride to prevent the hanging; and the recognition of the mistake just as the hangman is about to tighten the noose and the clock has begun to strike the fatal hour.

But none of these melodramatic moments is more exciting than, or as significant as, that when the will takes possession of the contemplative New England clergyman when he hears that Dick Dudgeon, the "devil's disciple" of the title, has been arrested by mistake for him. This is the author's description of the change that comes over the Reverend Anthony Anderson: "His fists clinch; his neck thickens; his face reddens; the fleshy purses under his eyes become injected with hot blood; the man of peace vanishes, transfigured into a choleric and formidable man of war."[4] He has become the will of the nation, and off he rides to the rescue of Dick Dudgeon. Dudgeon is a tearaway character who now, also, becomes possessed of the will. But his experience is different: the two men have seemingly exchanged personalities. Dudgeon tells the clergyman's wife of the nature of his acceptance of his wrongful arrest: "What I did last night, I did in cold blood.... I have been brought up standing by the law of my own nature; and I may not go against it, gallows or no gallows."[5]

General Burgoyne, in charge of the British troops, was plucked by Shaw from the pages of history. Known as "Gentleman Johnny," his elevated rank is derived from privilege, and he is not inspired by the will. He is well aware of the complacency that exists among his officers. Bitterly he says to his aide: "I suppose, sir, the British officer need not know his business: the British soldier will get him out of all his blunders with the bayonet."[6] History was to prove Burgoyne wrong in this respect: his army was defeated at Saratoga during the year in which the play is set. And imperialism was in this case to give way to the federation of states which was to be known as the United States of America.

The play has two pointers to American independence. The first comes when Anderson says to the British general: "Now tell them to take the rope from the neck of that American citizen."[7] The second comes when, accompanied by their military band, the British troops march away, followed by the town band playing "Yankee Doodle." In this context, imperialism has had its day.

The Devil's Disciple was first presented at the Hermanus Bleecker Hall, Albany, New York, on October 1, 1897, for one performance only. It was then transferred to the Fifth Avenue Theatre, New York, where it had a very long run. The play was performed in England at the Princess of Wales Theatre, London, on September 26, 1899.

CAESAR AND CLEOPATRA: A HISTORY (1898)

For lovers of Shakespeare, Egypt is the land where Anthony and Cleopatra acted out their immortal love story. But contemporary Egypt came into political prominence in 1875 when England acquired a major share-holding in the Suez canal. Since that time England's attitude had been both involved and ambivalent. Declarations had been made from time to time that England had no wish to annex Egyptian territory, but eventually Egypt became what was known as a "veiled protectorate."

To Shaw it was the ideal venue for a "lesson-in-history" play. It had its literary associations, its past history as part of the Roman Empire, and its relevance to the immediate present; most of all it had Julius Caesar, the man of a stature fit to govern an empire. He is possessed of the will.

In a didactic Prologue spoken by the Egyptian god, Ra, the author stresses the relevance of the Roman occupation of Egypt to the present times: "For Pompey went where ye have gone, even to Egypt, where there was a Roman occupation even as there was but now a British one."[8] And the British are not to think of themselves as any more fit to run an empire than the Romans were: "Men twenty centuries ago were already just such as you ... no worse and no better, no wiser and no sillier."[9]

Ra is speaking of humankind in the lump, but the play centers around Caesar, the Roman icon. Britain had its icon in General Gordon, who met his death in the neighboring territory of the Sudan in 1885.

In *Caesar and Cleopatra* the author follows his own precept, stated in the Preface to *Three Plays for Puritans*: "The playgoer may reasonably ask to have historical events and persons presented to him in the light of his own time."[10] Caesar, in the light of the late nineteenth century, becomes a precursor of Superman, an agent of the will, destined to be a leader of men, and the molder of an empire.

At a time when there was a belief in a multiplicity of gods, some of whom had human characteristics, Caesar is portrayed as resembling a godhead. When he first appears in the play he addresses the Sphinx in the following terms: "My way hither was the way of destiny; for I am he of whose genius you are the symbol: part brute, part woman, and part god—nothing of man in me at all. Have I read your riddle, Sphinx?"[11]

Caesar, unlike some latter-day imperialists, understands the importance of good governance, and he has the capacity for it. This point is well made in the following exchange with Apollodorus, the "art for art's sake" man, a familiar character in Shaw's plays. Apollodorus accuses Rome of purloining other countries' art treasures and producing none herself. Caesar replies: "What! Rome produce no art! Is peace not an art? is war not an art? is government not an art? is civilization not an art? All these we give you in exchange for a few ornaments. You will have the best of the bargain."[12]

The play is rich in imagery and spectacle. No one could describe it simply as a "play of debate," or "an easy play for a little theatre." It is a scenic play, with scenes embracing the mysterious darkness around the temple of Ra; the giant Sphinx that minimizes the stature of man; the great engineering feat of the huge crane in the harbor by which Cleopatra is hoisted (a reminder of the engineering skills of ancient Egypt); the exotica of Caesar's birthday party; and the splendor of a Roman army's farewell.

Caesar leaves behind him some messages for posterity. He speaks of "Rome, that has achieved greatness only to learn how greatness destroys nations of men who are not great!"[13] And "So, to the end of history, murder shall breed murder, always in the name of right and honor and peace, until the gods are tired of blood and create a race that can understand."[14]

Are these the burden of the play?

Newcastle-on-Tyne saw the first performance of *Caesar and Cleopatra* on March 15, 1899. The first London production was at the Savoy Theatre on November 25, 1907. In 1944–45 a film was made of the play. The filming took place partly at the Denham Studios in London and partly on location in Egypt. Shaw visited the Denham Studios and remarked afterwards: "What scope! What limitless possibilities!... Here you have the whole world to play with!"[15]

Captain Brassbound's Conversion: An Adventure (1899)

In his third play about imperialism Shaw gives no lessons taken from history. Rather he presents the "here and now" of imperialism, offering the nation a self-image and presenting the sort of incident and procedure that might well be a preliminary to the annexation of territory belonging to an undeveloped country. The play also shows how such countries may provide opportunities for exploitation to individuals, such as high-ranking officials, and drop-outs from the Western world.

The play is set in Morocco, and the opening scene overlooks the harbor of Mogador, useful, as it turns out, for the docking of the American gunboat which is of great significance in the play.

Captain Brassbound's Conversion was highly topical, but in some respects it was too late. Shaw began work on it on May 14, 1899, and finished it on July 7. The South African war broke out in October of that year. The play had its first performance at the Strand, London, on December 16, 1900.

Like *The Devil's Disciple* the play has a strong story line and the basics of the plot are familiar to the point of being hackneyed. The intrepid white woman and her companion, who is a man of standing and a judge, wish to explore the interior, and insist on doing so in spite of a strong warning from the resident (Scottish) missionary, also a stock character in this sort of story. They are escorted on this venture by a ship's captain, who is also a brigand, and members of his crew. The brigand's motive for doing this is to be revenged on the judge for his shameful treatment of his mother, now deceased. He betrays his charges to the local chief and they are taken prisoner. The judge and his lady (his sister-in-law) are rescued thanks to the timely arrival of the gallant captain of the American gunboat.

All this is "Boys' Own Paper" stuff, but as the plot unfolds there are revealed certain distasteful aspects of imperialism and also the unworthiness of those in high places, as exemplified by the judge.

Three different opinions are expressed as to the possible consequences if the native chief should harm the explorers of the interior: all are related to imperialism. The missionary says, "The Sultan would get into trouble with England if you were killed; and the Sultan would kill the chief to pacify the English government."[16] The judge speaks with pomposity and self-importance: "Her Majesty's Government, Captain Brassbound, has a strong arm and a long arm. If anything disagreeable happens to me or to my sister-in-law, that arm will be stretched out."[17] The captain gives a deflationary comment, which is probably nearer the truth: "Who are you," he asks the judge, "that a nation should go to war for you? ... You had better find a goldfield in the Atlas Mountains. Then all the governments of Europe will rush to your rescue."[18]

The judge's various misdemeanors and abuses of power are revealed, partly by Brassbound, and partly by himself in anecdote. The Judge and his sister-in-law, Lady Cicely, are duly taken prisoner and are released when a note is received from the American ship's captain saying that he

is coming to look for the two British travellers: "As the search will be conducted with machine guns, the prompt return of the travellers to Mogador
Harbor will save much trouble to all parties."[19]

The captives are released, and Captain Kearney sets up a so-called
court to "try" Brassbound and members of his crew who are brought in
as prisoners under armed guard. Captain Kearney, obviously, has no legal
right to do this any more than he had to issue threats about machine
guns; his status is ambiguous, and his ship is described in the text as a
cruiser. Nevertheless, his presence and his actions seem to indicate that
the American navy is now a force to be reckoned with.

When Captain Brassbound and his men are released (thanks to the
persuasive powers of Lady Cicely) the action of the play seems to have
worked itself out and we are left with the sort of situation that might herald the annexation of territory by one of the great Powers—if only there
were gold!

But what about the will? There is a surprise in store here. Lady Cicely
has subdued everyone by her charm. One suspects that this charm derives
from a self-confidence which is based on a certainty of her place in society, tinged with an almost unconscious feeling of superiority. This impression is reinforced when, on finding out that Brassbound is the nephew of
the judge, she offers to help him to find his true place in society. This
assessment of the lady is wrong. She tells Brassbound, with whom she is
now in rapport, that her ability to influence people depends on a renun-
ciation of selfhood. "How could I," she asks Brassbound, "manage people if I had that mad little bit of self left in me?"[20] Brassbound, who is
himself a leader, was once inspired by that great hero of empire, General
Gordon. More recently he has been motivated by his purpose of revenge.
Now Lady Cicely inspires him. At first he wants her for his leader, and
his wife. Then comes the moment of his conversion: "You can do no more
for me now: I have blundered somehow on the secret of command at last:
thanks for that, and for a man's power restored and righted."[21] Who can
doubt that Brassbound is now possessed of the will and is to take a new
and splendid part in the narrative of the British Empire?

But we have yet to hear the African point of view.

THE ADMIRABLE BASHVILLE
OR CONSTANCY UNREWARDED (1901)

The Admirable Bashville, which is based on Shaw's novel, *Cashel
Byron's Profession,* written between 1879 and 1883, is probably best known

for the fact that it is written in blank verse. But as far as Shaw's plays about empire are concerned its significance lies in the fact that here the African is (briefly) given a voice, the noble and dignified voice of Cetewayo, the Zulu chief, who, while visiting England, indicts the Englishman and the devastation he inflicts on a global scale.

The play was written in a hurry for reasons of copyright: Shaw claims that he chose blank verse as his medium because it was quicker to write. Sometimes the verse is parodic, but by no means always. Two speeches, in particular, stand out from the rest: both indict the white man, the first (by the boxer, Cashel Byron) for his cruelty to his fellow men, the second (by the Zulu chief, Cetewayo) for his mass slaughter and destruction.

The first professional performance of *The Admirable Bashville* was given by the Stage Society on June 7, 1903, at the Imperial Theatre, London.

10

Creative Evolution Comes to the Theatre: *Man and Superman*— A Comedy and a Philosophy

In the early years of the twentieth century a new philosophy began to emerge, that of creative evolution.

As a dramatist Shaw had already presented socialism, imperialism, and the working out of the will to the theatregoing public. Now, in 1902, he feels impelled to present the philosophy of creative evolution. In doing this he comes early on the scene, for Bergson's *L'Évolution créatrice* was not published until 1907; and as late as 1919 Shaw was saying: "A creed of Creative Evolution has been gathering into consciousness, and will soon inevitably proceed to organization. Man & Superman is the first attempt to dramatize it in English. My Life Force is Bergson's *élan vitale*."[1]

It was Shaw who introduced the word "superman" into the English language. It is a translation of *Ubermensch*, a concept of the German philosopher F. W. Nietzsche. Shaw's name began to be associated with those of Nietzsche and Schopenhauer, but it was not a matter of Shaw's being their disciple. It was rather that Shaw continued to occupy a *zeitgiest* role and tuned in to an ideology that was in the air. In explaining this Shaw once again identified himself as a European playwright: "I am rather an imposter as a pundit in the philosophy of Schopenhauer & Nietzsche.... I have often referred to them to remind my readers that what they call my individual eccentricities and paradoxes are part of the common European stock."[2]

When Shaw started to write *Man and Superman* he was faced with the problem of how to contain his tremendous subject within the boundaries of the theatre. He came up with a completely original solution and

48

invented a new literary form, which he described simply as a "volume which contains a play."

The volume, which consisted of five parts, contained a play, ingeniuosly structured, which in turn could be divided into two parts. Acts I, II, and IV are designed for the typical theatre audience, and provide the "comedy" part of the subtitle. The detachable Act III, which contains the philosophy, is intended for performance before what Shaw used to refer to as a "pit of philosophers."[3] The four acts can be played as an entity under suitable circumstances. Of course, the reader will wish to read the entire play.

Instead of the usual preface Shaw writes an Epistle Dedicatory addressed to Arthur Bingham Walkley, drama critic of *The Times*. Always a brilliant letter writer, Shaw writes as to a fellow man of letters, and gives the reader a sense of intimacy with the two confrères, closely sharing the author's thoughts. The contents of the Epistle illuminate and expand the thinking of the play.

The main body of the play, contained in Acts I, II, and IV, is a typical Shaw comedy, presenting a vignette of the English middle classes and their latest trends. It centers on who mates with whom and the nature of the forces that are exerted in the mating game. Act III, entitled "Don Juan in Hell," consists mainly of a dream sequence, and contains the dialogue concerning Shaw's creed of creative evolution, together with radical and controversial propositions which he sees as arising from that creed. Shaw had no expectation that Act III would be presented on the stage in the near future; but his readership was, of course, important.

The last part of the volume, like the first, is accessible only to the reader. Artistically it has a link with the first act of the play, for it consists of the "Revolutionist's Handbook" which in the opening scene is consigned to the waste-paper basket. The question of the authorship of the handbook is complicated. It was written by Jack Tanner, the play's protagonist. Tanner himself was generally supposed to be a representation of Shaw: Harley Granville Barker, who first played this part, was dressed to look like the author. Thus the handbook is a piece of persona writing, carefully distanced from the author. A similar situation arises in Act III when Tanner takes on the persona of Don Juan and utters some revolutionary thoughts. Shaw is a writer who speaks with tongues.

THE EPISTLE DEDICATORY

There is a sense in which the Epistle Dedicatory is almost as revolutionary as the Revolutionist's Handbook. For there can be few dramatists

who require the more serious members of their audiences to address themselves in some detail to serious issues of the day in order to fully appreciate a dramatic work of the theatre. Yet the purpose of the Epistle is to
enhance understanding.

In the first place, Shaw predicates an urgent need for the breeding
of a better race (that is, a race of supermen), and he thinks specifically in
terms of Britain. He identifies several matters of urgency: the inadequa-
cies, in practice, of political democracy, which, in his disillusionment he
describes as "the last refuge of cheap misgovernment"[4]; the need for the
reconstruction of industrial Britain: and Britain's responsibility for the
governance of a hugely expanded empire, which, in aspirational terms,
requires the construction of a practically international Commonwealth.

The author has moved away from his early Fabian enthusiasm for
universal suffrage, and he now looks to where the power lies: he sees it as
being vested in the middle classes. Most of Shaw's plays have had a middle-class ambience: now he gives this class a new significance. Certainly
he associates it with the decline of the aristocracy. Probably he associates
it with the continuing growth and spread of capitalism, for he uses the
term "bourgeoisie" in describing it: "Those forces of middle class public
opinion … are now triumphant everywhere. Civilized society is one huge
bourgeoisie."[5]

When he turns his attention to the breeding of a better race, Shaw
overturns the generally held view that the sexual initiative lies with the
male. (The idea that the woman might take some part in this initiative
was introduced, it will be recalled, in *You Never Can Tell*.) Whatever the
social conventions suggest, and however much the law relating to marriage and the owning of property may be weighted against women, it is
the woman who is impelled towards mating and motherhood. Later Shaw
is to argue that motherhood and marriage need not necessarily be associated, but, in the meantime, this is as far as he goes in the introduction
to his essentially bourgeois play.

The author points out that women nowadays have much more influence, partly because of recent legislation, but also because of the Nonconformist conscience, and its political influence. But Shaw's latest New
Woman is definitely not the Vivie of *Mrs Warren's Profession*, university-
educated, career-minded, about to become financially independent. Nor
is she a second Candida, whose mothering instincts are turned towards
her husband and her would-be lover. She is the woman impelled by the
Life Force to give birth to superman, and a new and imperial race; an
innocent forerunner, perhaps, of the women of Hitler's regime of the
1930s.

Standing firmly by his convictions, Shaw declares that the sexual initiative "is politically the most important of all the initiatives."[6]

After these predications there comes a tension which is fundamental to the argument of the play. It relates to the man rather than the woman, and it is based on the concept that the artist-philosopher, if he has creativity of the flesh as well as of the mind, has to make a choice between the two. Should he become the progenitor of a future race of supermen, or is he to be the begetter of creative thought which will be a beacon of light for present and future generations? The question arises of why Shaw regards these two functions as incompatible. It is addressed briefly in Act III.

MAN AND SUPERMAN, ACTS I, II AND IV

The successful pursuit of Tanner, the artist-philosopher, by Ann, who, Shaw tells us, is Everywoman, is the main theme of the play. It takes place within a society which is presented as being in the process of change. These changes relate to money, mobility, and manners rather than social mores and social institutions. The institution of marriage (which is becoming one of Shaw's favorite targets) is especially regarded as sacrosanct. Violet, who is wrongly suspected of carrying an illegitimate child, is incensed at both the suspicion and her consequent treatment. Tanner, however, unaware that the suspicion is not correct, tells her that she is entirely in the right. For this support he earns Violet's fury.

The comedy relates to the fact that in middle-class society the woman does not openly pursue her man. Ann does so covertly and her prey, Tanner, is, to begin with, unaware of this pursuit. The tension of the play is as described in the Epistle: Tanner, the artist-philosopher, holds the authorial view that marriage and parenthood are not compatible with creativity of the mind, and, until the ending of the play, he prizes mental creativity the most.

The climax comes when Tanner yields to the Life Force and tells Ann, "I love you. The Life Force enchants me: I have the whole world in my arms when I clasp you. But I am fighting for my freedom, for my honor, for my self, one and indivisible"[7]; he yields. There is an anti-climax when at the very end of the play, Ann says, "Never mind her, dear. Go on talking": Tanner replies: "Talking!"[8]

Acts I, II, and IV each show different aspects of middle-class society. In the first act the audience is presented with a stable situation in which the senior male is accepted as the head of the family. The male in question, Roebuck Ramsden, is eminent in public life and in business. His religion is Unitarian, which means that he is likely to be the possessor of the Nonconformist conscience to which Shaw made reference in the Epistle. He is presented in contrast to Tanner of the new generation. Rather like Mrs. Clandon of *You Never Can Tell,* but more dignified and more weighty, he is well versed in the forward thinking of his generation, but is reluctant to accept that there have been changes. In a head-on clash with Tanner he says, "You pose as an advanced man. Let me tell you that I was an advanced man before you were born.... I grow more advanced every day."[9] When he tosses Tanner's "Revolutionist's Handbook" into the waste-paper basket it is evident that the status quo in the Ramsden household will not easily be overturned.

In his home Ramsden's authority is unchallenged, possibly for a variety of reasons. His unmarried sister is, presumably, dependent on him. He is co-guardian (with Tanner) of the fatherless Ann, and Ann's mother is relieved to be able to transfer responsibility to Ramsden. Ann herself practices her manipulative skills on him, as she does on Tanner. Though Ann's wiles and subterfuges make good, conventional-style comedy, they add nothing to her personal dignity. She is certainly not everyone's New Woman.

It is within the stable setting of the Ramsden home that Tanner and the inevitable art-for-art's-sake character, Octavius, make their declarations of selfhood. Tanner describes to Ann the time when he became a man: "The change that came to me was the birth in me of moral passion; and I declare that according to my experience moral passion is the only real passion.... It is the birth of that passion that turns a child into a man."[10] Earlier he has defined to Octavius the creativity of the artist which is seen as antithetical to the creativity of the maternal woman:

> For mark you, Tavy, the artist's work is to shew us ourselves as we really are. Our minds are nothing but this knowledge of ourselves; and he who adds a jot to such knowledge creates new mind as surely as any woman creates new men.... Of all human struggles there is none so treacherous and remorseless as the struggle between the artist man and the mother woman.[11]

If the setting of Act I represents stability, that of Act II presents a new mobility, for, center stage, on the driveway of a country house, Tanner's motor car is parked. It is the car in which he is shortly to try and make his escape when he learns from his chauffeur, Straker, that it is he, and not Octavius, on whom Ann has set her sights. The chauffeur is himself a sign of upward mobility, for he has climbed the ladder of education in a way similar to, if more modest than, the waiter's son in *You Never Can Tell*: he is the product of the recently created polytechnics. Straker utters some famous lines: "Very nice sort of place, Oxford, I should think, for people that like that sort of place. They teach you to be a gentleman there. In the Polytechnic they teach you to be an engineer or such like."[12]

Ann and her party eventually arrive on the scene and Tanner makes a hair's-breadth escape.

Act IV also has a setting which relates to mobility, that of a holiday villa in Spain, where those in the pursuing party have caught up with the pursued, and where Hector Malone has caught up with his son, also named Hector, who, it transpires, is the husband of the maligned Violet. Hector senior is another symbol of upward mobility, for he left Ireland with his mother during the potato famine, and has since become a millionaire. Now he seeks social status for his son by buying an estate for him, so that he may become one of the landed gentry. Malone says of his son: "Let him raise himself socially with my money or raise somebody else: so long as there is a social profit somewhere, I'll regard my expenditure as justified."[13] To readers of Act III Malone also represents those aspects of international capitalism that are unacceptable and amoral. Like the ground landlord of *Widowers' Houses* he distances himself from his investments. Some of his income comes from the takings of the band of brigands whose activities precede the dream sequence in Act III.

Earlier in the play questions have been asked about the virtue of Malone's daughter-in-law. Nobody thinks to inquire about the sources of Malone's money.

ACT III: "DON JUAN IN HELL"

When, in his flight from Ann, Tanner crosses frontiers and arrives in the Sierra Nevada, there is a preliminary scene which serves as a prologue to the one in which Tanner is transported to an imagined Hell where there are no boundaries but those of the mind. This preliminary scene extends the area of the play's social commentary, exposing some of society's underpinnings and giving an indication of the unacceptable source of the wealth which is to make the millionaire Malone so very acceptable in the last act of the play. The band of brigands who hold up Tanner and his chauffeur bear some similarity to the motley crew in *Captain Brassbound's Conversion*.

The curtain rises on a debate by the brigands, entitled "Have Anarchists or Social Democrats the most personal courage?"

The story of the brigands is, in effect, a parable about the unjust distribution of wealth. It is epitomized in a famous exchange between Tanner and Mendoza, the brigand's leader:

> MENDOZA: I am a brigand: I live by robbing the rich.
> TANNER: I am a gentleman: I live by robbing the poor.[14]

The leader claims that the brigands redistribute among the poor the money that they steal from motorists whom they waylay. He makes a socialistic statement: "We naturally have modern views as to the injustice of the existing distribution of wealth."[15] However, it transpires that Mendoza belongs to a syndicate of capitalists "of the right sort" (which includes Malone senior) who draw income from the brigands' robbery. "Capitalism is theft" is an appropriate axiom.

When night falls on the Sierra, Tanner drifts into dreamland and adopts the persona of Don Juan as in Mozart's opera, *Don Giovanni*, and there comes a great expansion of his character. The artist-philosopher more fully expounds his philosophy. Having arrived in an imagined Hell, his vision expands to embrace eternity and he becomes the very embodiment of philosopher-man destined to embrace and pursue the purpose of the Life Force. He looks towards the eternity of Heaven where his joy will be to spend the aeons in contemplation and his purpose will be to help Life in its struggle for betterment.

But what about the persona of Don Juan, the notorious philanderer? This side of Tanner's character scarcely seems to exist in the main part of the play. It certainly exists in the dream sequence, where we learn how, as Don Juan sees it, the philanderer, the philosopher, and the husband may co-exist in harmony.

Don Juan has some noble and inspiring lines to speak when he looks back at prehistory and the forebears of man:

> Things immeasurably greater than man in every respect but brain
> have existed and perished. The megatherium, the icthyosaurus
> have paced the earth with seven-league steps and hidden the day
> with cloud vast wings.... These things lived and wanted to live;
> but for lack of brains they did not know how to carry out their
> purpose, and so destroyed themselves.[16]

The human brain is seen by Don Juan as the key to the evolutionary process. In the case of the philosopher, who is man at the highest level, his brain is "the organ by which Nature strives to understand itself."[17]

A brilliant metaphor, that of the mind's eye, is used to illustrate the growth of man's powers of perception. Don Juan says: "Just as Life, after ages of struggle, evolved that wonderful bodily organ the eye, … so it is evolving today a mind's eye that shall see, not the physical world, but the purpose of Life, and thereby enable the individual to work for that purpose."[18]

All this is said when Don Juan is in debate with the Devil, who, inevitably, does not accept the contention that humankind is making progress. He chooses a different metaphor, likening the successive phases in the history of mankind to the swing of the clockmaker's pendulum. Don Juan argues (as does Shaw in other contexts) that, in fact, progress is made by trial and error.

Earlier Don Juan has been in conversation with the Statue, Don Gonzalo of the opera, who is a dream version of Roebuck Ramsden. Dona Ana (alias Ann) is also present.

Masculinity flows freely in the blood of Don Juan, and in the dream sequence the sexual imperative belongs to him rather than the female. He foresees that in the course of time contraceptives will solve copulative man's dilemma. He speaks powerfully about this, regarding it as part of the evolutionary process. He dissolves into raptures about the benefits that contraception will bring:

> The great central purpose of breeding the race: ay, breeding it to heights now deemed superhuman: that purpose which is now hidden in a mephitic cloud of love and romance and prudery and fastidiousness, will break through into clear sunlight as a purpose no longer to be confused with the gratification of personal fancies, the impossible realization of boys' and girls' dreams of bliss, or the need of older people for companionship or money.[19]

As for Dona Ana her purpose remains the same as Ann's. She makes her departure from the scene crying to the universe: "A father! a father for the Superman!"[20] She makes the same demand, unspoken, when she returns to earth in Act IV.

"The Revolutionist's Handbook"

The Handbook is the obverse of "Don Juan in Hell." In Act III ideas about creative evolution flow freely, untrammelled by time and space. In this propagandist document the Tanner who belongs to the here and now looks in some detail at what, in his view, has to be done to further society's evolutionary progress.

But first he presents his argument as to why a superior race is required. In essence it accords with the Epistle. Social aggregation has reached a point where humankind, as it now exists, does not have the capability to manage that aggregate, and catastrophe threatens unless man has the will to breed a better race. But towards the end of the pamphlet an element of elitism creeps in. In the days when Shaw was writing about empire, elitism was, of course, inherent in the concept of an imperial race. Now Tanner perceives the need for an elitist corps within Britain. He writes: "The overthrow of the aristocrat has created the necessity for the Superman.... King Demos must be bred like all other Kings; and with Must there is no arguing."[21] Superman is very much in the singular here, as he was in *Caesar and Cleopatra*.

The author raises a question which has not been asked before: what qualities are we looking to produce when attention is turned to breeding? It is a question that remains virtually unanswered. For it is postulated that though certain deficiences could, and should, be eliminated by the practice of eugenics, "The proof of the Superman will be in the living; and we shall find out how to produce him by the old method of trial and error."[22] There follows a statement that smacks of the sinister, if "we" is taken to stand for some all-powerful State: "We are therefore driven to the conclusion that when we have carried selection as far as we can by rejecting from the list of eligible parents all persons who are uninteresting, unpromising, or blemished without any set-off, we shall still have to trust to the guidance of fancy (alias the Voice of Nature), both in the breeders and the parents, for that superiority in the unconscious self which will be the true characteristic of the Superman."[23]

It comes as no surprise that Tanner postulates the need for "the dissolution of the present necessary association of marriage with conjugation, which most unmarried people regard as the very diagnostic of marriage."[24] It was, after all, the obvious solution to Tanner's dilemma in the play, had it been viable under the given circumstances.

Almost at the end of the Handbook there comes a sudden change of climate. Tanner speaks in the manner of a contemporary politician, or possibly like a member of the Fabian Society: "A conference on the subject is the next step needed."[25]

But this is not the end. The Handbook is supplemented with several pages of aphorisms and witticisms, written, one might suppose, for the express purpose of providing material for those who love to quote Shaw or are bent on compiling anthologies of his sayings.

An interesting feature of this volume that contains a play is the number and nature of the parts that Shaw assigns to himself. As the writer of the Epistle a sophisticated Shaw is thoroughly at home with the literati and highly articulate about the state of the nation and the world at large. In the play he takes to the stage, so we are told, as Jack Tanner. Tanner as Shaw's stage persona is a follow-on to Charteris, the philanderer. Unlike Charteris, Tanner is not torn between philandering and philosophy: in his case moral passion rules. But in Act III the king of all philanderers, Don Juan, emerges from Tanner's subconscious. It is tantalizing to wonder whether Shaw introduced Don Juan partly as a means of self-expression. Finally, in the "Revolutionist's Handbook," we come to that aspect of Tanner that is revolutionary, speaking the sort of language that would be unsuited for Tanner's social environment and undiplomatic for Shaw to use in his political environment. Tanner returns from his dreams to his original persona: at the end of his revolutionary outpourings he returns to the respectability of the committee room. So, one may say, does the author.

Shaw as a playwright created many parts: and he was a man of many parts.

Man and Superman brought Shaw new fame and took him to new heights as a playwright. Hesketh Pearson records that when the play was published in 1903 the critics, for the first time, took Shaw seriously as a social critic and a philosopher. When the play was produced, in 1905, Shaw became the "idol of the rising generation of intellectuals.... His influence over the more serious young men and women in the early years of the century, and indeed in the years following the war of 1914–18, was far greater than that exercised by ... any other writer."[26] The play was first presented (without Act III) by the Stage Society on May 23, 1905, at the Court Theatre. "Don Juan in Hell" had its first showing, also at the Court, on June 4, 1907.

11

Aspects of
Twentieth-Century Society
Presented in the Drama

After the wide perspective of *Man and Superman* Shaw puts society under the microscope. He examines the various thrusts and counterthrusts which are at work, and their repercussions at the national and international levels. Dependency cultures; the interaction of a profession, such as medicine, with the rest of society; the spread of the tentacles of capitalism; the nature and significance of the institution of marriage, and the bringing up of children are all closely reviewed. These are true slices-of-life plays. The first three were written during the great days of the Vedrenne-Barker management at the Court Theatre.

JOHN BULL'S OTHER ISLAND (1904)

At the time Shaw wrote *John Bull's Other Island* there was agitation about home rule for Ireland. The play is intended as an example for all those countries whose basic right to self-rule is denied. He defines countries that are denied self-rule as those "in which the government does not rest on the consent of the people."[1] Except for the fact that Ireland was customarily regarded as part of the British Isles, this might well be classified as a play about empire.

The play was extremely popular with the British political establishment. The prime minister of the day, Arthur Balfour, attended four performances; on two occasions he was accompanied by future prime ministers, Sir Henry Campbell-Bannerman and Herbert Asquith. A special performance was arranged for King Edward VII. The king laughed so much that he broke his chair, which had been hired especially for the occasion.[2] The king's reaction highlights Shaw's supreme skill in presenting home truths of the utmost seriousness without raising the hackles of those most closely concerned. But was there a downside to this skill, a failure to strike home? Sometimes Shaw was upset by what he saw as the insensitivity of the audience rather than a defect of the author, but not, apparently, in the case of *John Bull's Other Island.* He wrote in a program note (dated New Year, 1913): "In all good plays tears and laughter lie very close together."[3]

Two comments in the text of the play should, in particular, have given any politicians in the audience cause to examine their motivation as regards Ireland and to turn their attention more closely to the true nature of Ireland's political status. Both are made by Broadbent, the English capitalist developer. Broadbent's attention is turned towards the prospects for development in Ireland; and, not by coincidence, he is seeking election to an Irish constituency as a Member of Parliament. He says, "I am an Englishman and a Liberal; and now that South Africa has been enslaved and destroyed, there is no country left to me to take an interest in but Ireland."[4] Later, with all the complacency of one who believes he belongs to a master race, he pontificates: "Home Rule will work wonders under English guidance.... We English must place our capacity for government without stint at the service of nations who are less fortunately endowed in that respect."[5]

When Shaw stepped into the arena of Irish political affairs, he centered his play on two related matters, both of which were relevant to Ireland's economy. The first was landlordism and the effect of Gladstone's Land Act of 1881, which gave tenant farmers (who were mostly smallholders) the "three F's" as they were known: Fair Rent, Fixity of Tenure, and Free Sale. The benefit intended for the tenant farmer was largely illusory, for the new law created a new class of poverty-stricken landowner who could barely scratch a living. Previously, as a tenant, if he fell behind in his rent he would have been evicted. Now if the tenant wished to buy the land which was for sale, the developer was on hand to offer a mortgage in the expectation that he would be unable to keep up the payments. At this stage the developer would foreclose, and, as under the previous arrangement, the defaulter would become a landless peasant.

The overall result in Ireland was a very significant change in land usage which affected the country's economy. For the developer belonged to a new capitalist class, intent not on cultivating a fertile land in the interests of self-sufficiency, but on providing leisure facilities, luxury hotels, golf courses and so on for the benefit of visiting tourists. Hence the Irish economy would become dependent on the prosperity of other nations, particularly the English. Ireland had no adequate power to prevent this since its only political voice was in the English Parliament and its land was being acquired by foreign capitalists. (Broadbent belonged to a Land Development Syndicate.)

This is the burden of the play: and, worthy, topical, and important though it is, it hardly seems the sort of stuff that even the most dedicated of prime ministers would wish to see again and again. And yet this is what happened.

It was perhaps inevitable that Shaw's sparkling wit should be at its very best when he wrote about Ireland. And there is nothing superficial about this: the wit is intertwined with the play's meaning and with its sadness. Shaw preserves the dignity of the Irish, deflates the standard image of the stage Irishman, and presents a believable picture of the Irish collectively and as individuals. Larry Doyle, the character who introduces Ireland to the audience from his office in England is himself an absentee Irishman about to accompany Broadbent on a visit to Ireland. He tells of the two great faults of the Irish, dreaming and laughter.

The play is multi-voiced. When Broadbent and Doyle, who are partners, arrive in Ireland, there is a key scene which the politically minded will easily recognize as a rendition of a party selection committee about to choose a parliamentary candidate. At the end of it the playgoer will find himself remarkably well informed about Ireland's culture. Broadbent presents himself as a prospective candidate for a vacant seat at Westminster.

Typifying characters bear witness to the effect of the recent legislation on Irish lives. The land agent (Doyle's father) is of less importance in the community now that there are fewer rents to collect because sales have been forced on landowners. The parish priest belongs to a church that has lost much of its income because the Act of 1869 disestablished the Protestant Episcopal Church in Ireland and thereby ended the payment of tithes. The one-time tenant farmer, now the owner even of a smallholding, is liable to be dispossessed because of debt. The small-time mill owner, whose financial viability depends on that of his farming neighbors, is not flourishing. At the bottom of the pile, and with no voice in community affairs, is the landless peasant, deemed to be unsuitable for the possession of a smallholding.

One might expect such a group to look for a candidate who would speak positively for Irish interests. This is not the case. They seek one who will make no demands on the individual purse, and who will "leave us alone." Broadbent gives these assurances, and, secure in the knowledge that he will acquire riches in his role as developer, talks of making substantial contributions to the community. Larry Doyle, who also stands as a candidate, turns his attention to the Irish economy and proposes the introduction of a minimum wage rate, but this falls on deaf ears: those gathered there are mostly self-employed. Doyle withdraws from his candidacy at an early stage. When he next talks politics, in the last act, he is not at all socially minded.

Broadbent is chosen as candidate.

So far, the question of Home Rule has largely been ignored, but a warning shot is fired by Matthew Haffigan, the peasant farmer, who, when he improved the fertility of his land, had his rent increased by the landlord to more than he could pay, and he was therefore dispossessed. Hodson, Broadbent's English servant, who believes that the English poor suffer more than the Irish, talks of "cutting the cable" with Ireland. Matthew Haffigan's reply prefigures the founding of the Irish Free State in 1922: "Take care we dont cut the cable ourselves some day."[6]

In the last act of the play the developers' intentions are given in some detail and their significance for Ireland's future becomes plain, as does the utter ruthlessness of those concerned. The dispossession of those smallholders who are described by Larry Doyle as "too small, too poor, too ignorant," is intended.

Broadbent opines that Haffigan, soon to be dispossessed, is too old to find other employment, and had better go to the workhouse. Doyle replies,"Pah! what does it matter where an old and broken man spends his last days? ... I say let him die, and let us have no more of his like."[7] (The "too old at forty" syndrome reappears in Shaw's next play, *Major Barbara*.)

The unfrocked priest, Father Keegan, is there to hold matters in balance by his perception of the spirituality of Ireland. He gives Doyle the ultimate reproof: "In the accounts kept in heaven, Mr. Doyle, a heart purified of hatred may be worth more than even a Land Development Syndicate of Anglicized Irishmen and Gladstonized Englishmen."[8]

Sadly, the impervious Broadbent is to have the last word. The continuing victim of self-deception (a quality which he may have shared with some of the distinguished audience), he responds to Father Keegan's eloquence as follows: "I feel now as I never did before that I am right in devoting my life to the cause of Ireland. Come along and help me choose the site for the hotel."[9]

The play was written at the request of W. B. Yeats for the Irish Literary Theatre, but, in the event, it was considered to be beyond that theatre's capacity. It was first presented at the Royal Court Theatre on November 1, 1904.

MAJOR BARBARA (1905)

Whereas *John Bull's Other Island* was concerned with a dependency culture that was related to the investment of foreign (English) capital, *Major Barbara* depicts three separate but conjoined dependency cultures with an archetypal capitalist (Undershaft) as the link between the three groups. The armament trade, which is Undershaft's main source of income, has more sinister connotations for the world at large than any plan of Broadbent's to make Ireland into England's playground. The earlier play probably left those members of the audience who were disposed to be serious with some grave uncertainties. This later play was to leave even the author in a moral maze. The dangers, the difficulties, and the complexities of the capitalist network are pushed to the extreme limits as far as personal responsibilities go. The moral problems that are presented have probably become even more complex with the passage of time.

The play's principal character—Undershaft rather than the Major Barbara of the title—is presented as one of three types of capitalist, two of whom, in typical Shaw fashion, do not appear on stage. Lazarus, Undershaft's partner, is described as a miser, seeing money not as a means to an end but as an end in itself. The third capitalist, Bodger, a personage in the whisky industry, is said to use money as a means of obtaining social prestige and overt political power. A portion of his wealth goes to endow good causes. Hence he has been created a peer of the realm and has a seat in the House of Lords. Undershaft's political power, on the other hand, is covert but immense. He makes this plain in a major statement which he addresses to his son, Stephen Undershaft:

> The government of your country! I am the government of your country: I, and Lazarus. When I want anything to keep my dividends up, you will discover that my want is a national need.... And in return you shall have the support and applause of my newspapers, and the delight of imagining that you are a great statesman.[10]

There is an interesting point of comparison between the source of Undershaft's money and Bodger's. At the time the play was written the abuse of alcohol left many poor families with insufficient money to buy food or pay the rent. In these circumstances drink was regarded as evil. Undershaft's armament factory, which he acquired rather than inherited, had the capability of destroying whole nations. Along with the factory went an armorer's code in which Undershaft took great pride. He quoted "the true faith of an Armorer" to his prospective son-in-law: "To give arms to all men who offer an honest price for them, without respect of persons or principles: ... to all sorts and conditions, all nationalities, all faiths, all follies, all causes and all crimes."[11] Cusins, a professor of Greek, will, because of some complicated clause in the will of the firm's founder, become a partner in the firm when he marries Undershaft's daughter, Barbara.

Cusins makes a major contribution to the debate of the play, especially in the last act. Like Undershaft he is motivated by a desire for power, but he puts somewhat of a gloss on it. When he says that he is selling his soul "for reality and for power," he quickly adds: "It is not for myself alone. I want to make power for the world."[12]

The three dependency cultures are presented in turn. The first is that of Undershaft's family who accept the benefits that their dependency brings as marital or filial rights. The second is that of the underclass who live in extreme poverty: they have no rights and are dependent on demeaning and uncertain charity. The third is that of Undershaft's employees, who are housed in a garden city where they work, live, and spend their leisure time. They have the dignity and security of earning their own livings in pleasant and cultured surroundings. Ultimately, however, their dependency relates to the destruction of others on an international scale.

In Act I, Undershaft is shown as having made a traditional marriage of convenience for the purposes of social prestige. Lady Britomart, seen in the comfort of her elegant home, requires Undershaft, from whom she is now separated, to provide suitable dowries for her two daughters on the occasions of their forthcoming marriages, and to use his influence to launch his son on a political career. To accede to Lady Britomart's requirements would arguably be to Undershaft's own advantage, for it would reinforce the stability of a sector of society that Undershaft knows well how to bend to his will.

The second dependency culture is presented in Act II. The yard of a Salvation Army shelter on a morning in January makes a bleak contrast to the comfort and elegance of the Undershaft home. The author says of this setting that it "would drive any idle rich person straight to the Mediterranean."[13] Here the bread of charity is available. Its recipients are the poor, the homeless, and the unfortunate.

Among these is one person of whom we are intended to take particular note, one who, like Haffigan of *John Bull's Other Island*, is deemed by employers to be "too old at forty." He represents a particular kind of two-way dependency to which reference is made in the Preface: "We allow our industry to be organized in open dependence on the maintenance of a 'reserve army of unemployed' for the sake of 'elasticity.'"[14]

When Undershaft visits this shelter at the invitation of his daughter, who is a major in the Salvation Army, he scarcely needs to be reminded of a reason, besides that of social prestige, for making large donations to organizations such as this. He understands very well what a shrewd Army Commissioner tells him: "There would have been rioting this winter in London but for us."[15] When he duly makes a substantial donation he is again helping to stabilize existing society to his own advantage.

But Undershaft has yet another reason for handing out his money. His lust for power extends to his daughter. He judges rightly that she will not admire his generosity, but the fact that the Army has accepted what she regards as tainted money will destroy her religious faith and break her spirit; she will then become susceptible to his influence. In this he presents an image of capitalism at its most ruthless. The Army's acceptance of the profits from the sale of arms poses a question which haunts the rest of the play, and continues to haunt the world at large: accepting the premise that money obtained from the (indiscriminate) sale of arms is tainted money, is it ethical to accept it for the purpose of doing good? The Army's answer is Yes; the money will be used for doing the Lord's work and is thereby sanctified. Having received it they march off in procession, and in triumph, with colors flying and Cusins playing the drums, a spectacle that was to add considerably to the play's success.

Barbara stays behind. For her, the immediate answer is No. She utters the lines, sometimes regarded as blasphemous: "Drunkenness and Murder! My God: why hast thou forsaken me?"[16] It looks as though Undershaft has achieved his aim as spoken to Cusins: "Barbara must belong to us, not to the Salvation Army."[17] Ironically it is to the too-old-at-forty man, Shirley, self-educated on the works of Thomas Paine and the like, that Barbara turns in her distress: but this distress is not to last. The ultimate sadness comes when not only Barbara's faith but her personality are destroyed and, in the last act of the play she really and truly becomes an Undershaft dependent.

This last act has its visual symbols: a cannon and some mutilated dummy soldiers. These are to be seen when the Undershaft family arrive at the firestep which overlooks the garden city of Perivale St. Andrews, where Undershaft's employees have their workplace and their homes, and where, as Undershaft tells his family, they are provided with every cultural amenity. One is reminded of the famous pioneer garden city of Bournville, but its founder, George Cadbury, was a Quaker and a man of peace; his city made chocolate, not guns.

Perivale St. Andrews is the scene of the play's great debate, which is chiefly between capitalist and potential capitalist, Undershaft and Cusins. Some powerful statements are made but none of these resolve the basic problem, of which St. Andrews is the symbol, about the conjoining of evil with good: is there an ethical justification for structuring an economy on an industry which is responsible for the death and destruction of others, perhaps on a global basis? Barbara does not address this problem although she makes a pious speech which contains the statement, "Let God's work be done for its own sake: the work he had to create us to do because it cannot be done except by living men and women."[18]

For those who cannot wrestle with the conundrum that Perivale St. Andrews represents, there is the sad fate of Major Barbara to ponder. At the end of the play she says, "I want a house in the village to live in with Dolly [Adolphus Cusins]." She clutches at her mother's skirt like a baby and says: "Come and tell me which one to take."[19]

Major Barbara had a brilliant audience when it was first performed on November 28, 1905. Once more Prime Minister Arthur Balfour was in the audience, this time accompanied by Beatrice Webb.

Many years later *Major Barbara* was filmed with Rex Harrison as Cusins. The play, and especially the film, enjoyed great popularity.

THE DOCTOR'S DILEMMA: A TRAGEDY (1906)

In a complex society various groups, such as the professions, are in a position to hold their fellow citizens to ransom, and in fact, frequently do so. This is the premise on which *A Doctor's Dilemma* is based. From this Shaw argues in the Preface that the moral standards of a person acting in a professional capacity may be lower than those of the individual.

The medical profession is chosen to illustrate this proposition for a variety of reasons, most of which have an element of topicality. The reason that actually sparked the writing of the play was extremely topical and had great potential for drama. This was the discovery of the antibody opsonin, which, if administered correctly, had the capability to cure tuberculosis. It was in extremely short supply. Shaw himself had been present when the discoverer of opsonin, Sir Almroth Wright, was asked which patients were to be selected for treatment.[20] Since it would be possible to choose patients based on questionable motives, this sort of decision-making could be used to illustrate Shaw's premise with great dramatic effect.

Among the subsidiary reasons for selecting the medical profession to illustrate his point was Shaw's very strong antipathy to vivisection (animal experimentation). He contended that not only was vivisection cruel in itself, it brutalized all those who practiced it or condoned its practice. This dictum applied to the medical profession.

There was also to hand an illustration of how members of this profession sometimes preyed upon the rich: it was a current fashion to remove by surgery, for no good reason, the vermiform appendix, which had been determined to serve no useful purpose. There was also the matter of so-called professional loyalty, whereby, if unnecessary treatment had been given, or there had been a blunder, this would not be revealed by another member of the profession.

On the positive side, Shaw cites in the Preface the recent practice of appointing Medical Officers of Health whose function was to keep people well by improving the environment and so forth, rather than tending the sick. This is mentioned only briefly in the play, but perhaps the point is sufficiently made.

The play has two great scenes in which Shaw puts across his playwright's purpose. The first is comedic; in true Shaw fashion, it is likely to amuse the very medics he lampoons as well as the laity. The second, most unusually for Shaw, is a deathbed scene, dignified and poetic.

The opening scene portrays a cluster of doctors celebrating the knighthood conferred on Sir Colenso Ridgeon, the dicoverer of opsonin. He is about to start on a moral decline, and to become, in effect, the murderer of a future patient. Those assembled have between them, as it transpires from their conversation, the faults already mentioned and more besides. Also present is an impoverished, worthy doctor, who is suffering from tuberculosis.

When this fraternity of doctors breaks up, two of them are left alone. Their dialogue epitomizes the author's thinking:

SIR COLENSO RIDGEON: We're not a profession: we're a conspiracy.
SIR PATRICK CULLEN [Ridgeon's future conspirator]: All professions are conspiracies against the laity.[21]

The time comes when a choice has to be made as to who is to be treated with the new drug: the worthy doctor who works among the poor, or a talented artist of dubious character whose wife has appealed to Ridgeon for help. This conundrum is often posed in hypothetical situations, and, no doubt, in real life. Who is to be refused a seat in a lifeboat? Who is to be thrown out of an overloaded balloon? To the impartial, high-principled decision-maker the question is almost impossible to answer. Ridgeon is not high principled, he is extremely devious, and he is not impartial: he is attracted to the artist's wife. He could, of course, save the doctor, leave the artist to die a natural death, and chance his luck with the widow. But Colenso Ridgeon is more devious than this. He rejects the worthy doctor, selects the artist as his patient, but leaves the complicated administering of the opsonin in other, bungling hands, thereby ensuring the death of his patient. Three typifing doctors are involved in the death of the artist, Dubedat: the malefactor (Ridgeon); the conniver (Sir Patrick); and the bungler (Sir Ralph Bloomfield Bonington). One assumes that all three have been knighted for their services to medicine.

A conversation between Sir Patrick Cullen and Ridgeon forms a defining moment in the play:

> RIDGEON: In short, as a member of a high and great profession, I'm to kill my patient.
> SIR PATRICK: Dont talk wicked nonsense. You cant kill him. But you can leave him in other hands.
> RIDGEON: In B.B.'s, for instance: eh? (looking at him significantly).
> SIR PATRICK (demurely facing his look): Sir Ralph Bloomfield Bonington is a very eminent physician.[22]

So the point is duly made. A doctor is able to commit a medical murder without leaving a shred of evidence against him: the patient dies by blunder and intent.

The character of Sir Colenso continues to deteriorate. He shows no remorse and continues to pursue Dubedat's widow. But the artist is enobled by the approach of death. In his death scene, which is the most powerful in the play, he is transfigured by his consciousness of his vocation as an artist. With his last words, which are taken, Shaw tells us, from Wagner's *End of a Musician in Paris*, he recites his artist's creed: "I believe in Michaelangelo, Velásquez, and Rembrandt; in the might of design, the mystery of color, the redemption of all things by Beauty everlasting, and the message of Art that has made these hands blessed."[23]

The unanswerable question (as to whose life to save) remains unanswered, but its answer was not the main issue of the play. In the death scene a powerful image is presented: whereas a man's profession may demean a man, the vocation of an artist uplifts him.

The play was first produced at the Court Theatre on November 20, 1906.

GETTING MARRIED:
A DISQUISITIONARY PLAY (1908)

At the time that Shaw wrote *Getting Married* there was public concern about the falling birthrate. The play gives an overview of marriage as an institution. It touches, in a fairly oblique way, on the question of the birthrate, and, less obliquely, on the position of those who remain unmarried.

The birthrate had been in decline since 1876. At first it had been a matter for rejoicing, now the contrary was true. The Fabian Society had conducted an inquiry into the causes of the decline, following which Sidney Webb had written two leading articles published in *The Times* on the 11th and 18th of October, 1906. They appeared later as Fabian Tract No. 131, "The Decline in the Birthrate" (1907). The inquiry found that the principal reason for the decline had been the use of contraceptives (as foreseen by Don Juan in *Man and Superman*), or, as Webb put it, the "deliberate volition of the married state." Some races and some religions did not practice contraception, but these apart, it was the prudent of all classes who were concerned with birth control.

The fact that a (supposed) major purpose of marriage was being sidelined suggested that a fresh look should be taken at that institution, and Shaw undertook this task in his play and in its Preface. The inquiry had also considered the numerical imbalance between the sexes and had come to the conclusion that, since there were so many more women than men, it would be to the nation's advantage to regard motherhood as an honorable status for single women, and that State support should be available. Similarly, since children were a valuable national asset, "child paupers," who were often the offspring of widows, should be given State aid.

This was the background against which *Getting Married* was written. These proposals are handled with tact in the play and are filtered into the text rather than dominating it. The Preface is less restrained than either the tract or the play, but it covers much the same ground as the former, thereby underscoring both the topicality of the subject of marriage and its social significance as an institution. There is, however, one important difference between the tract and the Preface. Shaw goes much further than Webb on the subject of single motherhood, seeing it not only as a service to the State but as a basic human right. In the play the aptly named Lesbia is the spokesperson for this point of view.

The play looks at marriage from a wide perspective. It has a host figure in the Bishop, an author-surrogate. He is knowledgeable about various forms of marriage, and is able to point out that within the British Empire monogamy does not have a monopoly. As a scholar he draws attention to a lesson of history when he warns that, unless the law relating to marriage is reformed, marriage as an institution will break down, as it did in Ancient Rome. The Bishop is one who has the ear of politicians. He has warned the past four Prime Ministers that "If they didnt make our marriage laws reasonable there would be a strike against marriage."[24]

The Bishop has an immediate personal interest in this, for the play takes place in his palace on his daughter's wedding day. It opens when preparations are afoot for the wedding breakfast and the guests, plus some others, are beginning to arrive. Each has his contribution of opinions and experience to make to the great debate which is about to take place. In total a comprehensive picture of marriage is given. There is one item, however, that is slightly lacking in credibility. Though the Bishop's role is that of mentor, it appears that his daughter and his future son-in-law are singularly unprepared for marriage. On their wedding morning they each receive pamphlets, the work of well-known activists, on the subject of the need for the reform of the marriage laws. The couple are informed, for example, that the husband is responsible for his wife's debts, and that a criminal offence is not grounds for divorce. They decide to call the wedding off.

In the meantime those assembled speak their minds. We are made aware that though they speak as individuals, together they represent society. The Bishop's brother, General Bridgenorth, spells this out when he asks the greengrocer who is helping with the wedding breakfast: "Why not dignify my niece's wedding by wearing your [alderman's] robes? ... I attach importance to this as an affirmation of solidarity in the service of the community. The Bishop's apron, my uniform, your robes: the Church, the Army, and the Municipality."[25]

Many of the characters can be seen in terms of casebook studies. Another brother of the Bishop, Reginald, has recently been divorced by his wife, Leo. For financial reasons he was not in a position to marry until he was middle-aged. The marriage is childless, and this accords with the current theory that older men tended to be less fertile: it was cited as one of the reasons for the decline in the birthrate. The actual circumstances of his divorce point specifically to the need to reform the divorce law and also the conventions associated with it.

In polite society, in order to spare the woman's reputation, it was customary, whatever the circumstances, for the wife to divorce the husband. If the husband divorced the wife, the only grounds required for divorce were adultery, but when the wife divorced the husband, it was necessary to cite cruelty as well. It was common practice, when an "innocent" husband was being divorced, for evidence of adultery to be faked, in a hotel bedroom, for example, with a woman engaged for the purpose and a hotel employee as a witness. A (feigned) assault in front of a witness was also necessary. This is how the Reginald Bridgenorths obtained their divorce. Such proceedings could lead to the sullying of the husband's reputation, as it does in the play, until an explanation is given.

There is a third party in the Reginald Bridgenorths' marriage, a traditional Shaw character, the "Sunday husband." He shares the matrimonial fireside, but not the wife's bed. When it comes to divorce there may be a certain amount of obligation on this "Sunday husband" to marry the divorced wife. The character who plays this part, St. John Hotchkiss, has no wish to marry the lady; he seeks, and finds, another fireside.

Lesbia Grantham, sister of the Bishop's wife, does not actually declare that she is a Lesbian. She puts the case for the single mother in general terms and also for herself. Coition for the specific purpose of producing a child would be acceptable to Lesbia: indeed she longs for motherhood. But she has her own particular brand of fastidiousness. She could not tolerate a man about the house, especially if, like the General, her perpetual suitor, he is a smoker. She is utterly opposed to that clause in the marriage law that allowed the husband "conjugal rights" which, if practiced nowadays without the wife's consent, would be classed as conjugal rape.

Another batchelor in the cast, the Bishop's chaplain, Father Anthony Soames, takes a positive view of celibacy, believing it to be part of his religious calling to the priesthood.

Mrs. Collins is by no means there simply to tidy up the plot. Hitherto no one, not even the Bishop, has spoken about the spiritual side of marriage. Mrs. Collins does not exactly do this but she takes the play into metaphysical regions and talks about the release of the spirit that relationships between the sexes may bring.

It is possible that Lesbia and Mrs. Collins are complementary to one another, each having something to offer to the wandering male. In Lesbia's case it is fatherhood shorn of marital and parental responsibility. Mrs. Collins, in her Lilith-like speech, offers the sort of sexual passion that moves mountains. But the recipient has to be acceptable to Mrs. Collins's husband!

The play not only makes a case for altering the marriage laws; it also recognizes those who, by temperament or through circumstances, are unsuited to marriage.

There are several anti-climaxes in the conclusion. The bride and bridegroom slip quietly away and marry, having made a private contract about various items. Reginald and Leo Bridgenorth agree to set aside their divorce and renew their marriage. And Hotchkiss, for all his ardent pursuit of Mrs. George, decides that he cannot "break the covenant of bread and salt,"[26] and hence may safely be taken into the Collins's home.

Getting Married was first performed on May 12, 1908, at the Haymarket Theatre, London.

MISALLIANCE (1909)

Misalliance is in many ways a companion piece to *Getting Married*, but its cast is smaller, its focus more intense, and it is concerned primarily with premarital backgrounds, especially the relationships between two fathers and their respective offspring, who are engaged to marry each other when the play begins. And whereas *Getting Married* gave a rounded view of a society which constituted a community, *Misalliance* shows two distinct cultures, brought together for strategic reasons.

As in *Getting Married* there is a host figure, the father of the bride, John Tarleton, a self-made industrialist. In the opening scene the author's spotlight is turned on the social milieu of Tarleton, who has moved from poverty to riches in one generation, and has almost achieved the lifestyle of the upper classes as expressed, for example, in the long weekend. This is demonstrated by the glass pavilion at the Tarletons' house in Surrey in which the opening scene is set. It has all the appurtenances for leisure activities, and when the play begins the Tarleton son is taking his ease there. The adjoining hall "suggests that the proprietor's notion of domestic luxury is founded on the lounges of week-end hotels."[27] Evidently the householder has not yet had access to the socially correct model. Nevertheless his daughter, Hypatia, is engaged to be married to the son of an aristocrat.

Tarleton is a seeming philanthropist, and this, as Shaw readers and others know, is an important factor in upward mobility. Like Andrew Carnegie's, his philanthropy is directed towards public libraries. He is himself a well-read man, but Shaw at this stage in his life has no enthusiasm for book learning: he hands his accolade to the aristocratic Lord Summerhayes, to whom the Governorship of a Dominion has brought knowledge of the world, and wisdom. (Lord Summerhayes is the father of Bentley, Tarleton's prospective son-in-law.)

The prospects of the second generation of Tarletons depend on gender. The son will inherit his father's business and has a role in life. On his sister are heaped all the disadvantages that can accrue from being the daughter of a self-made man.

Hypatia was sent to a very expensive school, unfortunately beyond the means of most of the aristocracy, so she did not acquire the looked-for peer group. She is now required to live the life of a young lady as envisaged by her parents (but probably outdated), which, according to Hypatia, means listening to people talk. Very clear-sighted, she sees her ultimate destiny, if she fails to marry, as being a companion to her parents in their old age. She has neither financial nor social independence. The irony of her situation is well illustrated when Lord Summerhayes, unaware of her relationship with his son, proposes marriage to her, offering as an inducement the prospect of early widowhood. Hypatia has already made a realistic appraisal of her situation and decided that, while she is still young, she will accept the best available offer, which happens to be Bentley.

Tarleton's feelings towards his daughter are probably bordering on the incestuous, and they are certainly possessive. He opines in general terms that relationships between parent and child are seldom innocent. When, towards the end of the play, there comes a break between them, and Hypatia attacks her father for his sexual wanderings, he becomes enraged, calls her and her generation "hard, coarse, shallow, cruel, selfish, dirty-minded,"[28] and tells her to clear out of the house. The suggestion about incestuous feelings accords with the implications of the Preface.

The aristocrat, too, has his problems with parenting. His elder sons were sent away to school (anathema to the author); as a result they became strangers to him. His youngest son, Bentley, "the tenth possessor of a foolish face," who runs to brain rather than brawn, was too frail for this treatment and remained at home. His father found it easier to run an empire than to bring up a son. Lord Summerhayes is seen at his worst in his bullying relationship with Bentley. The young couple are both ill-served by their fathers, as indeed, according to the Preface, are most of the population.

However, help is at hand from an unexpected source when a young couple, a pilot and his passenger, crash into that symbol of fragility, the glass pavilion. New values come from these intruders. The passenger, Lina Szczepanowska, who is a circus acrobat, represents a new kind of freedom for society in general, and for women in particular: she is significantly free from the bondage of the family, and in this respect is a role model for Hypatia. The latest of Shaw's New Women, she makes her declaration: "I am an honest woman: I earn my living. I am a free woman: I live in my own house.... I am strong: I am skilful: I am brave:

I am independent: I am unbought."[29] She is also the antithesis of the Mother Woman (Ann) of *Man and Superman*; she comes as a breath of fresh air. It is not to be supposed that she will marry Bentley but she does some remedial work on him by challenging him to accompany her on her return flight away from what she dubs the "stuffy house" of the Tarletons.

The airplane's pilot, Percival, is a bridge between two cultures (he is an old school friend of Johnny Tarleton's) and also an exemplar of the benefits of a liberal home life, having been blessed with two surrogate fathers in addition to his own. This sort of arrangement was admired by Shaw as having much more to offer than conventional parenting: he spoke from his own experience.

The pilot has a liberating effect on Hypatia, who now seems to become possessed of the Life Force. Her natural tendency towards realism is reinforced by his influence. When they plan to marry, Percival requires a sufficient marriage settlement from the father of the bride-to-be so that his present lifestyle can be maintained after marriage. The lady says to her father: "Papa: buy the brute for me."[30]

Escape from the Tarleton household is insufficient; there has also to be a cleansing. This comes from a second intrusion, not accidental but purposeful; one which looks to the past rather than the future, and is motivated by revenge. The armed intruder, Gunner, belongs to the class from whose labours Tarleton derived his wealth, and from whose women he derived his sexual pleasure. Gunner has come with the intention of killing Tarleton but he is disarmed. Instead his retribution comes from his exposure of Tarleton's previous callous and anti-social behavior. Like Shirley of *Major Barbara*, Gunner is well educated in the literature of the Left, but he lacks any social skills. It is clear that the aspirational working classes that Shaw knew in his younger days are now seen by the author as on their way out.

And yet Gunner does have his revenge and serves a purpose. His intervention answers the question as to why (apart from subsidizing public libraries) Tarleton can find nothing constructive to do with his wealth and spends it on aping the lifestyle of the aristocracy: he lacks any generosity of spirit. Also Gunner, by his very poverty, adds emphasis to the way in which money infiltrates the action of the play. Mrs. Tarleton buys her way, up to a certain point, into high society. Tarleton does the same on a grander scale. He almost buys his daughter into the aristocracy (though it would have been by alliance with a rather diminished member of that breed); next he buys her the gallant pilot of her choice. Lord Summerhayes seeks to buy himself a young wife with the promise of the future independence of widowhood. Lina, the icon of a free way of life, is happy to sell her sexual services to a suitable bidder, seeing this as an ordinary commercial transaction. And Bentley does not object to being involved in the traditional exchange of blue blood for new money, though this does not take place. Yet it is he who quotes Tarleton's opinion that "a marriage between a member of the great and good middle class with one of the vicious and corrupt aristocracy would be a misalliance."[31]

One of the questions posed by the play is Where do the boundaries of corruption lie?

Misalliance was first performed on February 23, 1910, at the Duke of York's Theatre, London. The action of the play takes place on May 31, 1909.

12

The Playwright
with the Fabian Touch:
Fanny's First Play

On March 3, 1911, Shaw decided that the time had come for him not to seek re-election to the Executive of the Fabian Society. He wrote to the Society's Secretary: "I think the moment has arrived for the old gang to make room for younger men."[1] He and three other members stood down, and *Fanny's First Play* may be seen as a recognition of the emergence of a new generation of Fabians.

In his most recent plays Shaw had been assessing and presenting recent changes in society, offering, as it were, evidence of Ibsen's "law of change." In *Fanny's First Play* he goes one step further, looking at these changes through the (imagined) eyes of a younger generation.

He chooses for the fictional author of the play a girl named Fanny who has studied at Cambridge University and was a member of the Cambridge Fabian Society. Shaw had been no lover of the older universities, seeing them as bastions of class privilege. But Cambridge had a special recent significance for him. In his Fabian Memorial Lecture (1951), Hugh Dalton records that from 1906 to 1910, when he himself was at Cambridge, the Fabian leadership—he mentions Shaw and the Webbs—was very influential with the undergraduate Left. "At that time to be a Fabian was as far Left as you could go at Cambridge.... I was much attracted by Shaw when he came to Cambridge."[2]

Here we meet Fanny, the aspiring young Fabian playwright, who gives herself a spokeswoman (Margaret) in her play, produces it anonymously in her wealthy father's home, and joins in the induction which precedes the play and the epilogue in which the critics have their say.

Fanny is an illustration of Shaw's long-held tenet that the value of a university education lies less in book learning than in the liberation of spirit which living in a community of one's peers can bring. This point is doubly underlined. First, Cambridge, especially in the political sense, is seen as having moved with the times. Second, had Fanny not left home she would have remained within the culture of the eighteenth century, to which her father, the Count, was addicted. A Cambridge man himself, he imagined that the climate would not have changed since his day, and hence had been happy for his daughter to study there. Fanny's own experience of life accords with her play's main thesis, that family life is stultifying. Young people need a wider world in which to grow to maturity.

Fanny's First Play is a continuation of Shaw's concentration on middle-class society. Here, using Fanny as his observer, he focuses on the prosperous suburbia that has developed around the outskirts of London. This is a one-class society, where respectability is the passport to social acceptance. The characters presented are rather lower class than, say, the Tarletons of *Misalliance*, and neighbors live more closely together; respectability is more important and more narrowly defined.

In classic *Romeo and Juliet* fashion the play centers around two households whose interlocking relationships are a microcosm of suburban society. The husbands are partners in the same retail business, and the son and daughter of the respective households are engaged to one another. It follows that any loss of respectability in either family will diminish the social standing of both. When the children of the two families each receive jail sentences for separate offences it is as if the whole world of the parents had fallen apart: each pair tries to keep their secret from the other.

These incidents give the author the opportunity to raise two topical issues, the ill-treatment of suffragettes in prison, and police brutality towards women. Margaret Knox is arrested merely for being present at a dance when rowdyism broke out. She gives the brutal policeman who arrests her as good as she gets, and finds the whole incident, including her time in jail, a liberating experience. She declares herself "a heroine of reality"[3] and announces the coming of her adulthood: "I know now that I am stronger than you and papa ... I've found strength. For good or evil I am set free; and none of the things that used to hold me can hold me now."[4]

One of the ways in which Margaret shows this new strength and understanding is by her acknowledgement of Dora, a prostitute or near-prostitute, who was her fiancé's companion on his night out. Dora also fell foul of a policeman and was Margaret's companion in jail. The passion that accrues around respectability, and its fundamental importance to their way of life, is spoken of by Margaret's father. He asks his wife, "Is she going to ruin us? To let everybody know of her disgrace and shame?

To tear me down from the position Ive made for myself and you by forty years hard struggling?" He entreats Margaret: "Theres only one thing I care about in the world: to keep this dark. I'm your father. I ask you here on my knees—in the dust, so to speak—not to let it out." Margaret, in her new-found strength, is not kind-hearted. "I'll tell everybody,"[5] she replies.

It is not just this passion for respectability that Fanny indicts. She also has something to say about over-protectiveness, but this is presented ironically rather than dramatically. The neighbor, Gilbey, says proudly of his wimpish son, Bobby, who bears a similarity to Bentley of *Misalliance*, but without the blue blood: "Ive done my duty as a father, Ive kept him sheltered."[6]

Though the play is patently an attack on "respectability" Fanny is fair-minded beyond her years when she has Margaret's mother make a statement as to why the derided respectability is so important; people must have shared customs and habits if they are to live together in social groups.

The play has several ironies, and some surprises that belong to melodrama. The French naval lieutenant, whom Margaret meets on her famous night out, praises the freedom accorded to English daughters. He also lets us know of the far worse despotism that the French practice on their sons: "In France we are not men: we are only sons—grown-up children."[7]

The Gilbeys' footman turns out to be the brother of a duke and so provides the opportunity for an outbreak of suburban snobbery: all due deference is now accorded to the footman. After the fashion of melodrama, he is to provide a husband for Margaret, while the sheltered Bobby, it appears, is to marry the near-prostitute, Dora.

But the complete turning of the tables comes when, after the news of the prison sentences and the reasons for them gets around, the young people, far from being vilified, are lionized, and Gilbey begins to boast about what a dog his son is. Respectability has changed its face, social mores have altered, the "law of change" has been recognized. And a new generation of Fabians is on hand to note and record these changes.

In the Epilogue the group of eminent theatre critics, invited by Fanny's father, and taken from real life, discuss the play and speculate as to who is the author. Fanny takes up a suggestion that the play might be by Shaw: "Oh, of course it would be a little like Bernard Shaw. The Fabian touch, you know."[8] That touch was the touch of reality.

Fanny's First Play was first performed at the Little Theatre, London on April 19, 1911.

13

The Drama in Brief

Shaw's first one-act play, *The Man of Destiny*, was by no means an immediate success and it brought the author several disappointments. The dialogue of the play is chiefly between Napoleon and the Strange Lady. Shaw had based the character of Napoleon on Richard Mansfield and had intended Ellen Terry to play the Strange Lady. Mansfield not only rejected the part, but did so in a way that caused Shaw to reply: "I was much hurt by your contemptuous refusal of "A Man of Destiny.""[1] Nor did Ellen Terry appear in the play, in spite of persuasive letters from Shaw telling her about "a beautiful little one act play."[2] *The Man of Destiny* was written in 1895; its first performance was at the Grand Theatre, Croydon on July 1, 1897. Hesketh Pearson described this first performance as "appalling, the applause at the end was like a groan."[3]

Undaunted by this, Shaw continued to write brief plays, ranging from sketches to one-act plays of substance. The sketches were often farcical: typically they presented some sort of situation between marriage partners and, possibly, a third party. A number of the sketches were intended for some particular occasion, or to support a good cause with which Shaw had an association. But however brief the playlet, and however farcical the content, somewhere in the text there would be a significant message.

The one-act plays are of a different and more serious matter.

THE MAN OF DESTINY: A FICTITIOUS PARAGRAPH OF HISTORY (1895)

This play was intended as a curtain-raiser. In it, the author writes about the nature of a man who was to have an imperial destiny rather than about the nature of imperialism. The play postulates that Napoleon is a man of destiny because he is possessed by the will.

Napoleon sees the will as a devouring devil, telling the innkeeper with whom he is lodged: "You have no devouring devil inside you who must be fed with action and victory: ... who is at once your slave and your tyrant, your genius and your doom: ... who shews you all the kingdoms of the earth and offers to make you their master on condition that you become their servant!"[4]

The plot is fragile and serves chiefly to show the reaction of others to the man of destiny: servility from the innkeeper; gross flattery, and some trickery, from the Strange Lady; and an oblique ackowledgement from his lieutenant that the present times require a leader: "The fact is, the Revolution was all very well for civilians; but it wont work in the army."[5]

Evidently Napoleon is the leader that the times require.

HOW HE LIED TO HER HUSBAND (1904)

This is the first of the many playlets in which Shaw addresses the subject of matrimonial relationships. Here the husband discovers that the wife has a lover—or perhaps he is merely an admirer?

The author presents a picture of conspicuous consumption as it existed in a fashionable part of London. This is described as follows: "The room is furnished in the most approved South Kensington fashion; that is, it is as like a shop window as possible, and is intended to demonstrate the social position and spending powers of its owners."[6]

Customarily the husband uses the wife, as well as the domestic scene, as a means of displaying wealth. Here the lady ("She") is wearing many diamonds. Convention also requires that the husband project a sexually superior image: the wife must have the appearance of beauty and be sexually desirable, arousing the envy of other men. An open avowal of attraction (provided that it is kept within limits) does not necessarily displease the husband. In the case of "She," the author is sufficiently ungallant as to draw attention to the fact that, stripped of her finery, "She" is very ordinary; and "hopelessly inferior in physical and spiritual distinction to the beautiful youth [known as 'He']."[7] "He" has mistaken the trappings for the reality.

And so has "Her Husband," who now takes his place on the stage with his wife and her admirer. He describes his wife (to no less a person than "He") in the following terms: "She's the smartest woman in the smartest set in South Kensington, and the handsomest, and the cleverest, and the most fetching to experienced men who know a good thing when they see it, whatever she may be to conceited penny-a-lining puppies who think nothing good enough for them."[8]

This outburst comes when "He" denies that he has addressed a book of poems, of which he is the author, to "She." (He makes this denial at her urgent request.)

The two men come to blows, but peace is restored when "He" declares his adoration of "She." Her husband, bent on retaining his position as an ultramasculine man, and seeking a further opportunity for conspicuous display, asks the poet if he may arrange to have the poems printed. The finest paper and the most sumptuous binding will be used. "I should like to shew them about a bit."[9]

The poet also has his self-image, that of the romantic lover. When left alone he nestles into the loved one's shawl and "presses his hands to his eyes to shut out reality and dream a little."[10]

It is the playwright's task to reveal reality.

The playlet was first performed at the Berkeley Lyceum, New York on September 26, 1904. It was written as a curtain-raiser for *The Man of Destiny*. The first London performance was at the Court Theatre on February 28, 1905.

PASSION, POISON, AND PETRIFICATION OR THE *FATAL GAZOGENE*: A BRIEF TRAGEDY FOR BARNS AND BOOTHS (1905)

The eternal triangle has another ironic working out in an entirely ludicrous melodrama in the barnstorming tradition. The husband administers poison to the lover, but has regrets when he learns of the possible consequences of what he has done. The wife avers that, when her lover is gone, she will cease to perform all wifely duties of the housekeeping kind. Instead she will bestow on her husband that romantic love which previously she had accorded to her lover who now lies dying. A desperate rescue attempt proves unavailing, and the lover dies. A doctor has been called and there is some irony at his expense, foreshadowing *The Doctor's Dilemma*. He exclaims: "Do you mean to say that an unqualified person! a layman! has dared to administer poison in my district?"[11]

As in the previous play there is an indication of the couple's social rating in the description of the set: "The general impression is one of brightness, beauty, and social ambition, damped by somewhat inadequate means."[12]

The playlet was performed several times in a booth in Regent's Park for the benefit of the Actors' Orphanage.

THE SHEWING-UP OF BLANCO POSNET: A SERMON IN CRUDE MELODRAMA (1909)

Shortly before this play was written there had been, as Shaw recounts in the Preface, a Select Committee of both Houses of Parliament set up to inquire into the workings of the censorship of stage plays.[13] Shaw, whose play, *Mrs Warren's Profession* was still under the Censor's ban, was among the many distinguished authors who gave evidence to this Committee: the list included William Archer (translator of Ibsen), Galsworthy, Professor Gilbert Murray (on whom Cusins of *Major Barbara* is based), Pinero, J. M. Barrie, and G. K. Chesterton. *Blanco Posnet* was to become a weapon in the battle against the way in which censorship operated at that time, and one can imagine that Shaw chose the subtitle with due deliberation.

Ostensibly the play was written to be performed at His Majesty's Theatre to benefit a children's charity, but, not unexpectedly, it was banned as blasphemous. The charge of blasphemy rested on a carefully crafted piece of anthropomorphism. The play's cowboy characters, who live in the Wild West of America, have no abstract conception of a creator God or Life Force. They think in terms of a personalized God with human attributes. Hence when Blanco Posnet experiences a conversion comparable with that of St. Paul on the road to Damascus, or with John Wesley's when he "felt his heart strangely warmed," he talks about God in homely terms which it would be possible for an over-zealous censor to construe as derogatory and therefore blasphemous. Posnet says: "He's a sly one. He's a mean one. He lies low for you.... And then, when you least expect it, He's got you."[14] But the story of Blanco Posnet is an extremely moral one: he risks being hanged on a charge of horse stealing in order to serve God's purpose and rescue a sick baby. His credo after conversion is simple and sincere, and accords with the doctrine of creative evolution: "You bet He didnt make us for nothing; and He wouldnt have made us at all if He could have done His work without us. By Gum, that must be what we're for! ... He made me because He had a job for me. He let me run loose til the job was ready; and then I had to come along and do it, hanging or no hanging."[15]

The play, having been duly censored, was produced at the Abbey Theatre, Dublin, where the English Censor's writ did not run: the date was August 25, 1909. The day after the first performance *The Times* reported: "Everybody today is enjoying the story of Mr. Shaw's cleverness and the Censor's folly."[16]

But there was shortly to be another engagement with the Censor.

THE GLIMPSE OF REALITY: A TRAGEDIETTA (1909–10)

When Shaw wrote this play he succeeded in capturing something of the atmosphere of fifteenth-century Italy, in which the play is set. At the same time he also imposes on the ethos of the period—which he frequently caricatures—the sort of thinking which is relevant to the present.

Primarily the playlet is about self-knowledge. The "glimpse of reality" comes when Ferruccio, the Italian aristocrat, under threat of death, does some inner probing and calls himself "a man who has found his soul."[17] His self-portrait is devastating: "Outside the life I lead all to myself—the life of thought and poetry—I know only two pleasures: cruelty and lust."[18]

A comment by Giulia and an exchange between Count Ferruccio and Sandro each have their political resonances:

> GIULIA: The poor often die that the rich may live.[19]
> FERRUCCIO [to Sandro]: Rascal: Have you then no soul?
> SANDRO: I am a poor man, Excellency: I cannot afford
>   these luxuries of the rich.[20]

Shaw began writing this playlet on March 8, 1909; it was completed on August 30, 1910. The text was mislaid for some time: the first professional performance was at the Arts Theatre Club, London, on November 20, 1927.

PRESS CUTTINGS (1909)

Soon after finishing *Blanco Posnet* Shaw wrote *Press Cuttings*. It too was a challenge to the Censor, so it was first performed at a "Private Reception" at the Royal Court Theatre. The date was July 9, 1909. Shaw described the play as "A topical sketch compiled from the editorial and correspondence columns of the daily papers during the women's war in 1909."[21]

Included among the play's characters were two caricatures of public figures who were given barely disguised names: Lord Mitchener (Lord Kitchener of military fame) and Prime Minister Balsquith, whose name was an obvious amalgam of Baldwin and Asquith. At first the play was refused a license on general grounds, but later the sole condition for a license was that the two leading characters be renamed. On the occasion of this censorship Shaw obtained publicity by drawing attention to the situation in *The Times*, the *Observer*, and several other newspapers.

The play, which is structured as a farce, is an excellent example of Shaw's ability to combine the farcical with the serious. In this case the farce relates chiefly to the women's suffrage movement and the seriousness to the portentous undertones of war, undertones which the German press was not slow to pick up. The prognostication is, in a sense, justified by fixing the date of the action as "three years later" when, in actuality, the first World War was only two short years away. The contest between the Government of the day and the women's suffrage movement is also depicted in war-like terms: there is a reference to "a declaration of martial law and a two-mile exclusion zone round Westminster." However, it is not difficult to keep in mind that all this takes place on the morning of April Fool's Day (1 April).

The play's social and political commentary is spoken chiefly by Mitchener and Balsquith. Since they are farcical characters, most of what they have to say has ironic overtones, but the impact is not necessarily lessened because of that. Mitchener speaks of the way the Government operates: "The one condition on which we can consent to grant anything in this country is that nobody shall presume to ask for it."[22] He displays an ability to speak in platitudinous epigrams (today's sound bites) when he says, "The real government of this country is and always must be the government of the masses by the classes."[23] He also has an awareness of the terrible sea battle that is to come, though he sees it in chauvinistic terms. In a Britannia-rules-the-waves announcement that reminds one of Lord Summerhayes of *Misalliance*, he pontificates: "The Germans have never recognized, and until they get a stern lesson they never will recognize, the plain fact that the interests of the British Empire are paramount, and that the command of the sea belongs by nature to England."[24]

There is an echo of *Major Barbara* and the suborning influence of capital when Balsquith remonstrates with Mitchener, who is proposing to throw a young soldier out of the army: "Steady, steady. His father has subscribed a million to the party funds. We owe him a peerage."[25]

The author takes the opportunity to draw attention to a matter which greatly concerned him: the loss of citizen's rights which the soldier suffered in peace and in war. It is the private soldier who speaks of this: "It's not fightin I object too: it's soljerin … it's bein made a bloomin sheep of."[26]

Even on April Fool's Day all is not tomfoolery.

THE FASCINATING FOUNDLING:
A DISGRACE TO THE AUTHOR (1909)

The joys of marriage without the encumberance of in-law relations are extolled in this brief farcical playlet. We meet Brabazon, who was made a ward-of-court in his infancy, and now looks to the Lord Chancellor to find him a wife who is also unemcumbered with relations and who will be a mother figure to him. While he is in the Lord Chancellor's office he meets Anastasia. He decides to accept her instant proposal of marriage when he learns that she too is a foundling. She is also a suffragette who has spent some time in prison.

The playlet becomes serious for a moment when she gives a message of rebuke to the Lord Chancellor: "For you, a man, politics meant the House of Lords. For me, a woman, politics meant Holloway Gaol and the hunger strike."[27]

The Fascinating Foundling was written for Elizabeth Asquith, daughter of the Prime Minister, to be performed at a charity benefit.

THE DARK LADY OF THE SONNETS (1910)

"The Quintessence of Ibsenism" contains a chapter entitled "Needed: An Ibsen Theatre." In *The Dark Lady of the Sonnets* Shaw argues the case for a national theatre (as a memorial to Shakespeare), stating plainly in the Preface: "A National Theatre is worth having for the sake of the National Soul."[28] This, it will be recalled, accords with the vision, as presented in *Fabian Essays in Socialism*, of a future socialist State where the arts were available to all. In the play, Shakespeare is the author's spokesperson; he presents the case to Queen Elizabeth I.

Shakespeare's argument has two aspects. First he refers to the influence of the theatre on human thinking and behavior: "This writing of plays is a great matter, forming as it does the minds and affections of men in such sort that whatsoever they see done in show on the stage, they will presently be doing in earnest in the world, which is but a larger stage."[29]

The second part of his argument relates to the failure of the commercial theatre to provide his greatest plays with sufficient public viewing.

Reminding the Queen—as Shaw was wont to remind his readers— of the days when the Church used the drama as a means for instructing the people, Shakespeare calls for the endowment of a theatre from public funds for the performance of his plays so that the worst of them will not drive out the better.

The Queen is disposed to be cynical about the willingness of her subjects to fund a national theatre. In her cynicism she throws out a challenge to future generations, a challenge aimed particularly at the playlet's first audience. Elizabeth says: "Of this I am certain (for I know my countrymen) that until every other country in the Christian world … have its playhouse at the public charge, England will never adventure." More hopefully she adds: "But this I will say, that if I could speak across the ages to our descendants, I should heartily recommend them to fulfil your wish."[30]

The play was first presented at His Majesty's Theatre, London, on November 24, 1910. This occasion was one of two charity matinées intended to raise funds for the projected Shakespeare Memorial National Theatre.

14

A Time of Definition

When, in 1911, Shaw stood down from the Executive of the Fabian Society, saying it was time to make room for younger men, he told only part of the story. Many years later, in an authoritative article about Fabianism, he wrote in general terms about the commitments and the fame that the talents of the Fabian leaders had brought them over the years and how these had competed with the Society for their time and energy. Shaw was one of those leaders for whom a wider vista had opened—that of the theatre. Fruitful though his years as a political activist and a political economist had been, the theatre offered him a wider audience, and a wider sphere of influence, than did the lecture hall, the debating chamber, and the rostrum in the park. He was, indeed, a playwright of international repute.

Also, since he had adopted Ibsen's practice of having his plays published, there was the matter of his readership. Those who would not be inclined to sit by the fire reading a Fabian essay might well enjoy reading a Shaw play. There would also be other readers who did not have access to the theatre who saw the play in their imagination. Indeed, when Shaw's plays were published the author always had the reader especially in mind.

To the man-with-the-message, the artist-philosopher, as Shaw declared himself to be, the drama was the ideal medium, appealing to the senses of sight and sound, multi-voiced, capable of moving through the centuries of the past, the present, and the future and offering in the theatre an expression of the life of the community. All this is common knowledge: to Shaw as an artist-philosopher and a propagandist it was very significant knowledge.

In 1911 when he made his decision to give priority to the theatre, it was truly a time of definition.

The journeying along the way had not been easy. There had been a number of critics, mostly professional; there had been difficulties over censorship both in England and America; and in the early days there had been financial difficulties about producing some of his plays. These had now been overcome and Shaw wore the mantle of success.

In his next phase Shaw was to run into difficulties of a different sort, and there was to be a different kind of criticism at a time when Shaw forsook the theatre for a while.

PART II

THE HORIZONS OF WAR:
A EUROPEAN PLAYWRIGHT
(1912–1919)

15

The Politics
of War and of Peace

For some time after Shaw left the Fabian Executive, the upward spiral of his fame as a dramatist continued, reaching a high point with his play *Pygmalion*, which was first performed in England on April 11, 1914. But later in the year, when Britain declared war on Germany, Shaw suddenly and dramatically changed course. He dedicated himself to the politics of war and peace for the duration; as far as drama was concerned, he completed only one full-length play and a few playlets. His immediate reaction was to retire to the Hydro Hotel in Torquay and write his highly controversial "Common Sense About the War." It was published as a supplement to a recently established periodical, *The New Statesman*, on November 14, 1914.

This was not, of course, the first time that Shaw had spoken out about war. But in the case of the South African War the occasion was of a lesser magnitude and the circumstances were very different. When Shaw wrote "Fabianism and the Empire" he wrote as the spokesman of a respected Society, whose members were persuaded to accept the views he presented because of his clarity of thought and his articulative skills. Now he wrote as a distinguished and famous author who spoke for himself alone—and who was about to become notorious.

Although Shaw acted with dramatic suddenness, he was one of the few people whom the war had not taken by surprise. Indeed he had written two previous articles on the subject. One of these, "Armaments and Conscription: A Triple Alliance Against War," had been published in the *Daily Chronicle* on March 18, 1913; the second bore a title to which the onset of war was to give an ironic twist, "The Peace of Europe and How to Attain It." This was published by the *Daily News* on January 1, 1914. Also it will be recalled that his farcical playlet *Press Cuttings* (1909) contained overtones of war—or so the German press thought.

91

Nevertheless, in spite of his early warnings, Shaw had feelings of guilt that he had not addressed himself sufficiently to the rumblings of war and the politics of Europe. He saw this guilt as belonging not only to himself but to the corporate body of the Fabian Society. He wrote about it in the introductory chapter of his anthology, *What I Really Wrote About the War*: "I ... had been too preoccupied with my colleagues of the Fabian Society in working out the practicalities of English Socialism, and establishing a parliamentary Labor Party, to busy myself with foreign policy."[1]

At the beginning of the war Shaw was very much a loner. But— particularly because there was so much rejection of his early wartime writing—it should be emphasized that he had a great deal of constructive thinking to offer with regard to the seeking of a lasting peace. His essays and articles contain basic reasoning similar to that of "Fabianism and the Empire." The earlier work argued that the South African War, and imperialism in general, was undertaken from unworthy motives; nevertheless, ultimately it might lead to a federation of (socialist) States. Similarly the World War which began in 1914, though evil in itself, could and should have an outcome that brought a concept of internationalism and lasting peace and unity to the nations.

This being the case, why did the first of Shaw's wartime political writings, "Common Sense about the War," cause mayhem? The pamphlet reads as though it were written in the white heat of passion, the sort of passion that the "Preface to Politicians" of *John Bull's Other Island* contains. Certainly Shaw's famous and brilliant tact in language either deserted him or was deliberately set aside. And whatever the truth of his arguments might be, in many instances it was hardly diplomatic to raise them at the onset of war.

When it was published, "Common Sense" aroused a furore particularly among the literary establishment. Some booksellers removed Shaw's works from their shelves. Some newspapers advised their readers to boycott his plays.

Certain members of the Dramatists' Club ostracized Shaw and at a meeting on October 27, 1915, the Secretary was instructed to write and suggest to him "that he should absent himself for the present."[2]

It is possible, however, that the opprobrium did not come from the generality of people, for Shaw stated that of the many letters he received after "Common Sense" was published only about six per cent were hostile, "mostly unprintable."[3] He told his well-wishers: "Many branches of the Independent Labor Party and ... Socialist organizations have passed resolutions which have been of the timeliest service to me publicly, and which have given me sincere personal gratification."[4]

But the ultimate accolade came in 1917 when the British Commander-in-Chief, Sir Douglas Haig, invited Shaw to visit the Flanders war
zone and give an account of his visit. He appears to have been treated as
an honored guest.

An earlier mention was made of the *New Statesman*: it had a convoluted significance in Shaw's life at about this time. It was the brain-
child of Beatrice Webb, who saw a need for a periodical which would be
an organ of the Left for politics and the arts. The Webbs and Shaw
founded the paper, and Shaw was a major shareholder.

16

A New Arena:
What I Really Wrote About the War

This anthology of Shaw's writings contains a selection of essays and articles written before, during, and immediately after the First World War, together with later comments written at the time of publication in 1930. A reprint of Fabian Tract No. 226 is also included: this is reviewed in a later chapter.

Shaw describes this collection as "[A] record of what I did with my pen in the Great War," about which no attempt has been made "to trim it into an academic history."[1]

The two articles written before the war, "Armaments and Conscription" and "The Peace of Europe and How to Obtain it" are evidence that Shaw perceived the possibility of war and had views as to how it could be avoided. They both contain a similar main precept, namely, that Britain should tell Germany and France that if either attacked the other Britain would join forces with the aggressor. The two articles served as a prelude to the controversial "Common Sense About the War." "Common Sense" is the longest piece in the book and certainly the most significant, the most controversial, and the most interesting. When it was first published it "provoked a flood of letters, almost all of them long and angry."[2]

In part it seems to have been written in the heat of moral passion, using language and metaphor designed to provoke indignation against the author. In the main it takes as its thesis a proposition that the twin causes of war are capitalism and militarism: socialism on a global scale could offer a world at peace. What is remarkable is that at the very beginning of the war Shaw is far-sighted, looking towards the ways and means by which a lasting, equitable peace might be secured. But amid all the sweet reasonableness with which in the later stages Shaw writes—in marked contrast to the beginning—two-edged statements and witty shafts are directed against individual people, institutions, and cultures, which were bound to be unacceptable to some readers.

Shaw gives some immediate reasons for the outbreak of war but asserts as a general principle that capitalism constantly seeks new undeveloped territory because, since labour is cheaper there, a greater rate of interest may be had. All capitalists have similar objectives and it is inevitable that eventually they will clash in their search for new territory.

It is when Shaw describes and compares capitalists in England and Germany that he becomes, it would seem, deliberately offensive. He starts by saying that the capitalists in both countries belong to a privileged class. He chooses the word "Junker" (a member of Prussia's nobility) to identify this class in both countries. Shaw names those whom he sees as English "Junkers," including Sir Edward Grey, Foreign Secretary from 1905 to 1916. We are told: "It is very difficult for anyone who is not either a Junker or a successful barrister to get into an English Cabinet, no matter which party is in power."[3]

A further classification is made, that of Militarists, who, like the Junkers, exist in both countries. They too belong to the privileged: they also belong to a culture that glorifies and romanticizes war. It is argued that since the motivation towards war belongs to these two classes, those on the outside are being used as "tools": not an argument likely to appeal to the establishment!

Some of the contentions that Shaw makes, though sustainable, could not have improved the general morale in the early days of war. For example, in condemning the tradition of secret diplomacy he opined that had Germany known, even at the eleventh hour, of Britain's intention to declare war if German troops were to enter Belgium, no such entry would have taken place. In an earlier famous passage he looks at the possibility of revolution among those that he had described as "tools":

> No doubt the heroic remedy for this tragic misunderstanding [caused by secret diplomacy] is that both armies should shoot their officers and go home to gather in their harvests in the villages and make a revolution in the towns; and though this is not at present a practicable solution, it must be frankly mentioned, because it or something like it is always a possibility in a defeated conscript army....[4]

The war is seen as an opportunity to further the cause of socialism. The Labour Party should have no hesitation in using the opportunities that the war affords. Specifically Shaw looks at the present contest as having the potential for a war of class against class rather than nation against nation. "In truth, the importance of the war to the immense majority of Englishmen, Frenchmen, and Germans lies in the possibility that when Junkers fall out common men may come by their own."[5]

Shaw is not always so supportive of the common man!

A greater part of the work is devoted to the question of how peace is to be secured and how it should be structured in order that it might be constructive and lasting. It is amazing that with the war scarcely begun the author can, in due course, set aside the passion that it aroused and write so constructively about the hoped-for peace. Essentials of which he wrote include the redrawing of the map of Europe, the redrafting of political constitutions in order to avoid future wars, and the need for a League of Peace which must be suitably armed so that it has the capability of maintaining peace.

Shaw writes a great deal about the common man in "Common Sense." Later when he visited the Western Front he showed great empathy with the soldiers. He writes (in an ill-titled article, "Joy Riding at the Front"), "Men torn from civil life of the most prosperous and comfortable kind, and engaged in the most perilous service ... say without affectation that they have never been so happy. They seek terrors and hardships more determinedly than warm clothes, comfortable firesides, and security."[6]

Shaw acknowledges the strange fascination that terror and suffering may sometimes have: he adduces that it is the comradeship that exists in wartime, together with the absence of those social evils that belong to peace, which bring this happiness. He becomes the practical socialist when he argues for "the purification of peace" in civilian life.

In another article, "Cataclysm," about the Russian Revolution and the demise of the Tsarist Russian Empire, Shaw writes some powerful words:

> Suddenly came the cataclysm. It was the crash of an epoch. The mountainous dyke within which western Capitalism had been working for centuries cracked and left a gap the whole width of Europe from the Baltic to the Black Sea.... And it began as an incident of the war.[7]

The saddest of Shaw's writings in *What I Really Wrote* relate to the peace rather than the war. Disturbed by the greed and rancour of the victorious nations which worked against Shaw's vision of a federation of States, he centered his hopes on President Wilson of the United States of America: "If he could secure federal government for Germany, Austria, Russia, Slavia, and the British Islands, it would be established as the rule for Europe instead of, as it was before the war, the exception; and the United States would immediately succeed to the political seniority of the world."[8] Shaw returns to his philosophy of creative evolution: "There is only one force that can beat both [greed and rancour]; and that force is the entirely mystic force of evolution applied through the sort of living engine we call the man of principle."[9] "Europe" says Shaw "is proclaiming President Wilson as that man."[10]

However, he also expresses forebodings as to whether President Wilson can hold out to the end. Unfortunately these forebodings were to prove true.

These views are expressed in the pamphlet, "Peace Conference Hints: Enter History: Exit Romance" which was published in 1919.

Despair and disillusionment continued to haunt Shaw. He described the Treaty of Versailles as "perhaps the greatest disaster of the war for all the belligerents, and indeed for civilization in general, [it] left nothing to be done in foreign affairs but face the question of the next war pending the consolidation of the League of Nations."[11]

In a cynical article with the eyecatching title "The Coming War with America," Shaw considers the dependency of the British Empire on sea power. He argues that there can be no security for Britain until "the American fleet has followed the way of the German fleet to the bottom of the sea."[12] The French fleet is likewise a threat and should receive the same treatment as the American fleet; and so forth and so on.

All this is blamed on Lloyd George (one of the main figures at the Peace Conference) whose demand, says Shaw, was for "security, security, security." This article was published in the *Daily News* on June 23, 1921.

Later Shaw takes a look at the economics of the postwar world and again all is gloom. "Here we are, more than five years after the order to cease firing, and no peace yet, only ruin and unemployment and starvation and bankruptcy...."[13]

In a detailed analysis of why the economy was in such a parlous state "The Practical Man of Business" (the title of the article) is the author's chief target. Among other things, according to Shaw, he sold off the nation's assets for a mere pittance and by demanding excessive and increasing hours from the workforce he had added vastly to the hundreds of unemployed whom he had gagged by the unemployment dole.

Shaw's final dictum is: "What a nation!"[14]

And this is Shaw's conclusion. When one thinks of the effort, the dedication, and the commitment that was involved, and when one realizes that the totality of his work seemed to fall on deaf ears, one shares Shaw's sadness: "They pretended not to hear me,"[15] he said.

But Shaw had other listeners who were to hear his voice as a dramatist at other times and in other places.

Two Plays Written
Before the First World War:
Androcles and the Lion
and *Pygmalion*

The last two plays Shaw wrote before the war are as different as chalk from cheese. *Androcles and the Lion* poses a question to which the war brought new poignancy: when will the world be ready to accept the teachings of Christ? *Pygmalion*, on the other hand, contains a last glorious expression of the exuberance and vitality of Cockney and middle-class London as it existed before the war, an exuberance which the world was waiting to share in the play, in the film that followed the play, and finally, in the musical comedy *My Fair Lady*, which was based on the play.

ANDROCLES AND THE LION:
A FABLE PLAY (1912)

Androcles seems to be a play that has different facets. Set in ancient Rome, it has links with the fable which tells how Androcles, a runaway slave, extracted a thorn from the paw of a lion. When subsequently the slave encountered the same lion in the arena of the Roman Colosseum, the lion showed its gratitude and refrained from eating him. It appears that Shaw's work was intended, in the beginning, largely as a children's play, for Shaw told Hesketh Pearson that he wrote it "partly to show Barrie [author of *Peter Pan*] how a play for children should be handled."[1] It was presumably for the benefit of any children in the audience that Shaw has the lion and Androcles waltz together.

As the play proceeds it grows beyond its beginnings. Its crux is contained in a statement by Ferrovius who sets aside Christian martyrdom and accepts honorable employment with the Roman Emperor:

> In my youth I worshipped Mars, the God of War. I turned from him to serve the Christian god; but today the Christian god forsook me; and Mars overcame me and took back his own. The Christian god is not yet. He will come when Mars and I are dust; but meanwhile I must serve the gods that are, not the God that will be.[2]

Images of Christ seem to be central to Shaw's thinking during the period of the war and in the early years of peace. In his addendum to the play Shaw writes, "The most striking aspect of the play at this moment is the terrible topicality given it by the war. We were at peace when I pointed out, by the mouth of Ferrovius, the path of an honest man who finds out, when the trumpet sounds, that he cannot follow Jesus."[3] He made a similar point in a letter published in the *New Statesman* in December 1914: "If the church would close its doors and say: 'Ye shall not enter into God's house until your hands are cleansed from your brothers' blood' the working classes would think a good deal better of it.[4]

But the preface to *Androcles*, written much later than the play, in December 1915, has a more positive message to convey. It is concentrated entirely on the teachings of Christ and how they may be applied to the society of the present age. (Shaw does not specifically say so but he is obviously looking forward to a world at peace.)

First the author is at pains to separate the teachings and sayings of Christ from those of his disciples. Setting the current war aside, he looks at Christ's dicta in terms of the politics of the day and opines that it is the community rather than the individual that has the potential to put into practice the teachings of Christ. He writes that in earlier times, "it was believed that you could not make men good by Act of Parliament, we now know that you cannot make them good in any other way. ... The rich man must sell up not only himself but his whole class; and that can be done only through the Chancellor of the Exchequer."[5]

He goes on to itemize how the Christianization of the community is to be achieved: municipal organization of the food supply, universal suffrage, equality of income, and "all sorts of modern political measures" are included in the program.[6]

We have heard in the play Shaw tuning in to the likelihood of war. We have read in "Common Sense" of Shaw's powerful response to the actuality of war. Here in the Preface, when the war is well under way, Shaw talks about how it is required of man as a corporate being, rather than as an individual, to put into practice the teachings of Christ: and how unless empires share a common bond, conglomerate government will remain impossible.

The Preface is twice as long as the play and is an important part of the sequence of Shaw's thinking during the war years: war was a rejection of Christ; postwar reconstruction should be based on an acceptance of the teachings of Christ, secularized and politicized.

Shaw's second phase of disillusion, which came, not from the war, but from a disastrous peace, was still a long way off.

PYGMALION: A ROMANCE IN FIVE ACTS (1912)

Playwright, public speaker, debater, journalist, and essayist: who better than Shaw to understand the significance and the subtleties of language and of speech? He was, indeed, hyperbolical about the English language, saying: "He who is master of the English language is master of the world. We Irish ought to know that, as we have done so much to forge the weapon to its finest temper."[7]

Here in *Pygmalion*, speech modes are looked at in relation to social class and economics, and the famous Cockney accent of London's East End is selected as a particular example.

The play also touches briefly, but with great significance, on speech as a means of communication between soul and soul, and as an ennobler of the spirit. Professor Higgins, expert in phonetics and teacher of acceptable speech modes, is not one who wears his heart on his sleeve, but he makes the most moving and significant statement in the play when he tells his mother:

> You have no idea how frightfully interesting it is to take a human being and change her into a quite different human being by creating a new speech for her. It's filling up the deepest gulf that separates class from class and soul from soul.[8]

The play begins in Covent Garden outside the Opera House, where, then as now, a mixture of classes is to be seen. (It has been famously described as the place where one has to step over the homeless on one's way from the opera.) First on the scene are a pathetic mother and daughter, belonging to the "genteel poor," whose income is insufficient to support the position in society which they consider to be rightly theirs. To the daughter, as we shall later discover, it is desperately important that she should mix with the right people in order to find a suitable husband to support her. Her brother, Freddy, unable to find a taxi in the pouring rain, is presented to the audience as a wimp.

In contrast is Eliza, the flower seller, a robust character with a strong Cockney accent, and, as it transpires, a determination to better her position by her own efforts. Her Cockney accent (but not Eliza herself) attracts the attention of Professor Higgins, author of Higgins' Universal Alphabet. In his conversation with Eliza he presents a boorish character. Again there comes a contrast, this time in the person of Colonel Pickering, also an expert in phonetics, who appears to the audience as a typical officer and a gentleman: he is as courteous to Eliza as he is to the Professor.

A selection of bystanders is present to provide local color and also a modicum of social commentary. For example, a Sarcastic Bystander has some words to say to the Colonel when he tells the poor flower girl she has a right to live where she pleases: "Park Lane, for instance. I'd like to go into the housing question with you, I would."[9] (This brings back memories of Shaw's first play, *Widowers' Houses*.)

Professor Higgins has a significant statement to make about the link between speech modes and upward mobility:

> This is an age of upstarts. Men begin in Kentish Town with £80 a year, and end in Park Lane with a hundred thousand. They want to drop Kentish Town; but they give themselves away every time they open their mouths. Now I can teach them....[10]

He also makes a boast that sets the whole business of the plot in motion, and brings to life a vital home truth:

> You see this creature with her kerbstone English: the English that will keep her in the gutter to the end of her days. Well, sir, in three months I could pass that girl off as a duchess at an ambassador's garden party. I could even get her a place as lady's maid or shop assistant, which requires better English.[11]

The scene moves to Professor Higgins's house where Eliza arrives to take him up on his boast so that she may better herself by obtaining a post in a flower shop. We learn from her initial treatment there something of the way the poor are despised and humiliated. Under the supervision of Higgins's housekeeper she is made to strip off her clothes and take a bath. She is reduced to tears: "I've never took off all my clothes before. It's not right: it's not decent."[12] And later: "Oh, if only I'd known what a dreadful thing it is to be clean I'd never have come."[13] With a little more experience she makes an important point for the audience to grasp: "Now I know why ladies is so clean. Washing's a treat for them. Wish they could see what it is for the like of me"![14]

Shortly after the compulsory cleansing of Eliza, her father, dustman Doolittle, arrives and thereby enters the Hall of Fame as spokesman for the poor of London, and more especially the "undeserving poor." He has come to claim, for what he supposes to be his daughter's services, the modest sum of £5; had they been of a sexual nature he would have asked for £50. It is Doolittle's function to remove from the current vocabulary the phrase "the deserving poor," which was then much used by charity organizations. Those who were classified as "undeserving" did not receive help. Doolittle throws contemporary charity workers into disrepute not by his humility but by his buoyancy. The term "deserving poor" is consigned to the dustbin.

We meet dustman Doolittle again, when, for some complicated reason, he has been named as a beneficiary in the will of an American known to Higgins. Doolittle had not wished to accept this money because he had no wish to become a "gentleman." He gives a moving account of why he did so and tells about the fear of poverty in old age:

> What is there for me if I chuck it but the workhouse in my old age? I have to dye my hair already to keep my job as a dustman.... I, as one of the undeserving poor, have nothing between me and the pauper's uniform but this here blasted three thousand a year that shoves me into the middle class ... it's a choice between the Skilly of the workhouse and the Char Bydis of the middle class; and I havnt the nerve for the workhouse.[15]

Something is also to be said about the family who live in genteel poverty whom we met outside the opera house. When Higgins arranges a trial run for Eliza before he launches her into society, he takes her to an at-home at his mother's house, where Mrs. Eynsford-Hill and her daughter Clara are present as guests. Eliza's speech mode is satisfactory but her small talk tends towards the unusual.

When Eliza uses the taboo word "bloody" in the immortal phrase "not bloody likely,"[16] it proves to be a show-stopper in the theatre. But it is a pathetic moment for poor Clara in her struggle to keep on the edges of fashionable society. She thinks the word must have become newly fashionable among those of her generation. She says, "It's so quaint, and gives such a smart emphasis to things that are not in themselves very witty. I find the new small talk delightful and quite innocent."[17]

In due course Eliza is taken to an Ambassador's reception where she acquits herself perfectly. Ironically, her English is so excellent that it is thought that she may be of foreign extraction and her demeanor gives rise to speculation that she may be of royal blood. Higgins has won his bet on Eliza's success.

When the little party of three returns to the Higgins residence there is the inevitable anti-climax towards which Higgins's mother had already pointed a finger: Eliza has been given the speech and manners of a lady but, in a highly class-conscious society, no suitable environment or occupation has been offered. Higgins chooses to be obtuse about the chasm that yawns in front of Eliza. In a true "slice-of-life" play this would be a problem on which the audience is left to ponder; and this was Shaw's intent. But Sir Herbert Beerbohm Tree, the actor-manager who took the role of Higgins when the play was first produced in England, had more romantic notions and played the part accordingly. To forestall any similar future interpretations, Shaw decided to introduce a romance between Eliza and Freddy, brother of Clara. A new ending was added, spoken by Higgins: "She's going to marry Freddy. Ha ha! Freddy! Freddy!! Ha ha ha ha ha!!!!!"[18]

For the reader of the play there is a continuum in which a few more "slices of life" are added as regards the younger members of the cast. They each reject the concept of dependency and their actions are, from an economic aspect, a working out of a maxim current at that time that "poverty should be prevented rather than alleviated. Eliza and Freddy become the owners of a flower shop. The two of them study at "shorthand schools and polytechnic classes,"[19] presumably run by the London County Council, and they even attend classes at the London School of Economics, of which Shaw was one of the founders. The vista of London is expanded. We also learn of changes in the social circles where Clara struggles to keep a foothold. Conversation now includes the works of H. G. Wells, writer of science fiction, promulgator of new ideas (and a former member of the Fabian Society). With a fresh outlook on life, she seeks financial independence, ceases searching for a husband, and obtains work in an old furniture shop. Again horizons are expanded.

In the addendum to *Pygmalion* Shaw projects his young people into a world that is still at peace. By the time the play was first published in book form in England, in 1916, the world was at war.

Both *Androcles* and Pygmalion were first produced abroad in German translation: *Androcles* in Hamburg, in July 1913, and *Pygmalion* at Berlin's Hofburg Theater, on October 16, 1913.

The first performance in England of *Androcles* was at the St. James's Theatre, London, on September 1, 1913.

Pygmalion was not performed in England until April 11, 1914, when it was presented at Her Majesty's Theatre, London. This was Shaw's most brilliantly successful comedy, yet he was far from happy at its reception: his unhappiness was focused on the reaction of the press and the critics to his use of the word "bloody." He wrote to Auguste Rodin who at that time was modelling a bust of Shaw:

> *J'étais occupé au théâtre, où je viens d'avoir un succès fou parce que ma héroïne, dans un cercle d'élite, se sert du mot "bloody" (sanglant) qui est très inconvenable (un peu comme "je m'en fous"). Tout le monde— tous les journaux—en parlent sans cesse: la politique, la science, l'art, la religion ne marchent plus en Angleterre: il ne s'agit que du bloody; et me voilà au comble de ma carrière.*[20]*

One has to ask whether the perceptive Shaw was entirely unaware of the sort of reaction his use of the word "bloody" would bring. Beerbohm Tree had asked him to delete the word and he had refused. Was there an element of perversity here? Whatever Shaw's reasons for his persistence may have been, the play epitomizes a major question about his dramatic works of which he had always been keenly aware: did the audience who laughed so heartily at Shaw's wit and humour—and in this case enjoyed being shocked—miss, as a consequence, the serious content of the play? Who can say? In fact *Pygmalion* is not a play of debate but of statement and images. Those images and those statements, which lasted so long and travelled so widely, must surely have had their effect.

[I was busy at the theatre, where I have come to have a tremendous success because my heroine, in an elite circle, uses the word "bloody," which is very improper (a little like "fuck me"). Everyone—all the newpapers—they use it incessantly: politics, science, art, religion no longer count; it's nothing but "bloody"; and here I am at the height of my career.]

18

Playlets About Marriage
and Sexual Deviance

The little group of playlets that Shaw wrote between 1912 and 1914 all relate to sex. The first contains marital infidelity and is the usual sort of sketch designed to keep people up to date with the latest trends in marital relationships; the second is concerned with sadism and the third with bondage. Since plays two and three were written around the time that his relationship with Mrs. Patrick Campbell was causing Shaw stress and distress, it may be that, indirectly, they contain a working out of Shaw's own inner feelings.

OVERRULED (1912)

In a fairly lengthy Preface this one-act play is described as "A clinical study of how the thing [polygamy] actually occurs among quite ordinary people."[1] In fact modern colloquialism "wife-swapping" seems to be more appropriate since after their dialogue the two couples concerned leave the stage to go into dinner as a foursome but give no evidence that they will continue through life as a polygamous union. However, the author does give a fairly convincing picture, presumably drawn from his experience aboard cruise ships, of the sort of flirtation that takes place especially when, as in this case, two married couples decide to take holidays without their respective partners: each of the four falls in love and by an amazing coincidence, when they return from their respective cruises, the four bump into each other in a hotel lounge.

The picture given relates very closely to the time of which Shaw writes: the language, the modes of address, the thought patterns, the conventions about marriage and relationships outside marriage. The dialogue is witty and is for the most part turned against the speaker, who, however articulate he may be, tends to be more self-revealing than he is aware.

Overruled was first performed at the Duke of York's Theatre, London, on October 14, 1912. It was part of a triple bill which included Pinero's *The Widow of Wasdale Heath* and J. M. Barrie's *Rosalind.* Only Barrie's play was successful. Shaw wrote to Pinero after the opening night: "They simply loathed us ... they were angrily disgusted."[2]

THE MUSIC CURE: A PIECE OF UTTER NONSENSE (APRIL 1913–JANUARY 1914)

"This is not," wrote Shaw, "a serious play: it is what is called a Variety Turn for two musicians."[3] There are two distinct parts to it. It begins in the same sort of vein as *Press Cuttings.* With the arrival of a second principal character it centers on sadism and masochism.

The male character is a wimp, but born to the purple, which entitles him to a post in the public service. In real life there had recently occurred the Marconi scandal, concerning the buying and selling of shares, in which a number of leading politicians were said to be involved. In the playlet Lord Reginald Fitzambey has been involved in a similar scandal concerning the British Macaroni Trust. Unable to see that he was at fault, he has had a nervous breakdown. His father has told him he has disgraced the family name and should resign from his clubs. His mother has told him that he will not now be able to marry for money, and his doctor says: "Well, all I can tell you is that if you werent a son of the Duke of Dunmow, youd have to resign...."[4]

When the doctor gives his patient a dose of opium and departs, the playlet moves into a different mode. Reginald's mother has prescribed a music cure for him and the lady musician who has been commissioned to bring about the cure shortly arrives. There is an instant bonding between the musician and the immature, opium-doped Reginald. He tells her, "Ever since I was a child I have had only one secret longing, and that was to be mercilessly beaten by a splendid, strong, beautiful woman."[5] The musician, Strega, responds, and Reginald says further: "But you would be angry sometimes.... You would throw down the thing you loved and trample on it as it clung to your feet."[6] The reply: "Yes—oh, why do you force me to confess it?—I should beat it to a jelly, and then cast myself in transports of remorse on its quivering frame and smother it with passionate kisses."[7] They agree to marry and the sadomasochistic pair play the wedding march together.

The Music Cure was first performed as curtain raiser to G. K. Chesterton's *Magic* at the Little Theatre, London, on January 28, 1914, in celebration of the hundredth performance of Chesterton's play.[8]

GREAT CATHERINE (1913)

When, in *Caesar and Cleopatra*, Shaw turned his attention to the great Roman Empire of the past he looked for some aspects of its history that would provide a lesson for modern times. This was not the case when he wrote about Catherine the Great of Russia, the German princess who married the future Peter III and ruled as Empress after his death, achieving great fame—and notoriety—in so doing. Here Catherine and the members of her court are reduced to stereotypical figures of fun, pretentious in their manners, dirty in their habits, and speaking a language that is full of phrases like "Little Mother," "Little Darling," "Little Angel of a Mother," and so on. The solitary Englishman, Captain Edstaston, is equally a stereotype of the sort the author loves to caricature. He is overwhelmed by the superiority of being English and the certainty that if the Russians should be hostile to him the British will come to the rescue.

The nub of the playlet comes when the Empress, in pursuit of her sexual desires and in display of her sexual—and imperial—powers, has the Captain bound, trussed, tied to a pole, and brought into her imperial presence. He is untied and thrown at her feet. She proceeds to indulge in sexual play which consists of tickling him with her toes, adding thereby to the pain which he already feels from his bonds. Catherine's sexual passion finds expression in sadism.

When the Captain's fiancée, Claire, daringly finds her way into the very room where the Empress and Captain Edstaston are alone together, and expresses her jealousy, it becomes clear that the Captain has masochistic tendencies and, in spite of his protests, is enjoying his bondage. Nevertheless, he is released and makes his departure.

What was spoken about in *The Music Cure* is practiced in *Great Catherine*.

The playlet was first produced at the Vaudeville Theatre, London, on November 18, 1913, sharing the bill with Hermon Ould's *Between Sunset and Dawn*. It ran for only thirty performances. Shaw's comment on November 21 was, "The sooner the wretched thing is taken off, the better."[9]

Playlets Written
During the War

A heading to part of the Preface to *Heartbreak House* reads, "The higher drama put out of action," and this is what happened to Shaw as a dramatist for the first two years of the First World War. His output consisted of only four playlets. Each of them had some significant comments to make, but apart from *O'Flaherty, V.C.* they tended to be trivial, and they were never overburdened with patriotism.

The Inca of Perusalem: An Almost Historical Comedietta (August 1915)

This play is about Kaiser Wilhelm II of Germany but, because it has a convoluted plot which unwinds itself in the manner of a fairy tale, it is some time before it becomes obvious that the Inca is a representation of the Kaiser. The Kaiser, as one would expect, has some significant statements to make. But from the beginning there is an intermingling of the fairy tale with reality.

A Prologue introduces the impoverished and widowed daughter of a clergyman, formerly married to a millionaire. How is she to maintain an acceptable lifestyle? The father suggests a classic answer: go abroad and become a lady's maid. She does so and finds employment with a minor princess who is staying at a hotel. Here a note of reality creeps in. The point is made that in time of war civilians, as well as the armed forces, suffer hardship. The waiter, for example, was previously a medical man but, due to the circumstances of the war, his patients could no longer afford his services.

When the Inca arrives we are back to the fairy tale again. Travelling incognito, as monarchs are apt to do, he is on a mission to judge whether the princess would make a suitable bride for one of his sons: he mistakes the mistress for the maid—or so it appears.

There comes the point where the audience is given the message that it was assembled to hear. The Inca speaks of the fascination that death and destruction have for mankind, a theme to which the author was to return in *Heartbreak House*:

> You talk of death as an unpopular thing. You are wrong: for years I gave [my subjects] art, literature, science, prosperity, that they might live more abundantly; and they hated me, ridiculed me, caricatured me. Now that I give them death in its frightfullest forms, they are devoted to me![1]

Coming nearer to the practicalities of war, the Inca has something to say about its economics which was to resonate in reality.

> Victorious as I am, I am hopelessly bankrupt; and the worst of it is, I am intelligent enough to know it. And I shall be beaten in consequence, because my most implacable enemy, though only a few months further away from bankruptcy than myself, has not a ray of intelligence, and will go on fighting until civilization is destroyed, unless I, out of sheer pity for the world, condescend to capitulate.[2]

In 1916, the year when the play was first performed, two statements concerning the economics of war were made, one by a German spokesman, the other by a Briton. On July 4 the German Admiral Scheer issued an official dispatch: "A victorious termination of the war within measurable time can only be attained by destroying the economic existence of Great Britain, namely, by the employment of submarines against British commerce."[3] In November the President of the British Board of Trade, Viscount Walter Runciman, stated in a memorandum that if British shipping losses continued at their present rate Britain would collapse by the summer of 1917.[4]

The playlet did not stay overlong in the land of fairy tale.

The *Inca* was first presented at the Birmingham Repertory Theatre.

O'FLAHERTY, V.C.: A RECRUITING PAMPHLET (JULY–SEPTEMBER 1915)

In an introductory passage to this play the author says that as an Irishman he best understood how to speak to the Irish on the subject of recruitment: "I addressed myself quite simply to the business of obtaining recruits."[5] It was read by Shaw to an audience of wounded soldiers. The author says: "They gave me three cheers, and laughed a good deal; but the best bits were when they sat very tight and said nothing."[6] It was first presented on the Western Front at Treizennes, Belgium, by Officers of the 40th Squadron, R.F.C.

The play was written the year before the disastrous Easter Rising in Dublin, of which W. B. Yeats was to say, "a terrible beauty was born." In writing it Shaw used all the skill and tact in language that had characterized *John Bull's Other Island*. Yet to read the play is to understand why the English establishment had reservations about its being produced in Ireland. For there was, as Shaw tells us, an enormous gulf between the English and Irish attitudes to the war.

The author does not seek to reconcile these attitudes. He simply makes a basic proposition that antagonism against English rule and England's king is not irreconcilable with joining in the war. It is every Irishman's dream to leave Ireland, and as a soldier he is released from the tyranny of the employer and the tyranny of the home.

The characters and their circumstances are selected so as to be ideally suited for the sequences of dialogue they have to sustain. O'Flaherty, recipient of the Victoria Cross, on leave from the front, has just been lionized by his fellow countrymen: he is able to speak man-to-man with the local landowner, who is also his employer, the Anglophile Sir Pearce Madigan. He talks to him about patriotism: "It means different to me than what it would to you, sir. It means England and England's king to you. To me and the like of me, it means talking about the English just the way the English papers talk about the Boshes."[7] He is moved to speak against patriotism in Ireland and in general. He says, "Youll never have a quiet world til you knock the patriotism out of the human race."[8]

As does the author, O'Flaherty rejects the idea that there is a Christian-like purpose in war: "No war is right; and all the holy water that Father Quinlan ever blessed couldnt make one right."[9]

To the mother of a holder of the Victoria Cross everything is forgiven. One minute Mrs. O'Flaherty is pouring out Irish blarney over the General, to whose son she was once a wet-nurse; the next she is berating her son when she finds out that he has been fighting on the side of the English and not, as she had supposed, against them.

Mrs. O'Flaherty is one of the reasons her son joined up. After a verbal battering from her and his girl friend he looks forward to his return to the front. They, for their part, make it clear how welcome army pensions, and the money attached to the award of the V.C., are to the womenfolk.

O'Flaherty philosophizes to the General: "Some likes war's alarums; and some likes home life. Ive tried both, sir; and I'm all for war's alarums now. I always was a quiet lad by natural disposition."[10]

But what O'Flaherty's experience at the war front had brought him was a different perspective on life. He speaks to his mother:

> Whats happened to everybody? thats what I want to know.... I tell you the world's creation is crumbling in ruins about me; and then you come and ask whats happened to me?[11]

The first professional performance of *O'Flaherty, V.C.* was at the 39th Street Theatre, New York, on June 21, 1920, by the Deborah Bierne Irish Players. The first presentation in England was by the Stage Society at the Lyric Theatre, Hammersmith, on December 19, 1920.

AUGUSTUS DOES HIS BIT: A TRUE-TO-LIFE FARCE (AUGUST 12–23, 1916)

On January 15, 1917, Shaw wrote to Frank Harris: "I am rehearsing a play, and there is some question of my going to the front immediately afterwards to see the show."[12] The play in rehearsal was *Augustus Does His Bit* and the "show" relates to Shaw's official visit to the Western Front. Lord Augustus's ilk had been on the stage before: on the previous occasion he was Lord Reginald Fitzambey of *The Music Cure*; he was younger then and more fragile.

Augustus is tricked by "the Lady" into parting with some secret information, but this trick has no serious consequence; rather, it serves the purpose of putting Lord Augustus out of countenance.

The playlet is extremely witty: most of the jokes are, as usual, against the privileged upper class, whom the author depicts as stupid, arrogant, and having a monopoly on the seats of power. As in *Common Sense About the War* it is suggested that they have German connections. In fact Lord Augustus has three German brothers-in-law. A note of farce creeps in when he tells the Lady: "If you had a German brother-in-law, madam, you would know that nothing else in the world produces so strong an anti-German feeling."[13] His next statement is less laughter-provoking: "Life affords no keener pleasure than finding a brother-in-law's name in the German casualty list."[14]

The author introduces a matter about which he feels very strongly:

the soldier's loss of his civil rights. When Augustus's clerk joins the armed forces his lordship takes the opportunity to kick him downstairs. "Theres no more law for you," he tells him; "Youre a soldier now."[15]

Augustus was first presented by the Stage Society at the Royal Court Theatre, London, on January 21, 1917.

ANNAJANSKA, THE BOLSHEVIK EMPRESS: A REVOLUTIONARY ROMANCELET (1917)

"A frankly bravura piece" is the way Shaw describes *Annajanska* in the Preface.[16] He explains that the modern variety theatre demands sketches of this kind so that some favorite performer (in this case, Miss Lillah McCarthy) may make a dazzling performance.

The sketch was written in December 1917 and presented the following month. The Russian Revolution, which Shaw had described so dramatically elsewhere as a cataclysm, had taken place in March 1917. Soon afterward, in May of that year, the Petrograd Soviet had called a Socialist Congress on War Aims and invitations had been issued to attend a venue in Stockholm. Its purpose was that "the work for peace started by the Russian Revolution be brought to a conclusion by the efforts of the international proletariat."[17]

The world-shattering event of the Russian Revolution and the noble aims of the Stockholm Conference are presented as subjects for buffoonery in a play which is set in the post–Revolutionary republic of Beotia, where the Panjandrum has recently been removed from his throne, replaced by a dictatorship; where people are shot in masses; and where those who spectacularly shoot themselves do so with blank cartridges.

The leading character in the sketch, and her actions, have a familiar ring about them. Annajanska, daughter of a former Panjandrum, has escaped from her captors, and is thought to be escorted by a young officer. This is not the case; she *is* the officer: under her cloak she wears the uniform of a Hussar. She presents a paradox which probably surprises no one. She has not escaped from the Revolution; she has escaped because she is a revolutionary.

The General who is Commander-in-Chief makes reference to the coming peace conference at Stockholm. His remarks are entirely deflationary. He says: "A third [revolutionary] orders me to go to a damned Socialist Conference and explain that Beotia will allow no annexations and no indemnities, and merely wishes to establish the Kingdom of Heaven on Earth throughout the universe."[18] He asks, "What can save a mob in which every man is rushing in a different direction?" The Grand Duchess gives a disturbing reply: "The war can save it.... Only a great common danger and a great common duty can unite us and weld these wrangling factions into a solid commonwealth."[19] She takes off her cloak, revealing her uniform, and is hailed as the Bolshevik Empress.

Was 1918 the time, was the Variety Theatre the place, and was a bravura piece the medium, for presenting a sketch relating to the Russian Revolution and talking about yet more war?

The author claimed that he received only one compliment on the piece. A friend said, "It is the only one of your works that is not too long."[20]

Heartbreak House:
A Fantasia in
the Russian Manner
on English Themes

As soon as war broke out in 1914 Shaw took up his pen as a political writer. But he laid it aside for a time as far as serious drama was concerned, writing only minor playlets. Then at long last *Heartbreak House* emerged[1] and Shaw became in a special sense a playwright of Europe. In the Preface Shaw explains that "Heartbreak House is not merely the name of the play which follows this preface. It is cultured, leisured Europe before the war."[2]

Chekhov is cited as the play's great precursor: three of his studies of Heartbreak House, namely *The Cherry Orchard, Uncle Vanya*, and *The Seagull*, had been performed in England. Tolstoy, author of *Fruits of Enlightenment*, is also mentioned. To Tolstoy Heartbreak House was "the house in which Europe was stifling its soul."[3]

However, the Heartbreak House of Shaw's play is also a metaphor for pre-war upper-class England, which a certain Ruth Cavendish Bentinck had described as lying behind deer park walls. She wrote about this in "The Point of Honour. A Correspondence on Aristocracy and Socialism" which was published as a Fabian Tract (No. 151) in 1910. The following extracts, the first from Shaw's Preface, the second from Mrs. Bentinck's tract, show very similar concepts of the country house lifestyle.

The Preface: These intensely Russian plays fitted all the country houses in Europe in which the pleasures of music, art, literature, and the theatre had supplanted hunting, shooting, fishing, flirting, eating, and drinking.[4]

> *The tract:* Most people in our class will do more good by keeping
> an oasis, where culture and beauty, art and literature, may find a
> home.[5]

The play itself abounds with metaphors—vast, interlocking, and interchangeable. The Heartbreak House in which the play is acted out is halfway towards being a ship. This is clearly seen from the set which represents the home of the eccentric Captain Shotover. And the ship is a metaphor for the ship of state, which is eventually seen as drifting on to the rocks. What is more, the metaphorical nature of the house keeps changing with the unpredictability and confusion of a nightmare, the nightmare of pre-war Europe, becoming now a madhouse, and then again the true house of heartbreak. Heartbreak House, as well as representing the construct of the play, is the dominant metaphor in which all other metaphors are enclosed.

The metaphor of sleep is introduced at the beginning when the young house guest Ellie dozes into slumber while she waits to be greeted by her hostess, the daughter of the house, Mrs. Hesione Hushabye, who has fallen asleep elsewhere in this house of dreams. In due course Ellie announces her symbolic marriage with the octogenarian Captain Shotover, her soul's "natural captain": he is fast asleep at the time.[6]

This is the sleep of inanition, the sort of inanition that, in Shaw's view, overtakes the Parliamentarians of the front benches, the sort of inanition to which Webb refers when he writes of the citizen's feeling of shame: "Shame for the lack of capacity of its governors, shame for the inability of Parliament ... shame for the supineness which looks on unmoved at the continued degradation of our race."[7]

Shotover, at his age, is entitled to his sleep, but when he takes the play into an area where sleep, dreams, and drunkenness intermingle, it is not to be supposed that he is talking only about old age: "To be drunk means to have dreams; to go soft; to be easily pleased and deceived.... But when you are old: very very old, like me, the dreams come by themselves.... You will never be free from dozing and dreams."[8]

Along with sleep and dreaming go forgetfulness, confusion, and non-recognition. This keeps happening throughout the play. The Captain does not recognize his daughter, Lady Utterword, newly returned from abroad. His other daughter, Hesione, does not recognize her sister. Mazzini Dunn is introduced to his own daughter, and so on. There is no certainty as to whether the confusion and forgetfulness are real or assumed.

But dreams, as well as bringing confusion, can also strip the soul bare to release an inner unacceptable truth. As with sleep so it is with hypnotism. And so, when Boss Mangan, the capitalist entrepreneur, is hypnotized he goes through a stage of self-revelation, and as a symbolic gesture, attempts to strip himself naked. Sleep, unawareness, confusion, and finally a possible awakening: these are the states that Heartbreak House induces, and this is the state of Europe before the war.

Heartbreak House, as has been said, is also a ship, the ship of state which is drifting onto the rocks. When the ineffectual Mazzini Dunn is misguided enough to remark that nothing ever happens, and refers to an overruling providence, he receives a powerful reply from Captain Shotover:

> At sea nothing happens to the sea.... Nothing happens, except something not worth mentioning.... Nothing but the smash of the drunken skipper's ship on the rocks, the splintering of her rotten timbers, the tearing of her rusty plates, the drowning of the crew like rats in a trap.[9]

As to what is to be done, Shotover's answer is clear: "Learn your business as an Englishman.... Navigation. Learn it and live; or leave it and be damned."[10]

The war brought Shaw a perception of a need in some men to experience danger. Shotover speaks of this in terms of his experience as a seaman, giving a memorable message to the sheltered people of Heartbreak House. He tells Ellie:

> I was ten times happier on the bridge in the typhoon ... than you ... have ever been. You are looking for a rich husband. At your age I looked for hardship, danger, horror and death, that I might feel the life in me more intensely.... You are going to let the fear of poverty govern your life; and your reward will be that you will eat, but you will not live.[11]

The Captain's words about a rich husband are a warning against sex-parasitism, a matter which had long engaged Shaw's attention. But Ellie has no thought of carving out a career for herself. She remarks that she is not "going to sit down and die of a broken heart ... or be an old maid living on a pittance."[12]

The last major metaphor of the play is dynamite, which carries at least three interpretations. First it presages the First World War, and draws attention to the folly of England's unawareness. Thus, when the Captain brings some of his store of dynamite from the gravel pit into the house, his daughter's only comment is: "Dont drop it about the house: theres a dear."[13]

Second, the atom bomb seems to cast its shadow a long, long way before it when Hector Hushabye gives his explanation of the Captain's intentions: "To blow up the human race if it goes too far. He is trying to discover a psychic ray that will explode all the explosives at the will of a Mahatma."[14]

Third, the Captain's own explanation, and Hector's response, suggest that dynamite represents the way of the dynamiter, which, when opposed to capitalism, is the way of the Impossibilist. Hector says: "They [the capitalists] will always be able to buy more dynamite than you."[15] The Captain claims that he will make a dynamite that the capitalists cannot explode.

The metaphor of dynamite is part of the play's construct: all three of its aspects come together in the catastrophic conclusion which might be the end of the capitalist's world—and of much more besides.

Dynamite is linked with the metaphor of gold, which has its own power of destruction. Shotover is willing to use dynamite against the mass of people in order to acquire riches. The Act ends with the Captain's evil statement: "Give me deeper darkness. Money is not made in the light."[16]

At this stage it is appropriate to look at a selection of the play's characters. The mighty Lear-like Shotover represents both the play's constructive and destructive principles, and stands, perhaps, for the darker side of Shaw. For the rest, most of them are recognizable stereotypes, and, as such, remain static. But two of them, Ellie and Hector, the philandering playboy husband, grow during the course of the play.

Superficially and initially Ellie represents the New Woman. She begins by talking as such, telling Shotover: "Oh, you are very very old-fashioned, Captain. Does any modern girl believe that the legal and illegal ways of getting money are the honest and dishonest ways?"[17] But she has not grasped, as Vivie Warren did, that there is room for women in the world of business. Her modernity, like that of Ann in *Man and Superman*, consists of actively looking for a rich husband. But as she becomes attached to a man in his eighties, she can scarcely be considered an agent of the life force. Under Shotover's influence she acquires new spiritual values, but it is not clear to what purpose. In this, does she represent an aspect of the spirit of England?

Hector Hushabye, who changes his identity to make conquests of women, is like an earthly Jove. But communion with the Captain brings a further metamorphosis and new powers of perception. He then identifies capitalism with theft, describing the capitalist agent, Boss Mangan, and the thief who breaks into the house, as "the two burglars." When he is awakened he sees England as "this soul's prison" and is determined to escape. He finds the prospect of death and disaster exciting; when immediate danger from the skies appears and then disappears at the end of the play his reaction is, "How damnably dull the world has become again suddenly."[18]

Lady Utterword, daughter of the Captain and wife of a British diplomat, is a wholly fantastic caricature of the bombastic upper-class lady whose self-image is inflated by her husband's unearned status. Another example of a sex-parasite, she has come to the wrong address, for by disposition she belongs to Shaw's alternative residence, Horseback Hall. "Go anywhere in England," says Lady Utterword, "where there are natural, wholesome, contented, and really nice English people; and what do you always find? That the stables are the real centre of the household ... everybody can see that the people who hunt are the right people and the people who dont are the wrong ones."[19]

Lady Utterword's brother-in-law, Randall Utterword, is a true denizen of Heartbreak House. We last met his like in *The Music Cure.* He is ill-fitted for the work that he was assigned to in the Foreign Office. He neither hunts nor shoots. He plays the piano, reads literary books and poems, and runs after married women. So says his sister-in-law.

The Captain's other daughter, Hesione, is a New Woman of a different kind from Ellie. She belongs to a Bohemian sub-culture which is signified by her appearance. "She is uncorseted and dressed anyhow in a rich robe of black pile that shews off her white skin and statuesque contour."[20] Something of a siren, she is the sort of woman on whom the idle rich men of Heartbreak House waste their lives.

The two remaining principal characters are concerned chiefly with the play's sub-plot, which is essentially an exposition of pre-war capitalism as perceived by Shaw.

Boss Mangan has been described by Mrs. Hushabye as "a Napoleon of industry and disgustingly rich."[21] He is considered to be a millionaire. But Mangan, whom at one time Ellie expected to marry, is not of this class; it turns out that he is an entrepreneur. When Mangan is unmasked in successive stages, the audience comes, step by step, to realize the significance of the divorce between the ownership of capital and its administration.

Ellie begins the Mangan story by telling Hesione how Mangan had financed her father when he started business and then bought him out when he went bankrupt. Mangan continues it when he feels impelled to tell Ellie his mode of operating as an entrepreneur. He waits on the sidelines for the inexperienced enthusiast with talent to go bankrupt. This can happen more than once:

> If it's really a big thing the third lot will have to sell out too, and
> leave their work and their money behind them. And thats where
> the real business man comes in ... I explained my idea to some
> friends in the city, and they found the money; for I take no risks
> in ideas even when theyre my own. Your father and the friends
> that ventured their money with him were no more to me than a
> heap of squeezed lemons.[22]

So Mangan is not the millionaire he was thought to be. Under hypnotism he spells it out. The factories "belong to syndicates and shareholders and all sorts of lazy good-for-nothing capitalists."[23] He makes
a further revelation concerning the infiltration of capitalism into the
processes of government (a matter addressed by Undershaft in *Major
Barbara*). Mangan, the capitalist tool, in his guise as the Napoleon
of industry, was asked to join the Government after the syndicate
had donated an immense sum to party funds, "without even going
through the nonsense of an election, as the dictator of a great public
department."[24]

Compared with Mangan, Mazzini Dunn, father of Ellie, is a financial innocent.

He is also a political innocent, and in this he seems to represent what
Shaw had come to regard as Fabian ineptitude, and the ineptitude of
thinking men generally, in the years before the war. Dunn makes just one
speech about his belonging to Fabian-style societies and then the matter
is dismissed, just as Praed's anarchism is dismissed in *Mrs Warren's Profession*. When Hector asks why he hasn't done anything to hinder the
powers of destruction he replies:

> But I did. I joined societies and made speeches and wrote pam-
> phlets.... Every year I expected a revolution.... But nothing hap-
> pened, except, of course, the usual poverty and crime and drink
> that we are used to. Nothing ever does happen.[25]

The phrase "Nothing ever happens," uttered shortly before the play's
catastrophe, has a terrible dramatic irony, which also belongs to the world
outside the theatre.

When Dunn enters Heartbreak House he is sucked into the upper-
class environment which he sees in the flattering mirror of illusion. He
describes it as "rather a favourable specimen of what is best in our English
culture." He tells the inhabitants: "You are very charming people, most
advanced ... democratic, free-thinking, and everything that is delightful
to thoughtful people."[26] Is Shaw saying here that the intelligentsia of the

Left were similarly sucked into the upper reaches of the political establishment?

However, judgment is about to fall on these delightful people, and all the major metaphors of the play, together with the sub-plot, are fused together in the play's climactic ending: a catastrophe from above creates earth-shattering explosions that blow up the dynamite in the gravel pit, killing Boss Mangan and the burglar, who have taken refuge there, and reducing the vicarage to a heap of bricks. The Captain sees this as a judgment, while Ellie, Hesione, and Hector experience a strange excitement.

There is an obvious reading of the catastrophe. Capitalism breeds war, and capitalists will be destroyed by war, or by the violence of revolution. And the Christian God, as Shaw has stated elsewhere, will give way to Mars for the duration.

Captain Shotover regards the turmoil as a Day of Judgment. Earlier he has made a savage remark to Hector: "Do you think the laws of God will be suspended in favour of England because you were born in it?"[27] Later he says: "Stand by, all hands, for judgement"[28]; and later still, "Turn in, all hands. The ship is safe."[29]

In fact it is Hector who makes the gloomiest predictions. They are to be echoed in Shaw's mighty pentateuch, *Back to Methuselah*: "Either out of that darkness some new creation will come to supplant us as we have supplanted the animals, or the heavens will fall in thunder and destroy us."[30]

But the last words of the play come from those who have found that they enjoy danger. In this they follow the previously quoted maxim of the Preface: "Those who do not know how to live must make a merit of dying." Under this heading Shaw observes: "Heartbreak House … did not know how to live, at which point all that was left to it was the boast that at least it knew how to die: a melancholy accomplishment which the outbreak of war presently gave it practically unlimited opportunities of displaying."[31]

The last words of the play are:

> MRS. HUSHABYE: But what a glorious experience! I hope
> theyll come again tomorrow night.
> ELLIE [radiant at the prospect]: Oh, I hope so.[32]

Heartbreak House was first presented by the Theatre Guild at the Garrick Theatre, New York, on November 10, 1920. In England it had its first performance at the Court Theatre, London, on October 18, 1921.

Shaw wrote about *Heartbreak House* in an article which appeared in the *Sunday Herald* on October 23, 1921:

> I am mysteriously impelled, like Garibaldi, to offer them [the the-atre audience] starvation, wounds and death; and they seem impelled to embrace their doom, and even to find a strange joy in their anguish.[33]

Back to Methuselah:
A Metabiological
Pentateuch

During the First World War Shaw argued that Christ had been set aside, and Mars had been ascendant. As the war came to an end, he became extremely aware of a new turning towards religion and towards Christ. He spoke about this in a lecture that he gave in November 1919 on the subject of Modern Religion:

> There has been a sort of rediscovery of Christ. People suddenly begin to discover that his religion is a universal religion, and ... that that spirit which was in Christ you will find ... among all sorts of persons, persons whom the evangelicals used to call heathen and idolatrous.[1]

Shaw had written extensively about the teachings of Christ, and suggested how they might be applied in a postwar democracy. Also he had long been familiar with the aspirations of the Christian Socialists towards establishing the Kingdom of Heaven on earth. And he was particularly aware that the ancient and universal religion of Theosophy had been "rediscovered," for among its adherents was his close friend, Annie Besant, who had left the Fabian Society to become a Theosophist.

For Shaw, creative evolution was a universal religion, but he went a step further than the Theosophists by blurring the line between religion and philosophy, calling the creative power of the universe the "Life Force" rather than "God." It was his elevated belief that he was himself "the servant and instrument of creative evolution" who ranked with the saints.[2]

It will be recalled that in his famous essay, "The Quintessence of Ibsenism," Shaw made a challenging statement: "The larger truth of the matter is that modern European literature and music now form a Bible far surpassing in importance to us the ancient Hebrew Bible that has served us so long."[3] Now, in *Back to Methuselah*, Shaw reaches to the heights and offers his own "quintessence," a latter-day bible, for so he regards it. He looks to the ultimate and constructs a world that goes beyond the boundaries of time and space, and presents it within the confines of the theatre: he tells the story of humankind from alpha to omega. Each of the five plays of the pentateuch relates to a postulated critical stage in the evolution of society and of humans as social beings.

At the end of the pentateuch, as in *Heartbreak House*, thoughts about the possible destruction of mankind arise. This time they come, not from one of the human race, but from the creative principle, Lilith.

PART I: "IN THE BEGINNING"

The moment when humans were first endowed with thought is selected as the beginning of the evolutionary journey. This starting point is held in common with that of the gospel of St. John. The gospel says: "In the beginning was the Word [logos], and the Word was with God, and the Word was God." The creative evolutionist, Shaw tells us, "believes in the thought [logos] made flesh as the first step in the main process of Creative Evolution."[4]

The creative power of the universe is ascribed to the mythical, androgenous Lilith rather than to the sectarian Judaic God of the Old Testament; thus a metaphor for a universal religion is provided. "In the Beginning" introduces the two opposing principles of creation and destruction, each of which has its part to play in humankind's evolution, and both of which are held in various states of tension until the end of the pentateuch.

The woman (Eve) is possessed of the Life Force, with which she has been endowed by the Creative Principle of the universe (Lilith). The man (Adam) is haunted by the fear of death, and by the opposite, the fear of immortality in the flesh. Procreation provides the answer. Their son (Cain) is possessed of the will to destroy, which is held in tension against Eve's will to create. Since warrior Cain's will to destroy is confined to man killing man (and man killing animals), it offers no threat to humanity's survival: woman, impregnated by man, can produce more of the species than man destroys.

Interwoven with creation and destruction is the matter of the use and misuse of word and thought. There is an implication that whoever abuses these abuses the godhead (the voice of creative evolution). Cain, who has a marvellous capacity for rhetoric, is guilty of such abuse. He tells his parents that he no longer listens to the voice; he decides what the voice shall say. Hence he abuses the word, and creates an anthropomorphic god.

"In the Beginning" is a prologue to "The Gospel of the Brothers Barnabas" and to the rest of the play series.

PART II: "THE GOSPEL OF THE BROTHERS BARNABAS"

Here Shaw demonstrates that contemporary civilization is at crisis point. World War I and its aftermath have shown what happens when the destructive principle, armed with new and terrible weapons, gets out of balance with the creative principle. Man now has the capacity for destroying humankind in the mass (including the mothers of the future race) together with his livelihood and his means of subsistence.

But warrior man has become a mere instrument of political man, who now occupies center stage together with thinking man. It falls to political man to control the destructive principle, but in a complex civilization he has so far failed to do so.

Two kinds of political man stand, as it were, in the dock. They are based on two Prime Ministers. Joyce Burge, the demagogue, represents Lloyd George; Lubin, the complacent aristocrat, represents Asquith. The mantle of Cain has fallen on them both as regards the word, which they abuse by using speech to destroy reality. Each is his own spin doctor.

Political man is held in tension with two kinds of thinking man. They are the brothers Barnabas: the man of religion (Franklyn) and the man of science (Conrad). Together they are symbolic of Shaw's universal religion in which there is room not only for the man of religion but also for the man of science. And together they represent the creative principle which, in Part I, was represented by Eve.

The brothers offer no political solution to what is, in essence, a political crisis. Indeed, they condemn political man root and branch, perceiving that the world's complexity is now beyond his comprehension and control. Instead, a biological concept of an evolutionary leap is applied to a political situation. If Man exerts the will with which he has been endowed by the Life Force, he could extend his life-span to a period of three hundred years or so, and with longevity would come the much-needed wisdom to deal with politics and government. He would become the founder of a new race, the race of the longlived.

PART III: "THE THING HAPPENS"

In the year A.D. 2170 a different crisis threatens. This relates not to war but to racial supremacy. It is not concerned with civilization in general, but with the English in particular (unless they are intended as a metaphor for the white races in general).

Center stage, at the beginning of the play, we meet political man and thinking man once more. Political man, Burge-Lubin, is the President of the British Islands. (Britain no longer has a monarchy, nor, apparently, an empire.) He has scarcely changed since the days of his ancestors: he is the snake who will not shed his skin. And in his institutional form he has gone backwards: Parliament has deteriorated into a refuge for the nearly insane. But thinking man, the Chinese Chief Secretary to the President (Confucius) is different, and has been assigned a different role: he is not part of the establishment, nor is he destined to play a constructive part in the evolutionary process.

Burge-Lubin, who combines the demagogue (as in Joyce Burge) and the playboy politician of the country house set (as in Lubin) is as false to the word as his predecessors, using speech to hide from himself and from others the truth that Confucius, who is supposed to serve him, is really the master, because *he* does the work and *he* does the thinking. This parallels the relationship that exists between the English and the colored races. The position is correctly described by the Archbishop, but given the false spin by the President:

> THE ARCHBISHOP: Our routine work, and what may be called our ornamental and figure-head work, is being more and more sought after by the English; whilst the thinking, organizing, calculating, directing work is done by yellow brains, brown brains, and black brains....[5]
> BURGE-LUBIN: I grant you we leave the most troublesome part of the labor of the nation to them. And a good job too: why should we drudge at it? But think of the activities of our leisure! Is there a jollier place on earth to live in than England out of office hours? And to whom do we owe that? To ourselves, not to the niggers. The nigger and the Chink are all right from Tuesday to Friday; but from Friday to Tuesday they are simply nowhere; and the real life of England is from Friday to Tuesday.[6]

In this part, too, Shaw takes the theory about longevity which he expounded in the second play and applies it only to the English. Other races, as witness Confucius, do mature. But not the English, who prefer games and weekending, as witness Burge-Lubin. He introduces the long-established precept, usually applied to the animal kingdom in general, that those with the longest period of immaturity rank highest among the species. From this it is deduced that since the English die before they reach a postulated state of maturity potentially they are a superior race. This argument is tendencious, it is certainly racist, and Shaw may well have had his tongue in his cheek, but it serves the purpose of the play.

It transpires that the Archbishop and Mrs. Lutestring, Minister for Domestic Affairs, are survivors from the second play where they were assigned the more modest roles of the curate and the housemaid. When they make their decision to become the begetters of a future race of (English) longlived they are clearly possessed of the Life Force: evolution is about to take another leap forward, side-stepping Confucius in the process.

PART IV: "TRAGEDY OF AN ELDERLY GENTLEMAN"

In Part IV Shaw constructs a world which is divided into two. One part, based in Ireland, is occupied by the longlived descendants of the Archbishop and the Domestic Minister; the other part is occupied by the original human race. The latter is the domain of two hostile empires: one of them is British with its capital in Bagdhad; the other belongs to what is now called the "undeveloped world." Thus two of the prophecies of the second play have come to pass: that a new race of the longlived would arise, and that the short-lived British would be threatened by the colored races.

However, the ultimate question in the third millenium A.D. does not concern rivalry between the short-lived, but relates to whether any of them should be allowed to survive. And the answer, in terms of creative evolution, seems to be that they should not: the short-lived are not compatible with the longlived.

The argument that the short-lived are unfit to survive is presented by having a party of them visit Ireland on a pilgrimage to consult a (false) oracle. The longlived have set this oracle up for the benefit of the short-lived; their purpose in doing so is not clear.

Those who visit the oracle are true descendants of Cain: political man is the British Prime Minister, warrior man is General Aufsteig, Emperor of Turania, "the greatest military genius of the age."[7] Both of them have the intention of falsifying the Word (as represented by the oracle, which is in itself a falsity) by claiming supernatural sanction for their intentions and actions. When the oracle says to the Prime Minister, "Go home, poor fool,"[8] he easily decides what he will tell the electorate, for the oracle has said this before. He will tell them "that the oracle repeated to me, word for word, what it said to Sir Fuller Eastwind fifteen years ago."[9]

Most importantly, thinking man makes his appearance in the person of the Elderly Gentleman, who is one of the visiting party. He is no match for the longlived. Sadly and symbolically, he dies of discouragement which comes to him at the touch of the Oracle.

When Shaw depicts the society of the longlived, he has the opportunity to let his imagination run riot. He does not do this: he keeps it strictly under control, drawing his projections from the trends of past civilizations and from various socialistic aspirations. The changes that are mentioned fall largely into three groups. In the first group are those which show a number of socialist objectives as having been achieved, such as the ending of landlordism and State acceptance of the care and nurture of children. The second group comprises technological changes, some of which are implied rather than fully described. Thus the disappearance of cities (originally destroyed by war and not rebuilt) suggests the advanced use of some sort of power, such as electricity, which has made urban conglomeration unnecessary. It has destroyed what was good as well as what was bad about urban man. In the third group are cultural changes. As a result of State intervention, family life has to a large extent disappeared. So have the arts, which may in part be due to the disappearance of the cities. Also, infanticide in cases where the infant is defective, is now the standard practice. There are to be no throwbacks to the short-lived.

What has happened to the voice? It is no longer a vehicle for dead thoughts and empty phrases. To achieve this the language of the longlived has been stripped of metaphor and rhetoric. At the same time there is no room in the speech of the longlived for imagination, or for poetry, or for inspiration from the past. At this stage in humankind's imagined evolution there is an imbalance between science, religion, and the arts. The arts have had to die in order that they may live again. In a sense the death of the Elderly Gentleman is symbolic of this. Though the longlived and the short-lived speak the same language the Elderly Gentleman could not make himself understood. Death by discouragement is the answer.

Is this also the intended fate of the ancient Hebrew Bible which the playwright seeks to replace?

PART V: "AS FAR AS THOUGHT CAN REACH"

The world of Part V belongs entirely to the longlived. And the society here constructed is based on two further evolutionary leaps. The first is that humans have become oviparous; and within the egg the normal recapitulation of the stages of evolution that hitherto took place in the womb are vastly extended so that the human being who emerges from the egg is fully grown and fully educated. Hence society is relieved of responsibility for the care of the young; parental relationships, with their joys, griefs, and responsibilities, no longer exist.

The second evolutionary leap is that humans no longer ingest food; they take nourishment from the elements. Hence they are no longer dependent on the food chain. (Humans have, in fact, destroyed the whole of the animal kingdom.)

These two profound biological changes have meant that what was previously the life of the idle rich is now available to everyone, except that the pleasures of Horseback Hall no longer exist. Enjoyment of the arts and of human love and companionship between adults are life's pleasures. The creation of works of art, together with study and contemplation, are its serious purpose. The arts, which had disappeared in the fourth play, have come alive again, and thinking man is an entire being.

In such a society there might be a tendency to elevate art to the status of religion, but the author makes it clear that it is the Life Force and not art that is truly sacred. "A dainty little classic temple" forms part of the set, but the altar outside the temple is reserved for the egg which is about to hatch. Later, when Pygmalion abuses the Life Force by creating a pair of automata, things go sadly wrong and he is killed by the female automaton.

The automata serve three useful purposes. They demonstrate some of the physical crudities and knee-jerk reactions which belong to them; this enables the youths and maidens to show their disgust at a more primitive way of life. They also give Shaw the opportunity to express his view that neo–Darwinism and determinism are contrary to the doctrine of creative evolution. And, in their death they give a dramatic demonstration that the destructive principle is still applied in the case of evolutionary throwbacks.

To return to art and its purpose in this society, it seems as though it is through art that humankind reaches maturity; but when maturity is reached, art is abandoned. There is a long and important discussion between Martellus and Arjillax in which they talk about how the artist progresses from depicting the ephemeral, fleshly beauty of mankind to the portrayal of the human psyche. They reach the conclusion that art is an illusion and life is the only reality. To the Ancients art has a diminished significance and has become the equivalent of dolls. "Ever since men existed, children have played with dolls,"[10] says the He-Ancient.

The Ancients seem to serve the purpose of taking audience and reader into a sort of hinterland between the world of the flesh and the mystery of eternity. When Shaw depicts them he takes another leap of the imagination, though others have been there before him. The Ancients have tired not only of the arts but also of human companionship. They remove themselves from society, returning only when their advice is needed. They have tired also of the flesh. They resemble the Therapeutae who, in ancient times, were renowned for the contemplative life they led, according to Philo, outside the walls of Alexandria.

We are to go one or two steps further along the road that the Ancients take. We are required to imagine that when the Ancients achieve their aim and discard the flesh they leave their home on planet Earth, and join the creative force of the universe somewhere in outer space and spend eternity in contemplation.

But there is more to be said about the destructive principle. In *Heartbreak House* it was mere man who contemplated the possible destruction of humanity. Here it is Lilith who looks with uncertainty at what she has created:

> They have accepted the burden of eternal life. They have taken the agony from birth…. Their breasts are without milk: their bowels are gone: the very shapes of them are only ornaments for their children to admire and caress without understanding. Is this enough; or must I labor again? Shall I bring forth something that will sweep them away and make an end of them as they have swept away the beasts of the garden and made an end … of all them that refuse to live for ever?[11]

Man is drinking in the "last chance" saloon. He has, Lilith reminds him, been there once before. "The pangs of another birth were already upon me when one man repented and lived for three hundred years."[12] Now Lilith makes another commitment: "I will not supersede them until they have forded this last stream that lies between flesh and spirit, and disentangled their life from the matter that has always mocked it."[13]

The metabiological pentateuch has its own artistic shaping. In the beginning the Word became flesh. At the ending the Word will cease to be flesh.

Back to Methuselah was first presented by the Theatre Guild at the

Garrick Theatre, New York, on February 27, 1922 (Parts I and II), March 6, 1922 (Parts III and IV), and March 13, 1922 (Part V).

It was first performed in England at the Birmingham Repertory Theatre in October 1923. The scenic artist, Paul Shelving, proved that it was possible to re-create on stage Shaw's imagined construct. It was described as "the most enterprising production ever put on in the city."[14] It brought no financial reward, however, to Barry Jackson, a philanthropist of the theatre who had financed the production: he lost £2500 on the Birmingham venture. *Back to Methuselah* was included in the opening program of the Malvern Festival Theatre in 1929. By that time Barry Jackson had been knighted for his services to the theatre.

22

A Widening of Vision

In his first phase as a writer Shaw's progress had been linear. At length there came a definitive moment when his status as a playwright impelled him to give priority to the writing of plays over the executive work of the Fabian Society.

In Shaw's second phase the definitive feature is a widening of vision. This applies to his political writing, but it applies much more to Shaw as a playwright and as a playwright-philosopher.

When the First World War broke out it became abundantly clear that Shaw had ceased to be the articulator of the Fabian Society: he spoke for himself alone. Yet he still spoke for the future, and for the future of humankind. His political vision expanded and he was one of the first to think in terms of a supranational association of nations, which was eventually to lead to the formation of the League of Nations.

However, this widening of Shaw's political vision had its darker side, and there were times when he was in despair at the political ineptitude of postwar statesmen.

Shaw came to a full flowering as a playwright-philosopher during this period. Three plays in particular are indicative of this. *Pygmalion*, a microcosmic play, full of the vitality and certainty of life before the First World War as experienced by Londoners, is a summation of the sort of world that Shaw portrayed in his early plays, though sometimes they contained a great deal more grief and sorrow than *Pygmalion*. This is to be compared with that other work depicting pre-war life, the macrocosmic *Heartbreak House*, which in its metaphors, its agonies, its uncertainties, and its heedlessness represents the world of pre-war Europe in a totally different context than *Pygmalion*.

More was to come. In *Man and Superman*, written in Shaw's first phase, he had introduced the concept of creative evolution. Now, as a playwright-prophet and a servant of creative evolution, Shaw offered his metabiological pentateuch, *Back to Methuselah*, and presented within the confines of the theatre the alpha and the omega of creation: human vision can extend no further.

Indeed, in his third phase Shaw set aside the universe and looked at the politics of government to which his name and fame had given him a particular access.

PART III

"ALL THE WORLD'S A STAGE" FOR THE POLITICAL PLAYWRIGHT (1920–1939)

23

The Years of Acclaim

During the 1920s Shaw was to reach a pinnacle of fame in England and in the world at large. Two milestones are to be noted. One was the international recognition given to Shaw when he was awarded the Nobel Prize for Literature for the year 1925. The other was the publication of his book with the slightly misleading title of *The Intelligent Woman's Guide to Socialism and Capitalism*, which the Prime Minister, Ramsay Mac-Donald, described as "the world's most important book since the Bible."[1]

The presentation of the Nobel Prize (in 1926) was made in Shaw's absence. At the ceremony Dr. Per Hallstrom, the Chairman of the Nobel Committee for the Swedish Academy, made an ennobling speech which recognized Shaw's continuing concern for the corporate good of humankind and rebuked those who persisted in seeing him only as a jester:

> [Shaw] showed in the novels of his youth the same conception of the world and the same attitude to social problems that he has ever since maintained. This provides a better defence for him than anything else against the long-current [mostly British] accusation of lack of honesty and of acting as a professional buffoon at the court of democracy.[2]

In fact there had been a change in Shaw's political status starting in January 1924, when the Labour Party became the Party of Government. Although this Government lasted for only nine months, there was a further period of office from 1929 to 1931. As a writer and a thinker Shaw was now within the circle of the political establishment. He set aside the drama for a while in order to write a textbook on socialism which was especially intended (despite its title) for the benefit of Labour Members of Parliament who had newly come into power.

In the wider world there was to be further acclaim in celebration of Shaw's seventieth birthday in 1926. Dan Laurence records that "a fanfare of acclamation" came from Germany. Those joining in the fanfare included Albert Einstein, Thomas Mann, and Bertolt Brecht.[3] At home, Ramsay MacDonald made the offer of a knighthood, which was rejected. Laurence says, "He had attained international supremacy in the theatre, and was probably the most famous person in the world."[4]

The cinema and the radio had, of course, played their parts in spreading Shaw's fame; he had also travelled abroad extensively. Sometimes, as when he visited Soviet Russia (with Lord and Lady Astor in 1931) and America in 1933, he gave memorable addresses.

In Russia it was he, rather than the Astors, who was lionized. When they arrived in Moscow there was a military guard of honor, and thousands of Russians were shouting "Hail Shaw" and carrying banners bearing his portrait. His seventy-fifth birthday was celebrated while he was there. In his birthday speech he told the Russians:

> When you carry your experiment [of Communism] to its triumphant conclusion—which I feel confident you will—then we in the West, we who are still just playing at Socialism, must follow in your footsteps—whether we will or no.[5]

Shaw also spoke of the Russians' ability "to understand and appreciate my dramatic works with a depth and a subtlety the like of which—I must confess—I have never found in Western Europe."[6]

However, Shaw did not enjoy undiluted admiration during the 1920s and '30s, largely due to his stance in favor of dictatorship and his apparent support of Mussolini and Hitler. It was many years since Shaw had first drawn a line of demarcation between socialism and parliamentary democracy. With the rise of Mussolini in Italy and, later, of Hitler in Germany, he was able to quote examples of the people having turned towards dictatorship as an alternative to democratic government: here, in the real world, were leaders possessed of "the will." An example of Shaw's attitude comes from a letter which he wrote to Dr. Friedrich Adler on October 14, 1927. He began in fairly measured terms: "I can now look back ... on a blameless career as a propagandist of Social-Democracy, with the success of the Socialism completely neutralised by the futility of the democracy." Later in the letter he makes a chilling statement: "Now we, as Socialists, have nothing to do with liberty. Our message, like Mussolini's, is one of discipline, of service, of ruthless refusal to acknowledge any natural right of competence."[7] Shaw wrote this letter in the same year he completed *The Intelligent Woman's Guide*, which was published in the following year.

As the above quotation illustrates, there was a new harshness in some of Shaw's writing at this time, including one or two of the Prefaces to his plays.

24

"The Most Important Book Since the Bible": *The Intelligent Woman's Guide to Socialism and Capitalism*

When *Fabian Essays in Socialism* was published in 1889, Shaw described himself and his fellow essayists as "communicative learners." In the next century, he wrote *The Intelligent Woman's Guide to Socialism and Capitalism* (1928) as an authority, and as a sage of international repute. The Essays were to make their way around the world. So did *The Intelligent Woman's Guide*. In the United States fifty thousand copies were given as bonuses by book clubs to their subscribers.

But in intention this was primarily a domestic work and its origins were comparatively humble. It was sparked off by a request that Shaw received from his sister-in-law, Mary Cholmondeley, for some ideas about Socialism for the benefit of a women's study group in Shropshire.[1] The request fell on fertile ground. Shaw looked at the situation around him and noted the vastly increased numbers of the electorate. At the time of the 1929 general election, almost the entire adult population, numbering nearly 29 million, were entitled to vote. Also there were about one and a half million more women than men on the electoral rolls.[2] Here was an opportunity to inform and advise the female electorate at large.

Shaw looked also at the possible candidates for election and judged that, with the probability of a Labour Government being elected, there would be many Members of Parliament with no previous experience in that capacity, who had insufficient knowledge of politics and economics. While the work was addressed to the "intelligent woman," he had

Members of Parliament very much in mind. Ramsay MacDonald's high regard for the work has already been mentioned; others were less reverential. Shaw's former editor, Frank Harris, for example, wrote that his socialist theories had been disproved and discredited yet he continued to give socialist advice, "fortunately to 'intelligent women' only."[3]

Some years later Shaw wrote two additional chapters for the book, one on Sovietism, the other on Fascism. They were published in the 1937 edition and the title was extended accordingly.

For the present-day reader the work encapsulates Shaw's political thinking and his views on the economy as of the late 1920s. When compared with his earlier works, the Guide demonstrates how his socialism and his political thinking in general had been modified in response to changing times and a changing political scene.

All the arguments about socialism in the Guide center around one major premise, namely Shaw's definition of socialism, which is not necessarily common ground with all socialists. He writes about how socialism is to be achieved, how it will affect social relationships such as marriage and what the subsidiary effects will be; and this is consistently related to what he calls the first and last commandment of socialism: "Thou shalt not have a greater or less income than thy neighbor."[4]

Another major precept, which enables the reader who has no special background in economics to follow Shaw's thesis, is his simple definition of capital as "spare money."[5] Spare money must not be left idle: it needs to be continually invested and re-invested. This is the reason there is a continual search for opportunities for investment and re-investment, a search which often takes the would-be investor to foreign undeveloped lands. In protecting such projects from attack, the investor's country of origin may find that it has acquired imperial territory almost unawares. Shaw uses a brilliant phrase to describe this continual search for investment: "the runaway car of capitalism."[6]

As to equality of income, Shaw discusses what the social impact would be. He raises one of his favorite arguments, that inequality of income (or, in earlier works, disparity of social status) leads to artificial selection in choosing a marriage partner, which is to the disadvantage of the race and hinders evolutionary progress.

Equality of income, Shaw points out, has to be introduced with care, and in carefully phased stages, bearing in mind the effect that each stage will have on the economy as a whole. The Fabian tenet of "gradualism" is here applied specifically to the economy.

Shaw's precise definition of socialism means that he is able to argue on this subject, without sidetracking. In particular he points out that not all those who call themselves socialists are (by his definition) committed to socialism. By the same token socialistic measures have been introduced by those who lay no claim to being socialists.

One finds in the text of this major work many fundamental points and references to topical issues which Shaw makes in his plays as well. This heavily underlines his serious purpose as a dramatist and his great gift—which he displayed particularly in the 1920s and 1930s—of dramatizing the political issues of the times.

The first of the added chapters, "Sovietism," presents a picture of a tremendous political crisis now happily mastered and turned to public good. There is a slight element of "holier than thou" in Shaw's discourse, since he does tend to say that if Russia had followed Fabian tenets rather than those of Marx, some of the tragedies might have been avoided. He also states challengingly: "But the process of trial and error by which this result was arrived at, though very much briefer and kindlier than the process by which England was starved into accepting the Capitalist development of modern machine industry, was pretty bad."[7]

Shaw refers to his visit to the USSR in 1931, by which time the tide had turned. He found no such horrors as he could have found in the distressed areas and slums of the capitalist west, but Russia had yet to accept the principle of equality of income: "Equality of income, which, as we have seen, is the final and essential diagnostic of Communism, is no part of the gospel of Marx."[8] For further reading on this subject Shaw recommends Beatrice and Sidney Webb's *Soviet Communism: A New Civilization?*.

The chapter on Fascism begins with a lament over democracy. The nearer the British (and others) have approached to political democracy the more its imperfections have appeared. Those political agitators who seek election to Parliament find, when they get there, that all they can do is debate. If they want to exercise influence they must turn their backs on Parliament and create a militant Fascist force.

The author describes the sort of person who might attach himself to an incipient dictator. The categories include Republicans, Trade Unionists, Socialists, and Bolsheviks. As to disposition, "They are patriotic, these people, by which they mean that God created them superior to the natives of other countries."[9] A description follows of the sort of organization that the dictator will wish to abolish. "This," says Shaw, "can be easily done by simple violence."[10]

Shaw presents a very powerful picture, and any impression that has been gained from his previous random comments about Fascism that he is a committed supporter of Fascist regimes is likely to be dissipated.

There follows an account, in more measured terms, of how, having gained power, the Fascist leader retains popularity.

The cruelty and the murder of the Fascist regime are set aside briefly when he makes an ironic comment: Fascism "sets up a national control of the press and platform which is at least less liable to abuse than the control of the millionaires."[11]

Shaw sees two great dangers in Fascism. The first "danger" is debatable. It is argued that where there is a powerful leader no provision is made for his death or downfall. A suggestion is made that scarcely seems tenable: "Hence a nation needs a constitution that will function harmlessly in the intervals between one able ruler and another."[12] (Somewhere along the way the Fascist dictator has become "the able ruler.")

The second danger, which is much more vast, accords with Shaw's persistent presentiment that the present civilization, like all its predecessors, will eventually fall into decline. Modern Fascism is seen as the latest mask of Capitalism. If it remains so it will follow the pattern of "the ancient Roman Fascism which perished and dragged down the European civilization of that time with it."[13]

The Intelligent Woman's Guide concludes with a chapter titled Peroration, the last words of which offer a courtly Irish compliment to the lady who "leaves the nation in her debt and the world a better world than she found it. By such ladies and their sons can the human race be saved, and not otherwise."[14]

The peroration is dated March 16, 1927. In 1939 would come the Second World War, in which many of those sons would perish.

"The League of Nations": Shaw Visits Geneva

In 1928 Shaw visited Geneva. He attended the League of Nations' annual Assembly and studied the workings of the League's other institutions, especially the Secretariat and the International Labour Office. He wrote about his visit in Fabian Tract No 226, "The League of Nations" which was published in 1929. His account of the League was printed in a number of newspapers.

A decade had passed since Shaw had written his "Peace Conference Hints." It will be recalled that this pamphlet had contained a great deal of advice and many observations intended for the benefit of the statesmen who were to attend the Versailles Peace Conference, from which the League of Nations emanated. The League first met in 1920. Now Shaw passes judgment on the League in action. He makes a very positive statement about its potential contribution to internationalism:

> The really great thing that is happening at Geneva is the growth of a genuinely international public service, the chiefs of which are ministers in a coalition which is, in effect, an incipient international Government. In the atmosphere of Geneva patriotism perishes.[1]

An example is given: young (English) diplomats, born and bred in the Foreign Office tradition, when assigned to Geneva, "suffer a lake change" and respond to the Geneva spirit.

In due course Sir Eric Drummond, the permanent (British) Secretary General is introduced: in charge of the Secretariat, he has a "splendid record as the first creator of the international staff."[2] But first the annual Assembly is described. It is obvious that the delegates, described as "deciduous" by Shaw, have no time to absorb the Geneva spirit: it is

also obvious that the Assembly is merely a front. "Roughly and generally," we are told, "it is a fact that the Pacifist oratory at the Assembly is
Christmas card platitude at best and humbug at worst."[3] M. Briand, the
French delegate, is presented as the exception to this: a more typical delegate is the "British Jingo Imperialist."[4]

Shaw enthuses about the International Labour Office. Unlike the
Assembly and the Secretariat, which are housed in former hotels, this
office occupies buildings that were built especially for it, "with Labour
glorified in muscular statues and splendid stained glass windows ...
and with every board room panelled and furnished and chandeliered
with the gift of some State doing its artistic best."[5] M. Albert Thomas,
the French counterpart of Sir Eric, but rather more magnificent, is
also more tuned to the future. "Here," says Shaw, giving him his international significance, "M. Albert Thomas reigns, not as a king ... but
as a Pope; for this is the true International of which Moscow only
dreams."[6]

It is easy to understand why Shaw is so rhapsodic: two projects of
the Labour Office that he mentions are at the heart of international socialism and thus at the heart of Shaw. The first is a project, undertaken by
the Howard Society, to obtain an international agreement about the
humane treatment of prisoners: "If the League of Nations did not exist,
such an object would be unattainable."[7] Similarly a second projected agreement to "eliminate sweating and limit the length of the working day would
not be possible without the League."[8]

At this stage Shaw is very confident about the future: "Take into
account the incipient international court of justice at The Hague, with
the body of international law which will grow from it, and the case for
maintaining the League becomes irresistible...."[9]

Many people, at that time, thought of the League in terms of the
prevention of war and were more aware of the Assembly than of the
other two institutions. It was Shaw's intention to adjust the balance of
public interest. After giving a brief account of some of the difficulties
that had arisen between nations since the end of the war, he repudi-
ates, in one sentence, the idea that it is the League's function to prevent
war: "Even were there no such question as that of war and peace, the
League would be able to justify its existence ten times over: indeed this
question is now rather the main drawback to the League than its *raison
d'être*."[10]

Shaw is not reneging here: in "Peace Conference Hints" (1919) after
discussing the pros and cons of disarmament, he pronounced: "The League
cannot make war physically impossible and should not try to."[11]

Tract No 226 was not the last of Shaw's writings about the League: his play, *Geneva*, was presented at the Malvern Festival in 1938. In the following year the Second World War broke out. The League of Nations was superseded in 1945 by the United Nations.

26

Shaw's Last Fabian Tract

In 1929 Shaw's last Fabian tract was published. It consisted of two articles that had appeared previously elsewhere: "Socialism: Principles and Outlook" in the *Encyclopaedia Britannica*, and "Fabianism" in *Chambers's Encyclopaedia*. Much water had flowed under the bridge since Shaw's first Fabian tract, "A Manifesto," was published in 1884, and Shaw was now writing, as in *The Intelligent Woman's Guide*, as an authority.

His definition of socialism, given in an opening statement, is rather more sophisticated than that which appears in *The Intelligent Woman's Guide*, but it is not incompatible:

> Socialism, reduced to its simplest legal and practical expression, means the complete discarding of the institution of private property by transforming it into public property and the division of the resultant public income equally and indiscriminately among the entire population.[1]

In this it is possible to perceive an example of the way in which Shaw adapts his style and his content to a different category of reader.

The Intelligent Woman's Guide and "Socialism" contain similar accounts of the rise of capitalism, but urbanity is set aside when the tract gives an account of the present political situation:

> Trade Unionism now maintains a Labour Party in the British Parliament. The most popular members and leaders are Socialist in theory … but the trade union driving force aims at nothing more than Capitalism with labour taking the lion's share, and energetically repudiates compulsory national service, which would deprive it of its power to strike.[2]

A categorical statement is then made with which it is unlikely that the majority of socialists would agree: "Compulsory national service is essential in Socialism...."[3]

Shaw moves next to a wider perspective and looks at capitalism through the lens of history to make his final pronouncement:

> It is a historic fact, recurrent enough to be called an economic law, that Capitalism, which builds up great civilisations, also wrecks them if persisted in beyond a certain point.... But though the moment for the change has come again and again it has never been effected because Capitalism has never produced the necessary enlightenment among the masses nor admitted to a controlling share in public affairs the order of intellect and character outside which Socialism, or indeed politics, as distinguished from mere party electioneering, is incomprehensible.[4]

"Socialism: Principles and Outlook" ends on a note of guarded optimism:

> Empires end in ruins: commonwealths have hitherto been beyond the civic capacity of mankind. But there is always the possibility that mankind will this time weather the cape on which all the old civilisations have been wrecked. It is this possibility that gives intense interest to the present historic moment and keeps the Socialist movement alive and militant.[5]

One wonders how the readers of the *Encyclopaedia Britannica* reacted to this article? Could there have been disappointment that no mention is made of socialistic aspirations as, for example, expounded in the Fabian Essays? No famous names are mentioned, such as the Webbs or William Morris, and there is no reference to Christian Socialism. Nothing is said about Ramsay MacDonald, the first Labour Prime Minister, who could surely lay claim also to being the first Socialist Prime Minister. The emphasis is on the presentation of socialism and capitalism as currently diametrical opposites. This is not the case in *The Intelligent Woman's Guide*, in which Shaw specifically states: "The steps to Socialism will not necessarily be taken by Socialist Governments."[6]

In "Fabianism" Shaw takes a different approach to his subject. An account of the history of the Society is given and its early leaders and important publications are named. We learn that the Fabian Society had its beginnings in 1884 when a body of English socialists came together to discuss social problems in general, and in particular those presented by a Scottish-American thinker, Thomas Davidson. Subsequently the group divided into two, one of which, "more matter-of-fact, militant, and political"[7] established itself as the Fabian Society. An indication as to the sort of individual who joined the Society is given and it is clear that the members are of the intelligentsia and determined to keep it that way. The original membership consisted of "educated persons of the professional and higher official classes, including civil servants of the upper division, stockbrokers, journalists, and propertied bourgeoisie generally, all under the age of thirty, with their careers still before them."[8]

A comparison is made between the Fabian Society and other societies of the Left to the disparagement of the latter, who looked to the "wage-workers" as a class from whom they would seek their recruits. Shaw becomes elitist when he describes these other societies as "hopeless and useless except for agitating and demonstrating against the unemployment and misery of the period of bad trade then prevailing."[9] Such associations had no attraction for "critical students of the great evangelists of the [socialist] movement, especially for the politically experienced ones, much less for upper division civil servants with a practical knowledge of government and administration."[10] When Shaw makes this reference to the civil service, clearly he had in mind Sidney Webb and Sydney Olivier, early leaders of the Society, both of whom were eventually raised to the peerage. The Fabian was, for them, "a Society of their own class."[11]

Membership for several years remained at less than forty. There was no recruiting and meetings were held in "one another's drawing rooms." The aim of the Society was declared to be "the re-organisation of society by the emancipation of land and industrial capital from individual ownership, and the vesting of them in the community for the general benefit."[12]

Shaw cites *Fabian Essays on Socialism* as an assertion of the Society's independence from Socialist dogma. Described here as "distinctively English," the Essays ridiculed the notion of a sudden change from capitalism to socialism, describing this as "catastrophic Socialism"[13]: the transition from capitalism to socialism should be by way of constitutional evolution.

Moving from theory to practice, Shaw describes how the Fabians introduced practical Socialism by means of municipal enterprise. This began in 1888 when the London County Council was first established. In their early efforts to influence politics at a national level the Fabians had pursued a policy of permeation, whereby they sought to imbue other bodies and political parties with socialistic objectives. Mention is made of the formation of an independent Labour Party led by Keir Hardie and Ramsay MacDonald. At the general election of 1906 the Labour Party became an accomplished fact; the Fabian Society was affiliated to it.

The year 1906 is taken as a benchmark from which Fabian achievements are reviewed. And here the horizon widens. During the twenty-two years of the Society's existence, the author claims: "Socialism had become Fabianised throughout Europe."[14] But the palm goes to Australasia where, we are told, "Labour parties had actually achieved parliamentary majorities, forming governments, and carrying into law many projects suggested and inspired by Fabian Essays and the long series of Fabian tracts which had supplemented them."[15]

Another benchmark year is 1922, when there was a general election, and Sidney Webb became a Member of Parliament. The general election of 1922 "marked the final transfer of the political activities of the Fabian Society to the front benches of Labour in Parliament."[16]

There is one significant event in Fabian history which Shaw mentions but does not stress: this was the formation of an International Agreements Committee. The war of 1914–18 had revealed, says Shaw, "the political futility of international Socialism, and the helpless nullity and ignorance of British Socialism and Labour in the sphere of foreign policy."[17] For this reason the Fabian Society turned its attention to supranational law, and, through its International Agreements Committee, produced plans for a supranational legislature and tribunal.

One of the most interesting features of this account of Fabianism is the mention that Shaw makes of the Society"s early leaders. Sydney Olivier (Lord Olivier), a one-time Secretary of the Society, had become Governor of Jamaica. Sidney Webb, together with his wife, Beatrice, had produced a monumental series of investigations into the history and structure of industrial democracy and had been involved in the foundation and development of the London School of Economics. Others are mentioned, including the author, of whom he says: "Mr Bernard Shaw, achieving success as a playwright, first in America and Germany and later on in England, substituted the theatre for the platform of the Fabian Society, and the prefaces to his published plays for Fabian pamphlets, as his chief means of propaganda."[18]

And that is the early Fabian story.

27

A New Politicization
of the Drama and
a New Theatrical Venue

The rise of the Labour Party to power gave Shaw, in his third phase as a playwright, a great sense of the immediacy of contemporary politics. Two of his plays are indeed central to British politics and in each of these the principal characters are close to the seats of power.

But first Shaw looks back in history to the days of Joan of Arc, seeing Joan as a leader at a time when Europe was beginning to move away from feudalism towards nationalism. Similarly, in an earlier phase, he had selected Julius Caesar as an examplar of leadership in the days of imperial Rome.

The phase ends as it began with a "lesson of history" play, this time set in the reign of Charles II.

These major plays are interspersed with a number of others, some set in fantasy land, some presenting snapshots of everyday life outside the political scene.

It was during this period that a new theatrical venue was provided for Shaw, the playwright of worldwide fame. This was in the heart of the English countryside at the spa town of Malvern. Here an annual festival of the drama was promoted which made a special feature of Shaw's plays. The Festival was the inspiration of Sir Barry Jackson, the patron and owner of the Birmingham Repertory Theatre, where a number of Shaw's plays had been produced. The first Festival (in 1929) was devoted entirely to Shaw's works, including *The Apple Cart*.

28

Saint Joan:
A Chronicle Play in
Six Scenes and an Epilogue

Saint Joan was the last play that Shaw wrote before he was awarded the Nobel Prize for Literature and it is probable that it was his most famous play. For this lesson in history Shaw chose the period when European civilization was emerging from the feudalism of the Middle Ages and when Protestantism was beginning to challenge the universality of Catholicism. Shaw argues—very effectively—that Joan was not a Catholic martyr but an early Protestant martyr. She, as an individual, and the Catholic church as an institution, stand at the crossroads of history. Likewise she is the harbinger of nationalism, whereby each man shall be loyal to his king and his country rather than to his feudal lord.

Joan is unaware that she is the voice of Protestantism, a mode of thinking that will evolve, for Shaw, into the secular religion of creative evolution. If one translates the voices of the saints, which Joan claims to have heard, into the secular language of Shaw, they become the voices of her own inspiration, or, in terms of creative evolution, the voice of the will or the Life Force.

Joan is presented as a country girl who speaks in the vernacular and addresses everyone, except the Archbishop, as an equal. (Shaw said that any dialect would do for the part of St. Joan.) But other characters in the play are representational, and speak of that which they represent: the Earl of Warwick for feudalism, Cauchon, the Bishop of Beauvais, and Lemaitre (the Inquisitor) for the Church and the Inquisition. In a brilliant passage in the Preface, Shaw explains how these representational characters must speak with a comprehension that they could not have possessed at the time: "It is the business of the stage to make its figures more intelligible to themselves than they would be in real life; for by no other means can they be made intelligible to the audience."[1]

151

In fact Joan's language seems to have presented Shaw with a problem. On significant occasions she drops the vernacular and speaks in an emotive fashion. She does this after the Dauphin's coronation when the Archbishop has chided her for conceit, ignorance, and presumption: "Do not think you can frighten me by telling me that I am alone. France is alone; and God is alone; and what is my loneliness before the loneliness of my country and my God? ... I will go out now to the common people, and let the love in their eyes comfort me for the hate in yours."[2]

Joan speaks in the same style after she learns that her recantation, though it would spare her life, would mean a sentence of life imprisonment:

> Bread has no sorrow for me, and water no affliction. But to shut me from the light of the sky and the sight of the fields and flowers; to chain my feet so that I can never again ride with the soldiers nor climb the hills: ... without these things I cannot live; and by your wanting to take them away from me ... I know that your counsel is of the devil, and that mine is of God.[3]

This is the language of near-poetry, it is not the language of Joan. Sybil Thorndike, who was cast as Joan in the first London production of the play, has a different view, however. She says: "The trial—I'd read the Records of it, and Joan's lines were word for word what she said. Except for the last big outburst, which was sheer poetry and pure Shaw."[4]

The nub of the play is, of course, the trial scene, both in drama and in argument. Shaw is at pains to demonstrate that the accusers, as well as the accused, are given a fair trial. The trial is conducted according to the precepts of the church at that time; indeed the Inquisitor bends over backwards to be fair and helpful to Joan.

However, the finger of blame is pointed—not unusually for Shaw— at the play's two English characters, the Earl of Warwick and his Chaplain, though neither of them has an active part to play in the actual trial. When the smooth-tongued Earl of Warwick makes his pronouncement before the start of the trial one may recognize in him the prototype of later politicians. "Her death," says the Earl, "is a political necessity which I regret but cannot help."[5] The Earl's Chaplain is the one member of the cast who is vengeful towards Joan and wishes her to be treated with the utmost rigour. After witnessing her terrible death at the stake he is overcome with remorse and self-hatred. He represents all those who are unable to conceptualize, and, for a time, substitute arrogance for understanding. (He just happens to be English.)

The last words of the play are spoken by the Executioner and the Earl. The Executioner, who has just disposed of Joan's ashes, says: "You have heard the last of her," the Earl replies, "The last of her? Hm! I wonder!"[6]

This ending might seem to be of an artistic sufficiency. But Shaw has something to say about Joan after her death, and he has a moral to point out. Hence there is an Epilogue, which takes place in the bedroom of the Dauphin, now Charles the Victorious. Time and space are set aside as Joan's contemporaries meet together and learn that Joan, more than four centuries after her death, has been declared a saint. They kneel in praise of her. But when Joan points out that as a saint she can work miracles, and asks shall she return as a living woman, each makes his excuses and departs.

The last words of the Epilogue are a reproach to the audience and to posterity: "O God that madest this beautiful earth, when will it be ready to receive Thy saints? How long, O Lord, how long?"[7]

The play was first presented by the Theatre Guild at the Garrick Theatre, New York, on December 28, 1923. It was produced at the New Theatre, London, on March 26, 1924.

29

Two Political Extravaganzas: *The Apple Cart* and *Too True to Be Good*

During the immediate postwar years much of Shaw's political thinking had centered on America. Would she take the lead in the formation of the League of Nations? How powerful would the American Navy be compared with that of Britain? How interested would she be in the politics of Europe?

In his play *The Apple Cart*, which he describes as a political extravaganza, Shaw presents some of his ponderings onstage when he has the American Ambassador inform the English King (Magnus) that it is America's intention to rejoin the British Empire, or, in less diplomatic language, to annex it. What is it that exists between America and Britain, kinship or rivalry, or a mixture of both?

The Apple Cart presents an imagined situation which takes place in the third quarter of the twentieth century; its setting is in the Royal Palace. The unities of time, place, and action are observed. It is concerned with the politics of a nation. *Too True to Be Good* is an extravaganza of a very different kind: it is concerned with the social mores of the individual, and is nebulous.

It is interesting that Shaw should link these seemingly so different plays together by a common subtitle, thereby inviting the reader to identify and examine the nature of that link.

THE APPLE CART: A POLITICAL EXTRAVAGANZA (1928)

Politics is not the easiest stuff out of which to create a play, and in order to do so Shaw fully exerts his playwright's art. The setting of the

King's palace provides a Ruritanian mirror and a perspective of distance to the action of *The Apple Cart*. Nevertheless the play is mostly about actuality: several of the stereotypical characters are based on politicians of the day.

The playwright's attitude towards socialism has not in essence changed since the days of *Back to Methuselah*. He continues to see socialism as an entity separate from democracy, and he continues to differentiate between thinking man and political man. But now, with the Labour Party in power, the scene has changed. With Ramsay MacDonald as Prime Minister (briefly in 1924 and again from 1929 to 1931) the thinking man of the Fabian Society has, in some cases, become the political man of the Labour Party.

And socialists have to address themselves to different questions. Previously the concern was to rectify social evils step by step. Now with Labour as the party in power, they have to look at the State as an entity, and at the major trends and forces which concern, and perhaps threaten, the State. This change of outlook is reflected in the subject matter of *The Apple Cart* and also in the later play, *On the Rocks*. To a certain extent Shaw was also part of the political establishment, but as befitted his status as an artist, he orbited around the political establishment and was not central to it.

The first night of the London production of *The Apple Cart*, together with later happenings and comments, illustrate the sphere of Shaw's political influence as a playwright, and its nature. The Prime Minister and the American Ambassador were seated side by side watching a play in which the independence of Britain and her traditional role as ruler of the waves was challenged by the United States. Later in the month Ramsay MacDonald was to attend a disarmament conference in America which was described as "a milestone in British foreign policy, marking the end of Britain's supremacy at sea and America's emergence as a naval power."[1] After the performance Shaw declared that he intended telling the Prime Minister that "he must refuse to take any young man into his Cabinet who hasn't seen 'The Apple Cart' at least six times."[2]

The thematic construct of the play involves a trio of inter-related political crises. The first is concerned with the issue of sovereignty. A democratically elected Government, which belongs to the political Left, finds itself in conflict with the hereditary principle of government, represented by King Magnus. The King proposes to exercise a (defunct) power of veto. In this respect he is a metaphor for the House of Lords, with its ability to frustrate the legislative will of the House of Commons. (When a Labour Government was in power with an entrenched House of Lords, this was a very topical issue.) The King is required to desist, at which point he offers a further challenge by threatening to abdicate; he would then climb the political ladder himself by standing for Parliament. His intention seems to be that, if he reached the top of the ladder, he would kick it away and would change the nature of sovereignty from the crown-in-Parliament to the crown alone, thus establishing a dictatorship. This aspect of the play shows a triangular relationship between three aspects of political man: the Prime Minister, who is at the apex of parliamentary democracy; the King, representing the hereditary principle and also dictatorship from the Right; and the demagogue, Boanerges, whose power base is the trade unions rather than the electorate, and who has the potential to be a dictator from the Left.

Political man is joined by political woman in the persons of two Cabinet Ministers, the Powermistress-General, Lysistrata, and the Postmistress-General, Amanda.[3] Boanerges's part in the construct is chiefly to provide an analogy to the dictatorship of the Right, but he also provides an object lesson about the ways by which, in the 1920s, the aristocracy exerted influence over the politicians of the people: by subtle flattery, by social intercourse, and by the mystique of the hereditary principle. If Magnus were to abdicate these would be the means by which he would make his political way. Like the two female Cabinet Ministers, Boanerges is also there as a matter of historical record: he is based on John Burns, the first artisan to become a member of the Cabinet.

The struggle between parliamentary democracy and the hereditary principle is played like a game of chess. It ends in stalemate when the Cabinet withdraws its objection to the King's exercising the power of veto on condition that he withdraw his threat to abdicate.

The second potential crisis relates to Britain's economy. In a capitalist world, Britain's self-sufficiency is threatened by the infiltration of international and foreign capital into key industries. Under the offstage influence of the capitalist firm Breakages Ltd., English manufactured goods consist chiefly of luxury items such as chocolate creams. As in *Heartbeak House*, capitalism has the will and the power to corrupt the representatives of the people in Parliament. It also, by creating a transient prosperity, lulls the electorate into an apathy which takes no thought for the country's long-term interests. The sinister power of capitalism is presented as one of the reasons for having a dictatorship. King Magnus postulates that he is beyond the sphere of influence of Breakages Ltd.

The third potential crisis demonstrates how weak Britain has become by her lack of self-sufficiency, her dependence on foreign capital, and her inability, if challenged, to keep her sea lanes open. Hence the threat of the United States to absorb Britain, which the American Ambassador diplomatically describes as America's rejoining the British Empire.

In brief, the argument of the play runs as follows: Political democracy, the aim of which is the socialist State, does not work. It is undermined by the forces of capitalism which operate on an international scale. The alternative form of government may be dictatorship because it would not be susceptible to the forces of capitalism. Dictatorship may be the result of political maneuvering, such as a redefinition of the nature of sovereignty. But national sovereignty, as well as international status, may be in jeopardy, threatened with engulfment by a superior power operating from a capitalist base.

The artistic construct of the play is as notable as its three-pronged theme. Mention has already been made of Shaw's use of distancing effects to give artistic perspective. An equally important feature is the play's near perfect symmetry, from which much of its elegance springs, and which enhances and enlarges the argument of the play.

In the first scene, which serves as a prologue, the balance is between the two secretaries of the King. Their talk is about two kinds of men, the non-thinker (Sempronius's father) and the thinker (King Magnus). Magnus is thereby shown to be more than an aristocrat by birth: he belongs to the aristocracy of the intellect.

In the rest of the first act, which builds up to a point of suspense about the veto and the abdication threat, the artistic balance is chiefly between Boanerges, the bluff politician of the people, and the elegant Magnus. Both are powerful men in their own spheres. The rest of the Cabinet, with the Prime Minister at their head, represent a third element in the balance. The artistic balance is also a balance of power.

At the end of the act the audience is left in suspense, which is maintained by the divide of the Interlude, acted out in the Palace boudoir of the King's mistress. This scene is counterpoised with the opening of the play, since it suggests that, in the private places of his life, Magnus remains the thinking man who is devoted to the passion of the mind rather than the passion of the body. (He talks of "our strangely innocent relations.")[4]

Later in the day, in Act 2, we see briefly another facet of the King's private life. The Palace gardens replace the boudoir and the Queen replaces the mistress. With the entrance of the American Ambassador, and his dramatic announcement, the play takes an unexpected turn which alters its perspective. It is now the Ambassador who is held in balance with the King, as Boanerges was in Act 1. And the two men, Boanerges and the Ambassador, represent two different cultures, and two different power bases, with which the King has to contend, just as in his private life he is poised between his mistress and his wife.

Shaw extracts the full dramatic potential of this final threatened crisis. The audience, together with thinking political man, sees the nation walking towards a disaster which is beyond the range of vision of its duly elected political leaders.

A special word needs to be said about the pivotal figure of Magnus, for the play is weighted heavily in his favor. In all the dual relationships in the play, apart from the introduction, Magnus is one of the duo, and in the triangular relationship of the first act (the Prime Minister, Boanerges, and Magnus) the King is the key figure. In all these relationships, public and private, Magnus is shown in a superior light, and he is never the subject of satire: satire is reserved for the representatives of political democracy. Hence the argument of the play is supported by the artistic construct, and this support forms part of the play's unity.

The Apple Cart was first presented at the Teatr Polski, Warsaw, on June 14, 1929. That was the year when the Malvern Festival began. At the Festival "it delighted the Malvern audiences and gave distinction to the first year of the Festival. Cedric Hardwicke as Magnus and Edith Evans as Orinthia put up performances of high distinction. They set a standard of acting that at once established the Festival as a players" as well as a playwrights "occasion."[5]

During the play's London run at the Queen's Theatre Hesketh Pearson challenged Shaw as to whether Magnus was a veiled portrait of the reigning monarch, George V. Shaw replied: "The real King Magnus is sitting within a few feet of you. Never having been offered a throne, I have had to seize one and crown myself."[6]

TOO TRUE TO BE GOOD: A POLITICAL EXTRAVAGANZA (1931)

In the Malvern Festival Book for 1932 Shaw writes of how, in the First World War, the shock to common morals was enormously greater and more general than in previous wars. The terror it invoked had been counterbalanced by subsequent indulgence: "For four years, it was taken as a matter of course that young people, when they were not under fire, must be allowed a good time."[7] The bright young things had sought to continue this pleasure-loving way of life after the war was over. *Too True to Be Good* presents this situation.

The play is set for the most part on a sunny beach in an unnamed mountainous country which, the text vaguely suggests, may be part of the British Empire. (Why else would British soldiers be permitted to search for some non-existent brigands there?) This is the land of uncertainty in an uncertain world. It is also the land of improbability, where strange coincidences bring together an assortment of people, including father and son, mother and daughter, who are bound together by uncertainty. The play has an overriding metaphor, that of a bottomless pit into which humankind is falling, falling.

There is no immediate perception of this, however, for the play starts elsewhere, in "one of the best bedrooms in one of the best suburban villas in one of the richest cities in England." A young lady (the Patient) lies in bed there with the Monster in a chair by the bedside. The Monster serves to ridicule the treatment the Patient is being given and also—a favorite topic with the author—the state of medicine in general. The Patient, so the Monster tells us, is suffering from German measles. The Monster is in fact a microbe, and it is the Patient who has infected him and not vice versa. The Patient's mother (the Elderly Lady) and the doctor enter the scene and it becomes obvious that the Patient is being mollycoddled. They depart, and the Nurse (Sweetie) enters: she opens the window to admit her conspirator, the Burglar (Aubrey). This is no ordinary burglar. He is also a clergyman who was ordained when he was at university.

The Patient (Miss Mopply) is persuaded to leave her home and join forces with the conspirators, taking with her the valuable jewelry the couple had intended to steal, and which she will sell to bring the three of them a life of leisure.

The Prologue is now over and the story of a distressed postwar world unfolds. In part it is the story of the generation of the Jazz Age, as it came to be known, a generation immortalized in the novels of F. Scott Fitzgerald; but Shaw also depicts an older generation and presents their reactions in a postwar world.

The three young people of Act 1 are now leading a life of luxury and leisure on the sunny beach of the mountainous country and on the proceeds of the sale of the Patient's jewelry. Because the Nurse and the Burglar are liable to pursuit as the (suspected) kidnappers of the Patient, the party is in disguise. The Nurse has adopted the persona of a Countess while the Patient poses as her native maid. The Countess is a true hedonist; her life is centered on the pleasures of the flesh, especially those of sex. She needs a continual change of sexual partners, and she looks around for someone other than Aubrey. On the beach she is stripped down to the bathing wear of the period. One of the mighty images of the play relates to the stripping of the flesh, which is bearable, and the stripping of the soul, which is infinitely less bearable.

As for the Patient, she has been set free from respectability, and, she tells Aubrey, "I revel in all your miracles of the universe: the delicious dawns, the lovely sunsets, the changing winds, the cloud pictures, the flowers, the animals and their ways, the birds and insects and reptiles."[8] But this is not enough for the Patient. She must have something to do: "If I do nothing but contemplate the universe there is so much in it that is cruel and terrible and wantonly evil, ... that I shall just go stark raving mad and be taken back to my mother with straws in my hair."[9]

Aubrey no longer has any attraction for her, and indeed she loathes the human condition. She describes herself and her two companions as "inefficient fertilizers. We do nothing but convert good food into bad manure."[10]

Aubrey speaks of "the lower centres":

> Our lower centres act: they act with terrible power that sometimes destroys us; but they dont talk. Speech belongs to the higher centres. In all the great poetry and literature of the world the higher centres speak. In all respectable conversation the higher centres speak.... Since the war the lower centres have become vocal. And the effect is that of an earthquake. For they speak truths that have never been spoken before—truths that the makers of our domestic institutions have tried to ignore.[11]

Later in the play Aubrey's father, the Elder, makes his appearance and meets his son, from whom he has long since been parted. The Elder is the voice of the atheist who has lost his faith. The Elder had believed in determinism but this belief has been destroyed by Einstein. "Nothing can save us from a perpetual headlong fall into a bottomless abyss but a solid footing of dogma; and we no sooner agree to that than we find that the only trustworthy dogma is that there is no dogma."[12] He utters the cry that haunts the play: "I am falling into that abyss, down, down, down. We are all falling into it; and our dizzy brains can utter nothing but madness."[13]

Joining the atheist's chorus is the man of religion, the Sergeant, assigned to the mountainous country to help in the search for the missing Patient. He is a devout student of Bunyan's *Pilgrim's Progress*. His grief does not come from lack of faith but from a conviction that part of the doom of which Bunyan writes is being enacted in the present age. The atheist and the man of religion share a joint sense of doom.

The son Aubrey has something to say to his father, who is shocked to learn that he became a clergyman and even more shocked to learn that he is a burglar. Aubrey tells how he became a sky pilot (clergyman) while at university and later became a pilot in the air force. He speaks of his experience as a bomber pilot:

> I was hardly more than a boy when I first dropped a bomb on a sleeping village. I cried all night after doing that. Later on I swooped into a street and sent machine gun bullets into a crowd of civilians: women, children, and all. I was past crying by that time. And now you preach to me about stealing a pearl necklace![14]

The play has its rhythms: the Patient encounters the Elderly Lady who has come in search of her daughter. The mother speaks of the culture that had been forced upon her regarding the bringing up of her family with excessive care and shielding. She has lost two of her children and has come to hate her daughter on whom she lavished so much protection.

However, the Patient, having no wish to pursue a life of idleness, has decided that it is her purpose to form a sisterhood (from which the poor are to be excluded). The mother, having discovered in her liberated daughter a new being, is to share in this enterprise and become liberated herself.

As far as the army is concerned, mention has already been made of the Sergeant. There remains the Colonel and the amazing Private Meek. The Colonel has taken to its extreme the well-known precept that those in command should practice delegation: all responsibilities are handed over to Private Meek, a former Colonel who finds greater fulfilment in belonging to the lower ranks. He has won the scarcely mentioned battle of the maroons and the non-existent brigands have been thwarted. For this the Colonel has been awarded the K.C.B. As for the Colonel, he spends his time painting in watercolors. He gives the Countess his reason: "I paint pictures to make me feel sane. Dealing with men and women makes me feel mad. Humanity always fails me: Nature never."[15]

The author has one more irony to utter, together with a last jibe at the British, before the play reaches its culmination. Private Meek has been commissioned by the Patient and others to obtain visas for Beotia, where the governing body is The Union of Federated Sensible Societies. But, says Meek, they won't admit any more English. "They say their lunatic asylums are too full already."[16] But one exception can be made. They admire the English school of watercolor painting and would be glad to admit the Colonel and make him head of their centers of repose and culture.

It seems that there is nothing left for the expatriots to do but to return to their own country. They proceed to move away. Their departure is hastened when the Elder turns to his son and urges him, "Preach, my son, preach to your heart's content."[17] And Aubrey makes a powerful speech, but it is not a sermon of certainty. As the characters drift away, apparently to conduct their various affairs, they are seen by Aubrey as following in his father's footsteps: "They are all, like my father here, falling, falling, falling endlessly and hopelessly through a void in which they can find no footing."[18] He speaks again to the present generation about nudity of the flesh and of the spirit:

> Throw off the last rag of your bathing costume; and I shall not blench nor expect you to blush. You may even throw away the outer garments of your souls: the manners, the morals, the decencies.... But how are we to bear this dreadful new nakedness: the nakedness of the souls.... Our souls go in rags now.[19]

The play ends with a final repetitive metaphor of uncertainty. The mist that arose from the sea whilst Aubrey was speaking now engulfs him: his ending can barely be heard.

Too True to Be Good was written especially for the Malvern Festival and had its English premiere there in the 1932 season. When it was transferred to London it was not a commercial success, and Shaw used this as an argument for the establishment of a National Theatre.

Two More Plays in Partnership: *On the Rocks* and *The Simpleton* *of the Unexpected Isles*

In the years that followed Shaw's writing of *The Apple Cart* there had been a great darkening of the political scene. The collapse of the American stock market had reverberated throughout Europe. In England there had been a massive rise in unemployment, and in the summer of 1931 Ramsay MacDonald's Labour Government was in serious difficulties. In an effort to meet this situation, and partly at the instigation of King George V, in August 1931, a new coalition government was formed, though MacDonald remained as Prime Minister. In Europe there were dictatorships in Spain, in Italy, and in Germany.

The new political scene Shaw presents in *On the Rocks* is infinitely harsher than that of *The Apple Cart*. Again it centers on a possible dictatorship, but this potential dictator is not a king but a politician. Like King Magnus, however, when it comes to the point of making a decision he lacks the necessary will.

Like *The Apple Cart*, *On the Rocks* was followed by a brief, highly introspective drama. *Too True to Be Good* ended with uncertainty and miasma; *The Simpleton* ends with the Day of Judgment.

ON THE ROCKS: A POLITICAL COMEDY (1933)

The construct of *On the Rocks* has a major difference from that of *The Apple Cart*. The earlier play is set in the future chiefly as an artistic device, for it is almost entirely concerned with the present. But the reasons for setting *On the Rocks* in the (very near) future are thematic. Features of contemporary life at the time of writing are projected into a credible version of what may happen in the immediate future.

The thematic construct of the play relates to the possibility of a dictatorship overturning the present form of government. This possibility is much closer than it was at the time of *The Apple Cart* and it is of a much more threatening kind. There is now no prosperity to lull the electorate into quiescence, and the unemployed have taken to the streets rather than the ballot box. The attitude of the Government is to quell violence rather than to seek to eliminate the causes of violence. The fear of violence begets violence, so that violence becomes part of the theme of the play.

The solution that was tried in real life, that of National Government, is shown to be no solution. The Cabinet consists of a group of disparate politicians who are likely to put loyalty to the old school tie ahead of loyalty to the national interest. The Government shows an incapacity to deal with unrest.

In this situation the question that arises is How can unrest be put down? rather than how it can be prevented. Should democratic government be set aside and superseded by dictatorship? There is a further question which Shaw has often asked before and will ask again in the future: What qualities are required in a leader?

In the situation depicted in the play there is the familiar tension between political man, thinking man, and the man with the will to be a leader; and a corollary question: Can these qualities be combined?

The play centers around the Cabinet Room in the Prime Minister's official residence at No. 10 Downing Street. It is here that he meets members of his Cabinet, his secretary, an official deputation, a mysterious Lady, and—occasionally—his wife and children. It is here, too, that the Prime Minister is to be heard rehearsing a speech which is full of platitudes, or what Shaw calls "dead thoughts." It is from inside this room that we hear the protests of the unemployed outside in Downing Street.

The Prime Minister (Sir Arthur Chavender) is presented first as a political man with a typical politician's disadvantaged background, which, in Shaw's book, means that he has been educated at a major public school and one of the older universities, and is proud of it. Such men are seen (by the author) as not having the capacity to think, and, in any case, if they are of Cabinet rank, they are so overworked with trivialities that they have no time to think.

However, this Prime Minister is different. In spite of his misguided education, he has the capacity to think, but not the time. There comes an occasion when, on the initiative of his wife, he is whisked away by a mysterious Lady to an offstage retreat, which is at once so restful and so conducive to thought that he returns with a legislative program that even the author could not better: he has recovered his power to think.

When the Prime Minister emerges from his retreat he makes a speech at the Guildhall which hits the headlines. Not surprisingly it is unfavorably received by members of his Cabinet, who are outraged. It is his intention to introduce his program, which includes nationalization of the land and compulsory work for all, by having the King prorogue (suspend) Parliament for as long as it takes to get his proposals under way. The police are to be the instrument for enforcing this program. Bearing in mind that the River Thames provides handy access to the Houses of Parliament, the navy is to be used to keep its Members in order. It is clear that what the Prime Minister is planning is a dictatorship of the Left.

But what happens when the Prime Minister receives a deputation of the Left, mostly of working-class origin, led by the Mayor of the Isle of Cats? This is the most lively and the most satirical scene in the play. The proposed nationalization of the land is objected to because the deputation does not understand, and therefore does not approve of, the intention to compensate the landowners concerned even though the source of money for compensation will be the taxation of other landowners. Only an actual landlord who happens to be present, the Duke of Domesday, can see advantages in it. Great exception is taken, also, to the proposal that work should be compulsory, on the grounds that this is not compatible with the right to strike. (This was a bone of contention that Shaw had in real life with the trade unions.)

Two characters stand out in this scene. One is the Duke, who is there to tell us that Dukes are not what they were and have moved with the times. The other is Old Hipney, who makes an elegiac speech lamenting the failure of democracy and accepting the advent of the dictator.

The situation dredges up another supporter besides Old Hipney: the foreign capitalist, Sir Jafna, looks forward to cheaper labour when the landlord is eliminated. And the aforementioned Duke of Domesday notes that the elimination of death duties will prevent the extinction of his class.

But this brave new world is not to materialize. The Prime Minister admits (to his wife): "I'm not the man for the job, darling; and nobody knows that better than you. And I shall hate the man who will carry it through for his cruelty and the desolation he will bring on us and our like."[1]

Thus the leader remains to be identified. As the play finishes, "Unemployed England," as the text has it, sings outside the Prime Minister's house the words of Edward Carpenter's verses: "England, arise! the long, long night is over.... Arise, O England, for the day is here!"[2]

In fact there was to be another "long, long night," which Shaw prefigures in his play, *Geneva*.

On the Rocks was first presented at the Winter Garden Theatre, London, on November 25, 1933.

THE SIMPLETON OF THE UNEXPECTED ISLES: A VISION OF JUDGMENT (1934)

In the Preface to *The Simpleton* Shaw explains why, in presenting his theory of liquidation in the text of his latest play, he takes it into the realm of fantasy. The vision of the Last Judgment is a way of helping the audience to appreciate the significance of exterminating those who make no contribution to society. In the following comment he is none too complimentary to the playgoer: "To me this vision is childish; but I must take people's minds as I find them and build on them as best I can."[3]

In *On the Rocks* the Prime Minister proposed that work should be compulsory for all able citizens. Now, in *The Simpleton*, it becomes a matter not of the law but of the judgment of heaven. The idea contained in *The Simpleton* was not new to Shaw. He told Hesketh Pearson: "Almost all my life as a playwright I have hankered after a dramatization of the Last Judgement."[4]

The setting of the play—a tropical island that rose unexpectedly out of the sea and became part of the British Empire—owes something to Shaw's need to seek out pastures new for his writings. Again Hesketh Pearson was his confidant: "I could not have written it [*The Simpleton*] exactly as it is if I had not been in India and the Far East."[5] He also said, "I have already written plays on all the subjects that lay near to hand.... I must go ever further and further afield except when I am coming nearer and nearer home."[6]

In *The Simpleton* he achieved both these aims as to distance and nearness, for though the venue of the Unexpected Isles is in the tropics, most of the key characters are either British or partly of British extraction. And when the Day of Judgment arrives it creates greater mayhem in England than on the island.

The play centers on a polygamous group of people, some of whom are natives while others belong to the British administrators of the Isles. An unfortunate latecomer to the scene is a simple-minded clergyman by the name of Iddy, who was captured by pirates and left stranded there.

The subject of polygamy is central to the play, and so is racial intermarriage. The parental expectation of the polygamous group is that the progeny of this inter-racial breeding would inherit the best characteristics of both races. Unhappily, apart from the fact that they are outstandingly beautiful, this does not prove to be the case.

When the unfortunate Iddy arrives on the scene and falls in love with one of the offspring, he is required also to take a second bride if he wishes to marry: in some sort of mystic way the two wives are to be regarded as one.

This is the scene when the Day of Judgment comes to the Unexpected Isles. An Angel appears in the skies, and later, Iddy gives an elegiac account of what happened:

> Heaven and earth shall pass away; but I shall not pass away. That is what she said. And then there was nothing in my arms. Nothing. Nothing in my arms. Heaven and earth would pass away; but the love of Maya would never pass away. And there was nothing.[7]

All of the four offspring of the polygamous marriage are taken, and they are soon forgotten: their parents forget their names, and forget how many children they had. Iddy forgets Maya and wants to return to England and the Anglican church. It is as if the four young people had never existed.

Lady Farwaters, one of the polygamous marriage group, makes a pronouncement as to why they were taken. She says: "We have taught them everything except how to work for their daily bread instead of praying for it."[8] In the context of the play this seems an extraordinary statement, since the island seems too far from reality for work to be a major issue. We have to turn to the Preface for an explanation:

> The four lovely phantasms ... embody all the artistic, romantic, and military ideals of our cultured suburbs. On the Day of Judgement not merely do they cease to exist like the useless and predatory people: it becomes apparent that they never did exist.[9]

It is at this point that the reader needs to remind himself of Pra's statement that "There is no Country of the Expected. The Unexpected Isles are the whole world."[10] And it is at this point that words seem to lose their meaning.

However, when the Day of Judgment reaches England and reports begin to come through to the Unexpected Isles about what is happening there, the author's choice of targets brings no surprise and (probably) some laughter. The Stock Exchange has closed, only two members are left. The House of Commons is decimated; only fourteen Members are to be found, none of Cabinet rank. The House of Lords has fifty Members but not one of these has ever attended a sitting. Others on the "hit list" include the congregations of churches, the medical profession, leaders of fashion, famous beauties, and the readers of novels. The newspapers are proclaiming the end of the British Empire.

Hugo Hyering, Emigration Officer and a member of the polygamous group, is perceptive enough to defend what is happening in the playwright's terms:

> The angels are weeding the garden. The useless people, the mischievous people, the selfish somebodies and the noisy nobodies, are dissolving into space, which is the simplest form of matter. We here are awaiting our own doom.[11]

The angels did not, you will notice, visit the theatre.

The Simpleton was first presented by the Theatre Guild at the Guild Theatre, New York, on February 18, 1935.

31

Life Outside Politics: *Village Wooing* and *The Millionairess*

On two occasions in the 1930s Shaw set aside the wider aspects of politics and presented in his plays the changing social scene around him. In the first play he writes about the changing nature of class distinctions and class habitats: in the second he turns his attention to an individual capitalist—the methods she employs to obtain her riches, and the nature of her personal relationships. Both the style and the subject matter of these two plays take us back to Shaw's earlier days as a playwright.

VILLAGE WOOING: A COMEDIETTA FOR TWO VOICES (1933)

Village Wooing looks briefly at the everyday life of the English Midlands. In *Fanny's First Play* Shaw looked at the new suburbia; now he records that urban man, impelled by some centrifugal force, is spreading beyond suburbia into the villages. In this particular instance the urbanite takes over that focal point in the community, the village shop. But the play is not about the community, it is about class meeting class.

The two characters in the play, known succinctly as A and Z, are shown at leisure as well as at work. And, whereas previously holidays were spent at the seaside (as in *You Never Can Tell*), the fashion now, for the more affluent, is the holiday cruise.

The playlet consists of three conversations, the first of which takes place on the deck of a cruise ship. It is based, as the author told an associate, on a self-induced experience of his own. When Shaw was on a cruise it was his practice to do some of his writing sitting on deck. In order to avoid interruption he would look for "the unprotected lady who is ripe for friendship with a celebrity."[1] He would place his chair next to hers and ask her if she would mind if he wrote rather than talked. She would then ward off other passengers so that Shaw was left in peace.

The two characters A and Z are fringe people as far as the cruise is concerned, A because he does not wish to socialize, and Z because by reason of class distinctions, others do not wish to socialize with her. Z does not belong to the monied classes and is there only because she won a prize in a newspaper competition.

A asks a significant but impertinent question: "Have they found out here that you are not a lady?"[2] Z (who is a telephone operator) gives a significant answer: "The Americans dont know the difference: they think my telephone talk is aristocratic; and the English wont speak to anyone."[3] These two representatives of a changing society have a conversation from which it becomes clear that the closer they come together the more noticeable are their differences. A whole alphabet lies between A of the intelligentsia and Z of the workaday world.

In the second conversation, A arrives at the village shop where Z, as well as operating the telephone, works behind the counter. It becomes increasingly clear from Z's persistent comments that speech continues to be the great divide that it was in the days of *Pygmalion*: but the nature of the divide is different. For though the telephone has tended to take the rough edge off local accents—especially in the case of trained telephone operators—the use of what are perceived as genteelisms and vulgarisms may remain as giveaways of low social origins. Such people as Z may also have a lack of tact in language and may be guilty of a certain crudity of thought. A tells Z with a condescension that is fairly typical of him: "I am a man of letters and a gentleman. I am accustomed to associate with ladies. That means that I am accustomed to speak under certain well understood reserves which act as a necessary protection to both parties."[4]

The play is, in a literal sense, a comedy of manners.

By the time that the third conversation takes place, events have moved on. A has become the owner and manager of the shop, thus indicating a change in social conventions: a gentleman may now become active in the retail trade. There is a second more momentous event: the Life Force has appeared on the scene, though it remains unnamed. At the beginning of this episode A and Z are addressing each other (rather repulsively) as "boss" (A) and "slave" (Z). But soon the Life Force and the will become involved and are triumphant. Social nuances become minimal when Z tells A: "I must and will have you."[5] A tells Z: "We shall get quite away from the world of sense. We shall light up for one another a lamp in the holy of holies in the temple of life."[6]

This sounds very much like Mrs. George in *Getting Married*, and it looks as though the Life Force is moving A and Z towards a union of the spirit as well as the flesh.

However, there is a dumbing down at the playlet's ending. When the rector's wife places an order for artichokes over the telephone, Z says: "Oh; and theres something else."[7] She asks to speak to the rector about the reading of the marriage banns.

THE MILLIONAIRESS (1934)

T.C. Kemp of the Birmingham Repertory Theatre suggested an alternative title for this play, "The Intelligent Woman's Guide to Capitalism,"[8] and in some respects it sounds very appropriate. For the accent is placed on the personal acquisition of capital, and a detailed account is given of two very significant ways in which the millionairess, Epifania, makes her money.

There are also pointers to other aspects of wealth besides the making of it. There used to be a phrase, "the battle of the sexes"; here there seems to be some sort of link among money, physical violence, and sexual attraction. One gets used to a certain amount of sadism and masochism in the sexual relationships that are acted out in Shaw's plays. Here the violence reaches new proportions when the future millionairess attacks her lover in their chosen meeting place, throws him downstairs, and says to the doctor who arrives on the scene (and is to be next in line for her sexual favors): "If he has broken every bone in his body it is no more than he deserves."[9]

Epifania is married to a boxer!

Shaw makes the point—and underlines it—that a capitalist in the making may be motivated by reasons which, sociologically speaking, are trivial. In Epifania's case she is required by the terms of her father's will to demonstrate her ability to make money starting from scratch before she may marry the (unfortunate) man of her choice. In any case, to Epifania, "Money is power. Money is security. Money is freedom."[10]

In the first example of moneymaking Epifania enters the world of the London sweatshops via a basement in the East End's Commercial Road, where the "sweaters" are themselves among the sweated. This scene is notable because it is the only occasion on which Shaw actually portrays poverty in the workplace. One may wonder how such conditions continued to exist; times had changed since Beatrice Webb and others did their pioneering work and there were now Factories Acts to prevent exploitation. An answer is given in the play: if the Factories Inspector were called in the establishment would be closed down, which would put both the employers and the employed out of work.

Epifania has no thoughts of improving conditions or increasing output. What she does is to eliminate one link in the chain and take the consequent savings to herself. She issues a dictum: "Mr Superflew [who collects the orders] is superfluous. We shall collect not only our own stuff but that of all the other sweaters."[11]

Thus is sweating perpetuated.

She has a different, more constructive, role to play in her second venture, but this too has its darker side. It takes place in the Pig and Whistle, the pub where she threw her one-time lover down the stairs. Starting as a scullery maid Epifania shortly becomes the proprietor of what she converts into "a very attractive riverside hotel," which is renamed "The Cardinal's Hat." We hear about the negative side of the project from the son of the previous proprietor. Although the refurbished inn is a credit to the neighborhood and gives employment, his parents have fared badly. "The change was too much for them at their age. My father had a stroke and wont last long, I'm afraid. And my mother has gone a bit silly. Still, it was best for them; and they have all the comforts they care for."[12]

The play reaches its conclusion when various characters come together in The Cardinal's Hat. Adrian, who was thrown downstairs, arrives intent on suing Epifania but finds it is no easy matter to sue a millionairess. Epifania displays the arrogance of wealth—or has her arrogance helped her to acquire her millions? She instructs her solicitor concerning her husband's mistress: "Mr Sagamore: take an action against Patricia Smith for alienating my husband's affections. Damages twenty thousand pounds."[13] Her next instructions concerning her future second husband are not only arrogant, they are ludicrous: "Mr Sagamore: my mind is made up: I will marry this doctor. Ascertain his name and make the necessary arrangements."[14]

As for the doctor, he decides that Epifania has a pulse of a hundred thousand. He cannot give it up: he consents to the marriage.

Does the play end there? Yes and no. It is usually the case that when Shaw writes about capitalists and other anti-social people he does not lay blame on the individual but on the society and the culture within which they find themselves. He has not done so in this case, so he offers an alternative ending for when the play is performed in Russia and other countries with Communist sympathies. In this version Epifania tells how different she would be in such different circumstances: "I am a capitalist here; but in Russia I should be a worker. And what a worker! My brains are wasted here: the wealth they create is thrown away on idlers and their parasites, whilst poverty, dirt, disease, misery and slavery surround me like a black sea in which I may be engulfed at any moment by a turn of the money market."[15]

Village Wooing was first presented at the Little Theatre, Dallas, Texas, on April 16, 1934.

The Millionairess was first presented in German at the Akademie Theater, Vienna, on January 4, 1936. In 1937 it was the opening play of the Malvern Festival.

32

A Minor Playlet:
The Six of Calais;
and Two Major Plays:
Geneva and *"In Good King Charles's Golden Days"*

THE SIX OF CALAIS:
A MEDIEVAL WAR STORY (1934)

The Six of Calais is unique among Shaw's plays and playlets in that it has no moral to impart to audience or reader. This, says the author, in his Prefatory Note, is "an acting piece and nothing else."[1]

The playlet retells and deromanticizes the story of the siege of Calais in which six burgesses of the city, with halters around their necks, submitted themselves to King Edward III in order to save the besieged city. According to tradition they themselves were saved by the intervention of Queen Philippa with her husband, the king.

In the playlet one of the burgesses proves to be aggressive and there are times when the playlet descends into farce, as for example when the burgess and the king, each in turn, bark and growl like dogs.

The work derives its inspiration from a statue by Rodin, "The Six of Calais," which Shaw had seen while visiting France shortly before the First World War. It was performed in the open in a London park in 1934.

GENEVA: ANOTHER POLITICAL
EXTRAVAGANZA (1936)

A Committee of Intellectual Cooperation was set up by the Assembly of the League of Nations in 1921. Its declared purpose was "to foster appropriate international activity within the broad realm of art, science, literature, and learning."[2] The general public had little knowledge of this committee, and it would appear from Shaw's correspondence that little use was made of it. When Shaw wrote his play *Geneva* in 1936, he had two particular points of focus: to make this committee better known, and to suggest that it might undertake an additional function, namely to draw the attention of the International Court of Justice, now in operation at The Hague, to injustices of international significance so that the Court could take them within its jurisdiction.[3]

It will be recalled that in Shaw's 1929 tract, "The League of Nations," he referred to "an incipient Court of Justice at The Hague." Now he writes a play in which the last act presents a session of this Court in which characters representing three European dictators then in power state their cases.

It goes without saying that Shaw regarded the Committee of International Cooperation and indeed the International Court with the utmost seriousness; but this did not prevent him from offering the audience lots of laughs at the expense of the Committee—and the dictators. His friend Professor Gilbert Murray was one of the founding members of the committee and became its chairman.

In this play above all others, who can doubt Shaw's dedication to supranationalism? The Committee of Intellectual Cooperation—as represented by Begonia Brown—runs like a thread through the whole of the play and duly finds its way to the International Court. The Court is equipped with various buttons connected with telephone apparatus signifying that the audience—and indeed the world at large—are required to join the Judge in making judgment.

The play opens in the (imagined) office of the Committee of International Cooperation, which is staffed by the notable Begonia Brown. She is one of those English prototypes in which Shaw specializes: ignorant, but unaware of her ignorance; badly educated, but proud of her education; blindly patriotic and imperialistic, with a certain strange capability for making herself heard—indeed, it is her voice that is heard rather than those of the intellectuals. For her services she is made a Dame of the British Empire.

Into Begonia's office at the beginning of the play come several typifying characters, most of whom are seeking a justice that they cannot find in their own country. And so we have the German Jew complaining of racial persecution and the Widow complaining that crimes (in this case the murder of her husband) go unheeded by the law when the perpetrator is in a position of public power. In these circumstances private vengeance may then be the alternative, especially in a country where the culture demands that retribution be exacted. A third character, the Newcomer, complains that his right to function as the elected representative of the people has been denied him because, on the instructions of the Prime Minister of his country he has been barred by the police from entering the Parliamentary building. Begonia, on her own initiative, does what in real life others have failed to do: she addresses these complaints to the International Court of Justice at The Hague.

Two other characters present themselves at Begonia's office, but the author does not intend that their complaints should be proceeded with; they are to serve a different purpose. The Bishop represents the sort of person that Shaw says in the Preface (and in his tract) should not be in Geneva. His complaint is that communists are invading his diocese: his footman has been converted. He has an argument with the other character, the Russian Commissar, who has rather more advanced views than the Bishop. "This man does not seem to know," says the Commissar, "what sort of world he is living in."[4] In fact the Bishop collapses on the stage and dies. It looks as though he might well be a victim of that same "future shock" which caused the death of the Elderly Gentleman in *Back to Methuselah*. The Commissar lives on to join in the dialogue of the court scene.

In Act 2 the play moves to the office of the Secretary to the League of Nations. Here we meet two individuals from "The League of Nations" who have become fictionalized. Sir Eric Drummond is now the anonymous secretary of the League, while the tract's Sir Austen Chamberlain of Birmingham has become Sir Orpheus Midlander of the play.

There is a satirical opening to this act, when Begonia arrives to see the Secretary. He tells her that there have been massive repercussions from the letters that she sent to The Hague. The British Empire has declared a war of sanctions on Russia, Japan is now in military alliance with Britain, and the little Dominion of Jackson has declared itself an independent republic, to name but a few events. "It was your hand that started the series of political convulsions which may end in the destruction of civilization."[5]

Begonia is flattered.

There is also serious purpose in the scene. When Begonia departs and Sir Orpheus arrives, the Secretary has some devasting things to say about internationalism and about the League:

> Pushing all the nations into Geneva is like throwing all the fishes into the same pond: they just begin eating one another.... When the nations kept apart war was an occasional and exceptional

thing: now the League hangs over Europe like a perpetual war-cloud.[6]

We remain in Geneva for Act 3, which is a sort of prelude to the great trial scene of Act 4. In a restaurant by the side of the lake a number of characters come together and express their views at a more personal level. In particular the Judge and the Secretary make some fundamental observations which complement each other:

> THE JUDGE: When the International Court was moved to action by the enterprise of my friend Dame Begonia, it found that the moment the League of Nations does anything on its own initiative and on principle, it produces, not peace, but threats of war or secession....
>
> THE SECRETARY: It is too true. Yet it is not altogether true. Those who think the League futile dont know what goes on here.... When I came here I was a patriot, a Nationalist, ... But the atmosphere of Geneva changed me. I am now an Internationalist.[7]

The act ends with the news that the trial of the three dictators of Spain, Italy, and Germany has been fixed to take place two weeks hence.

And so the play reaches its culmination. Those gathered together at the Court include the Jew, the Widow, the Newcomer, the Commissar, Sir Orpheus, and, of course, Dame Begonia. The latter two continue to represent those with restricted vision for whom there should be no place at Geneva. Begonia was to know a fictional life beyond the stage. In *Everybody's Political What's What?* Shaw wrote: "Begonia becomes the first female Prime Minister, too late for inclusion in the play."[8]

The charges brought by the Jew range from racial persecution to genocide. The former is described by the Judge as "An accusation ... of unlawful arrest and imprisonment, assault, robbery, and denial of his right to live in the country of his birth."[9] The latter is described by the Jew as "An attempt to exterminate the flower of the human race."[10]

The Widow presents herself as a personification. "My name is Revenge," she says, "My name is Jealousy. My name is the unwritten law that is no law."[11] But what she seeks is the return of the rule of law.

The complaints of the Newcomer which relate to dictatorship are not addressed directly to the Judge and he receives no official response. This may indicate that Shaw is not opposed to dictatorship per se, but only to what he regards as its abuse.

Nor are the charges brought against the three dictators answered directly. For the most part the three are satirized, and shown as bursting with grandiosity and self-importance. But when Bombardone (Mussolini) describes his past achievements and his vision for the future, parody is at a minimum and he almost echoes the playwright's own world vision:

> The nations [says Bombardone] are the bricks out of which the future world State must be built. I consolidated my country as a nation: a white nation. I then added a black nation to it and made it an empire. When the empires federate, its leaders will govern the world; and these leaders will have a superleader who will be the ablest man in the world: that is my vision.[12]

Battler, the German, when he states his case, darkens the scene by adding to a concept similar to Bombardone's his own sense of being divinely called to leadership and his belief in genetic superiority.

Blanco (General Franco of Spain) is rather less articulate. When the Judge tells him that he is charged with "an extraordinary devastation of your own country and an indiscriminate massacre of its inhabitants," he thinks it sufficient to reply: "That is my profession. I am a soldier; and my business is to devastate the strongholds of the enemies of my country, and slaughter their inhabitants."[13]

Blanco is not a man to indulge in the intricacies of debate.

Eventually the matter of human rights goes out of focus. The point is not made that continued aggression by the dictators will lead to further diminution of human rights; and the question is not raised as to how aggression is to be controlled without the use of force. Instead the bombast of the dictators arouses the aggressive imperialism of Sir Orpheus and Dame Begonia, who are prepared to drop bomb for bomb. Together with the dictators they demonstrate the capacity to wreck civilization to which Shaw made reference in his tract.

The political argument of the play is transcended when the Judge suggests that the International Court of Justice may come to replace the judgment seat of God. "Since people no longer believe that there is any such judgement seat, must we not create one...?"[14] He reinforces this opinion when, in response to a Deaconess who appears from nowhere and intervenes in the proceedings, he rules that "Jesus is a party in this case."[15]

The argument of the play concludes with the judgment of the Judge:

> There is no reason why you should not be good neighbors....
> Unfortunately when any question of foreign policy arises you confront me with a black depth of scoundrelism which calls for nothing short of your immediate execution.... I give you up as

hopeless. Man is a failure as a political animal. The creative forces which produce him must produce something better.[16]

Thus does the Judge make his pronouncement not only on those brought before him but on humankind as well.

Following this first judgment two pieces of news are received by the Judge over the telephone. The first item is, "Mr Battler's troops have invaded Ruritania."[17] The second item (which proves to be false) reports that the orbit of the Earth is jumping into its next quantum. The consequence of this is said to be that all forms of life will be frozen to death.

The Judge and the Secretary are left alone, and the Judge gives his second, and more moderate judgment. The Secretary calls the trial a farce. The Judge replies: "Not a farce, my friend. They came, these fellows. They blustered: they defied us. But they came. They came."[18]

Thus the audience hears the Judge pass a judgment on humankind which has overtones of that passed by Lilith at the end of *Back to Methuselah.*

Geneva was first presented, in Polish, at the Teatr Polski, Warsaw, on July 25, 1938. It was part of the Malvern Theatre's 1938 Festival Programme.

"*IN GOOD KING CHARLES'S GOLDEN DAYS*": A TRUE HISTORY THAT NEVER HAPPENED (1938–39)

When Charles II came to the throne in 1660 there was not only a restoration of the monarchy but also a restoration of the theatre, which had been under a cloud during the Puritan regime. And when, in 1938, Shaw turned his thoughts towards the past and produced his third "lessons of history" play, "*In Good King Charles's Golden Days*" was written very much after the manner of Restoration Comedy—at least in the first act. Restoration Comedy reflected the elaborate manners, the costly, exotic dress, and that special symbol of fashionable artificiality, the flowing wig, which belonged to the period. The themes of these plays were often based on the complexities of extra- and intra-marital intrigues and the like, but they were comedies of manners rather than of passion.

Charles II, with his elaborate wigs, his many mistresses, and his numerous bastard sons, fits ideally into his period, and into the comedy of his times.

All these elements are presented in this play about Charles II, but

Shaw writes also of the great intellectualism that existed at that time. Indeed, the play's first act is set in the library of the house of Isaac Newton, and it is in this unlikely setting that three of the King's mistresses, two of them duchesses, chance to call, as also does the King (visiting incognito), his brother James, George Fox the Quaker, and the painter Godfrey Kneller.

The time is 1680, a time when Isaac Newton, philosopher and mathematician, had propounded his theory of gravitation (in 1666), a time when the Royal Society had been founded and granted a Royal Charter (in 1662), a time when the Religious Society of Friends (popularly known as the Quakers) was in existence (having been founded by George Fox in 1652), and a time when the art of painting flourished.

During the conversations which take place in Newton's home, Shaw is at pains to show not only the strengths of these great characters but also their weaknesses. Thus, Sir Isaac Newton, that great mathematician and scientist, who had applied his mathematics to the universe, makes a strange statement about "creation." He tells Fox, the Quaker, who is arguing about the transmutation of metals: "I am as certain of them as I am of the fact that the world was created four thousand and four years before the birth of our Lord."[19] In support of this statement he says, "But the archbishop has counted the years! My own chronology of the world has been founded on his calculation."[20]

Fox (the wearer of leather breeches) also has his weakness. Reasoned in argument, unimpressed by the world's vanities and materialism, he suffers a personality change when he hears the church bells ring and proceeds to typify the intolerance of his times: "When the bell rings to announce some pitiful rascal twaddling in his pulpit, or some fellow in a cassock pretending to bind and loose, I hear an Almighty Voice call "George Fox, George Fox: rise up: testify: unmask these imposters: drag them down from their pulpits and their altars; and let it be known that what the world needs to bring it back to God is not Churchmen but Friends, Friends of God, Friends of man, friendliness and sincerity everywhere, superstition and pulpit playacting nowhere."[21]

Even when he rants Fox has something to offer to humankind!

A conversation between Sir Isaac Newton and Godfrey Kneller, the painter, centers on the significance of the straight line and the curved line: it becomes—seemingly—a signifier of the difference between the scientist and the artist. To the artist the curved line is the right line, the line of beauty. But Newton argues that the right line is a straight line, the line of gravity.

Eventually, in real life, as Shaw kindly reminds us in the Preface,

Einstein's theory of relativity superseded Newton's theory of gravitation. In the play Newton is chagrined at the possibility that he, a learned and dedicated mathematician, may be mistaken. Meanwhile, in the Preface Shaw addresses his readers: "Let me admit that Newton in my play is a stage astronomer: that is, an astronomer not for an age but for all time."[22]

Fox has two more important points to make, the first of which relates to the author's commitment to the concept of the continuous process of evolution, a point made by Shaw in other contexts. Fox says, "I am not one of those priestridden churchmen who believe that God went out of business six thousand years ago when he had called the world into existence and written his book about it. We three sitting here together may have a revelation if we open our hearts and minds to it."[23]

Fox also makes reference to "the new so-called Royal Society which the King has established, to inquire, it seems, into the nature of the universe."[24]

There comes a time when the glamorous mistresses and the men of intellect, of art, and of religion depart the room, leaving the King and his brother James on their own. And then a different sort of conversation takes place, relating to intolerance, to treachery, to plotting, and to pragmatism. The established Church rejects, on the one hand, Catholicism, and on the other, Puritanism. Charles himself is a Catholic but if he were to declare this publicly he would lose his throne; he is perforce a pragmatist. James, also a Catholic, refers to the divide that exists and speaks as brother to brother: "You are no king, cleverly as you play with these Whigs and Tories. That is because you have no faith, no principles."[25] An example of intrigue is given when they talk about the famous Titus Oates, the fabricator of the Popish Plot. When James talks about how Oates should be treated he epitomizes the cruelty that lay below the outward finery of the age. He tells Charles, "Flog him through the town. Flog him to death. They can if they lay on hard enough and long enough. The same mob that now takes him for a saint will crowd to see the spectacle and revel in his roarings."[26]

The other guests return and the general conversation resumes. The three mistresses continue to serve the purpose which Shaw ascribes to them in the Preface, namely, "to relieve the intellectual tension."[27]

But Shaw has more to say about King Charles, who in the second act ceases to be the spokesman of his age.

Alone with the Queen in her boudoir, and without his wig, he and his wife become spokespeople for Shaw's theory about marriage, sexual relationships, and progeniture. It was, of course, a long held view of Shaw's that the ideal partner in marriage was not necessarily the ideal partner for a sexual relationship or for procreation. And he had pointed out, in *Getting Married* for example, that polygamy is a widely practiced form of marriage, which suggests that Shaw believed that a multiplicity of sexual partners is no bad thing. He presents King Charles and his Queen as an example taken from the pages of history. Catherine finds her husband's conduct totally acceptable. She refers to his concubines and says, "They have set me free to be something more to you than they are or can ever be. You have never been really unfaithful to me."[28] There is no direct reference to the fact that their marriage is childless and so has not produced a legitimate heir to the throne.

A little later, still in the confidentiality of the boudoir, and still not wearing his wig, the King becomes the voice of the author when he talks of a country's need for a leader and the difficulty of selecting one with the necessary qualities of leadership (that is, in Shaw's terms, someone possessed of the will). Charles says, "The riddle of how to choose a ruler is still unanswered; and it is the riddle of civilization."[29]

Shortly Charles steps back into his place in history. He resumes his wig and his persona, and proceeds to the Council Chamber where, so his wife tells him, he would not be recognized without his wig.

"*In Good King Charles's Golden Days*" was first performed at the Malvern Festival on August 11, 1939. This was the last play that Shaw completed before the start of the Second World War.

33

A Critical Question
Remains Unanswered

In all Shaw's major plays during his third phase his attention is focused on the question of leadership. It was not a new question for him, as it arose in part from his philosophy/religion of creative evolution. What manner of man was fitted to lead humankind along the evolutionary road to betterment? He must surely be possessed of the Life Force and the will. This question had been presented on a global scale within the boundaries of eternity in *Back to Methuselah*. Now in the 1920s and '30s it took on a new political significance and a new urgency.

Shaw's own political thinking had, of course, been modified over the years: he now took the view that political democracy had been a failure, and indeed it was proving to be so over much of Europe. The 1920s and '30s had seen the rise of the dictators in Spain, Italy and Germany, as represented, it will be recalled, in Shaw's play *Geneva*. But Shaw was not merely concerned with presenting dictators; he was probing, seeking, searching to find what qualities constitute leadership and how they were to be recognized and popularized. As the political scene steadily darkened, the question became more and more urgent.

In *Saint Joan* Shaw seeks a lesson from history. The conclusion is that Joan has the necessary qualities but the world is not yet ready for such as St Joan. *The Apple Cart* presents King Magnus, who through heredity is blessed with high-ranking status (the "awe" factor, Shaw sometimes calls it). He has the intellect and the understanding, but he allows himself to be minimized by a superior power. *On the Rocks* sees a newly awakened Prime Minister beginning to think in terms of a benign dictatorship of the Left, but there comes a time of self-recognition: he has not the harshness that belongs to the present times; he lacks the courage.

But the playwright does not give up. Having begun this phase with a "lesson of history" play, in *Saint Joan*, he ends it with another of the same, presenting Charles II, the supreme pragmatist who sat successfully, if uneasily, upon his throne. Like the author, Charles ponders the question of leadership: how are potential leaders to be recognized and brought into the light of day? Like the author, he can provide no answer, though he does suggest that most of them may be found in prison.

Soon after "*In Good King Charles's Golden Days*" was produced at Malvern, the world embarked on its own tragic way of dealing with dictators: the Second World War broke out in September 1939.

PART IV

A RELUCTANT ICON
(1940–1950)

34

The World's Mentor

The onset of World War II marks the beginning of the last period of Shaw's long life; and at first his patterns of behavior and of writing resemble his attitudes and his work during the First World War. In fact he promptly wrote an article with the resonant title of "Uncommon Sense about the War" which was published first in the New York *Journal-American* on October 6, 1939, and then in the *New Statesman* on the following day.[1] However, in order, as Shaw said, to avoid embarrassing the editor of the *New Statesman*, he mostly sent his articles and letters to *Forward*, a Glasgow socialist weekly.[2] As in the First World War, Shaw was greatly concerned that there should be early negotiations for peace. He wrote to Gilbert Murray on October 23, 1940: "Why does not the League of Nations take the initiative? ... The fact is that when Chamberlain declared war it never even occurred to him that he should have referred the case to the League. So much for the Assembly." Later in the letter he observes: "It is for the intellectual elite to demand in the name of civilization why they [the belligerents] are disturbing the peace of the world."[3]

But, to judge by a letter which Shaw sent to the Prime Minister, Winston Churchill, in June 1940, some of his suggestions were somewhat bizarre: "Why not declare war on France and capture her fleet (which would gladly strike its colors to us) before A.H. recovers his breath?"[4]

It was perhaps inevitable that Shaw and his opinions should generate some hostility, which was not always expressed in measured terms. For example, when Shaw was invited by the BBC to give a talk about a statement he had made that "the British must fight to the last ditch," the text of his talk bore a note from the Minister of Information, Alfred Duff Cooper (later Viscount Norwich of Aldwick), "I won't have that man on the air."[5]

It was also the case that, as in World War I, Shaw gave up playwriting for the duration and concentrated his energies on writing a political treatise, *Everybody's Political What's What?*, but it is unlikely that his motivation for doing this was related to the war.

Shaw's wartime writings were not necessarily central to his image at this time, for irrespective of these he was venerated as a sage and an icon. In 1942 this veneration was formalized when the Shaw Society was founded by a new disciple, Dr. F.E. Loewenstein. Shaw was, in fact, an extremely reluctant icon. When Loewenstein asked his permission to form the Shaw Society, his reply was scarcely encouraging: "Go ahead; but dont bother me about it. I am old, deaf, and dotty. In short, a Has Been."[6]

Shaw's ninetieth birthday in 1946 gave further opportunities for celebration and veneration. A birthday exhibition was arranged by the National Book League: again Dr. Loewenstein was the instigator. Shaw also became an honorary citizen of Dublin at a ceremony held in his apartments at Whitehall Court, which were now little used. An unofficial offer of the Order of Merit was declined. He received masses of congratulations by post on his birthday. He gave instructions about his letters: "Throw away all the birthday ones. They make me sick."[7]

In fact, more and more, he began to resemble the Ancients that he had portrayed in *Back to Methuselah.* In July 1941 he had resigned from the Council of the Royal Academy of Dramatic Arts and from the Executive Committee of the Shakespeare Memorial National Theatre, Stratford-upon-Avon.[8] In the following year he told St. John Ervine, one of his biographers: "I have resigned everything, committees, chairmanships, etc., and work at my book [the *What's What?*] as hard as I can lest I should not live to finish it."[9]

During the 1940s death took its toll on many of Shaw's distinguished Fabian confrères: Lord Olivier, one of the "Big Four" of the early Fabian days and a Fabian Essayist, in 1943; Beatrice Webb, distinguished social reformer and joint author with her husband Sidney of several sociological works, in 1943; Sidney Webb, Baron Passfield, in 1947; and H.G. Wells in 1946. Wells was a one-time Fabian and an influential writer; Shaw wrote his obituary for the *New Statesman.* Shaw had written to Webb the day before Beatrice's death: "You and I are now the sole surviving Essayists."[10]

Increasingly Shaw sought solitude, using his village home at Ayot St. Lawrence as a refuge. He wrote to an over-persistent would-be visitor, Gabriel Pascal: "I do not want to see you. I do not want to see ANYBODY.... Keep away EVERYBODY."[11]

However, everybody did not keep away. Into the later years of Shaw's life came three newcomers, each of whom had something to contribute, and each of whom was determined to take something away. One of these was the previously mentioned Dr. Loewenstein. He became Shaw's "authorised bibliographer and remembrancer." Dan Laurence records how Loewenstein raided Shaw's papers for his own collection, which he sold in 1953.[12] Stephen Winsten, with his wife, moved in next door to Shaw. He was editor and organizer of *G.B.S. 90*, a collection of essays by various distinguished people who wrote about different aspects of Shaw's life. He was also the author of some inaccurate books about Shaw; Laurence says he also "departed with only a few of Shaw's unpublished manuscripts."[13]

John Wardrop was a genuine Shaw enthusiast who thrust himself on Shaw and gave him a great deal of help with the proofs of the *What's What?* and other matters. However, "he assumed," said Shaw, "not only the position of my literary agent but of my son and heir."[14] A final request for money (£3000) came from him when he emigrated to America. "I tore the letter up,"[15] wrote Shaw to his secretary, Blanche Patch.

The nearness of death preoccupied Shaw in his later years, and he addressed it with practicality and with a concern for the community. He followed the precept which he had laid down in Fabian Tract No. 107, "Socialism for Millionaires," that bequests should not be made to help the ratepayer, since as a consequence the landlord would increase rents. During his lifetime he donated his inherited estate to Carlow Urban District Council; but to ensure that such gifts would be used constructively, he persuaded the then Prime Minister, Eamon De Valera, to introduce the Local Authorities (Acceptance of Gifts) Bill which was enacted in 1945.[16] There were other bequests of a philanthropic nature.

Death began to come very close to Shaw. He wrote to Dean Inge on May 28, 1948, "I sleep well, always in the hope that I may not wake again; but I am not in the least unhappy."[17] A letter to a neighbor about smoke from a bonfire, written in September 1950 ends, "I shall be burnt up myself presently; but the fumes will get no farther than Golders Green...."[18] Shortly afterwards Shaw had an accident in his garden which led to his death. He died on November 2, 1950. Cremation at Golders Green followed on 5 November.

It was Hesketh Pearson, biographer of Shaw in his old age, who said: "Nothing short of death could stop Shaw's pen or shut his mouth."[19]

35

Everybody's Political What's What? A Political Finale

In his last years and in his last writings Shaw became more and more preoccupied with the eternity of creation and the fragility of humanity. This preoccupation had been made manifest in the drama some twenty years before in his metabiological pentateuch *Back to Methuselah*, wherein Lilith ponders the universe and wonders whether to allow humankind to continue in existence.

In *Everybody's Political What's What?* this sense of the imponderable finds its way into the world of everyday politics, where at times Shaw seems to speak as one of his own He-Ancients: it is crammed full of thoughts, suggestions, criticisms, and knowledge. There hangs over it like a cloud a sense of the inability of man.

The author's account of socialism and the way it has changed over the years is of particular interest. Reference has previously been made to some of the changes; for example, the divorce (as Shaw sees it) of democracy from socialism. But the essence of the author's concept of socialism remains the same: there must be equality of income and State ownership of land and capital. His definition of income equality runs as follows: "Equality of income up to the point at which all sections of the community are intermarriable is a fundamental necessity for a stable civilization."[1]

He looks back at the socialism of the nineteenth century and says, "Nineteenth century Socialism was too much preoccupied with the abolition of poverty and too little with the employment of leisure and culture."[2] The term "scientific humanism" is now more appropriate.

Looking at current attitudes towards politics, Shaw sees a tendency to merge political themes and principles. Political eyes had been opened by the Fabian Socialists "to the enormous possibilities of commercial

190

enterprise aided by the financial resources and political power of the State."[3] The current situation is defined thus: "This policy, called Fascism in Italy, National Socialism or Nazidom in Germany, is in growing and vigorous practice in England and the so-called Western democracies, where it is left unnamed. Properly it is State Capitalism."[4]

It had been some years since Shaw repudiated parliamentary democracy. On re-examination, he utterly condemns it. It was, he says, the ineptitude of parliamentary democracy in Germany and Italy that led to the rise of the dictator: the people wanted a strong man.

For England he has some constructive suggestions to make about Parliament and the election system which owe something to the ideas of Beatrice and Sidney Webb. Two new bodies would replace the existing Houses of Parliament, one a legislative assembly and the other a debating chamber. Persons standing for election would be required to hold suitable qualifications; those for the legislative body would be higher than those for the debating chamber. The candidates selected would be listed on a panel from which the electorate would make their choices. The electorate would themselves be required to pass tests as to their qualifications to vote. The function of the debating chamber would be to keep the legislative assembly in touch with the views of the electorate.

All this sounds eminently reasonable, though it might place overmuch power in the hands of those who make decisions about eligibility. But Shaw has some very chilling things to say about citizenship, and also about statesmen, which relate to the use of lies. The statesman must be on his guard against being taken in by lies, but the lie, according to Shaw, is an essential tool of government: "The most honest statesman has to govern the people by telling them what it is good for them to believe, whether it is true or not."[5] If this sends a chill down the spine, worse is to come when the author writes about extermination, using that euphemism that we have heard from Shaw before, "weeding the garden." He talks about "the Inquisition" which he sees as being the instrument of the future State. After a preamble about the cruelty of hanging and flogging, Shaw describes how an Inquisition would pass judgement on those members of the community who were considered to be unfit to rank as citizens. Such a person would simply be liquidated. He would go to bed one night and not wake up the following morning. Refusal to work when fit to do so would be one reason for this treatment.

As the *What's What?* was written at the time of the Second World War, Shaw expresses himself on the general subject. He introduces the subject of war by describing it as another way of killing people. He sees the present war as a continuum of the First World War, an inevitable consequence of human nature. In a chapter headed "Collective Scoundrelism" the author observes: "Killing is a necessity, a duty, which no State, however humanitarian, can escape or leave unregulated.... Wolves and man-eating tigers must be exterminated. There are men and women quite as dangerous. They also must be killed...."[6]

Shaw does not believe the objectives of the war will succeed. As he has said before, it would be more realistic to kill off the women, the bearers of the next generation, rather than the men.

A mood of fantasy overtakes Shaw: "If I were an Omnipotent Creator I could stop the war in a week by letting loose a few billion locusts and white ants in every acre of territory in the countries of the belligerents."[7]

Everybody's Political What's What? contains such a vast amount of thinking that in reviewing it a great deal has to be left unsaid. Perhaps in this case too much emphasis has been placed on Shaw's ideas about "weeding the garden" and destroying whole species. But Shaw is not expressing here the darker side of his imagination; this is the darker side of his political thinking. What he is talking about is now known as ethnic cleansing.

Shaw ends his work with touching modesty, at the same time giving a snub to his readers: "My Everybody's What's What is only an attempt by a very ignorant old man to communicate to people still more ignorant than himself such elementary social statics as he has managed to pick up by study and collision with living persons and hard facts in the course of a life (long as lives go, but too short for this particular job)...."[8]

36

The Last Years
of a Playwright

In 1945 Shaw turned his attention to an unfinished play which was subsequently published as *Buoyant Billions*. On the title page of the limited edition (1949) were some poignant lines that began:

> Only in dreams my prime returns
> And my dead friends forsake their urns
> To play with me the queerest scenes
> In which we all are but have-beens.[1]

But Shaw in these last years was by no means a "has-been," for though his writing of plays was almost at a halt, his name and fame as a dramatist certainly were not. Indeed many of his earlier dramas were enjoying a great boom. Dan Laurence records that during the week of Shaw's ninetieth birthday there were performances of his plays in nearly every State in Russia.[2] His work was being featured in the London theatres and on the radio. Film versions of *Pygmalion* and *Major Barbara* were extremely popular.

There was also an extensive reading public for his plays. A Penguin edition of a selection of these, *The Shaw Million*, was produced to celebrate his ninetieth birthday. Ten titles were published simultaneously in editions of 100,000: they were sold out in six weeks.[3] Shaw attributed some of this popularity to Hesketh Pearson's work, *Bernard Shaw: A Biography*, which was published in 1942. "The success of your book has driven the whole trade mad," he told the author. "They all want a book about me, a film about me, anything about me."[4]

It appears that everybody wanted to pick up a Penguin: this can't have been entirely due to Shaw's biographer!

37

Two Post-Atomic Plays: *Buoyant Billions* and *Farfetched Fables*

The Second World War gave Shaw's imagination as a playwright two images. One was the peacetime use of the atomic bomb; the other came from the revival of his idea of a gas that was lighter than air and could destroy, say, the inhabitants of a city while leaving its buildings and services intact.

In *Buoyant Billions* Shaw briefly iterates what he envisages as the positive aspects of splitting the atom and then moves in other directions.

In *Farfetched Fables* the concept of a gas that is lighter than air sparks off a series of playlets which trace the future of a new post-atomic race after the manner of *Back to Methuselah* but without its gravitas.

BUOYANT BILLIONS: A COMEDY OF NO MANNERS (BEGUN AND ABANDONED FEBRUARY 1936–AUGUST 1937; RE-BEGUN AUGUST 1945 AND COMPLETED JULY 1947)

Buoyant Billions gets off to a very promising start. In a dialogue between Father and Son (Junius), the son looks at what he calls the post-atomic age and sees a new, wonderful world opening up for humanity as a result of the benefits that the splitting of the atom may bring. At a time when there was much examination of the public conscience about the dropping of the atomic bomb Junius observes:

> When atom splitting makes it easy for us to support ourselves as well by two hours work as now by two years, we shall move moun-

194

tains and straighten rivers in a hand's turn. Then the problem of what to do in our spare time will make life enormously more interesting.[1]

He sees an all-embracing Atomic Age. He tells his father: "In your time the young were post–Marxists and their fathers pre–Marxists. Today we are all post–Atomists."[2]

The first step will be to rid the world of tropical insect pests. As a potential world betterer Junius intends to investigate this with the Panama Canal as his starting point. His father gives him his fare. This first act is entitled "The World Betterers."

Unsurprisingly "The Adventure" (Act 2) takes place in Panama; but there is no mention of Junius's atomic purpose, nor is it ever mentioned again. He (Junius), the traveller, meets She who is a resident. They have the sort of conversation which in a Shaw play means that probably the couple are sexually attracted to each other. There is also a Native in the cast whose fluency of thought and speech serves to highlight the mental arrogance of the "pink" race, to quote Shaw's term.

"The Discussion" (Act 3) takes us to a completely different environment, in the home of the owner of the Buoyant Billions, namely Bastable ("Old Bill") Buoyant. The scene is a drawing room in Belgrave Square which has been converted into a Chinese temple. The only link with the previous act is that She of Act 2 turns out to be the daughter of the host figure of Act 3, Old Bill Buoyant. Junius also arrives on the scene, not as a world betterer but as one who wishes to marry the said daughter.

The main dialogue of Act 3 relates to a discussion between Buoyant's grown-up offspring and his solicitor, who has been appointed to explain their financial prospects after their father's death: new legislation will probably relieve Bastable Buoyant and his heirs and successors of some of his billions. Their reactions, for the most part, are entirely self-centered. World betterment does not enter the thinking of those born to riches.

So what are audience and reader to make of this play which seems to have no common theme and whose characters are linked only by coincidence? In the Preface Shaw gives the perfect answer which is no answer: "If I am asked why I have written this play I must reply that I do not know.... When I write a play I do not foresee nor intend a page of it from one end to the other: the play writes itself."[3]

Buoyant Billions was first presented in German at the Schauspielhaus, Zurich, on October 21, 1948. It was presented at the Festival Theatre, Malvern, for six performances beginning on August 13, 1949.

FARFETCHED FABLES (1948)

The first of the six Fables is concerned simply with the implanting of an idea in the fertile brain of a young man who works in a chlorine gas factory. He meets by chance a young woman in a public park. They hear a middle-aged man with a newspaper shouting that there is to be no more war: the United Nations have abolished it. The young man reads the headlines in the newspaper: "Atomic bomb manufacture made a capital crime. Universal security guaranteed."[4] He does not believe that war can be prevented. The young woman observes, "Somebody will discover a poison gas lighter than air! It may kill the inhabitants of a city; but it will leave the city standing and in working order."[5] The young man thinks that the atomic-bomb people may be barking up the wrong tree. Left alone, he ponders: "Lighter than air, eh? Ligh—ter—than—air?"[6]

The second Fable is set in the War Office, London. The play leaps through time to a point at which this new gas has not only been invented, it has been used to kill off the entire population of the Isle of Wight (the Isle proves to be a convenient venue for some future Fables). Even as the staff are being told about what has happened in the Isle of Wight, the deadly gas begins to seep through the office window.

Time has moved on again before the tale of the third Fable is told. A new population has established a new culture as indicated by a building at the back of the stage labelled Anthropometric Laboratory.

All the residents are required to submit to anthropometric tests in the course of which their body fluids and secretions are analyzed. From these tests judgements are made as to the citizens' suitability to undertake various tasks and duties, and as to whether they are acceptable members of society. It will be recalled that this matter of eligibility for citizenship was raised in *Everybody's Political What's What?*.

Refusal to take these tests or failure to reach a satisfactory standard of usefulness to society can have draconian consequences: compulsory labour or liquidation are the alternatives.

The fourth Fable gives an account of a fundamental physical change: there has been a shift in diet from that of the carnivore to vegetarianism. Eventually people have moved to a diet of leaves and nettles, and finally to air and water only. We hear this from a character called a Commissioner, who is dictating copy for his book on Human Diet. He sits outside the building which is now inscribed DIET COMMISSIONERS. The

Commissioner observes in his text that the ending of the food problem meant that men were no longer the slaves of nature. They were free to do what they liked instead of what they must: "The supergorilla became the soldier and servant of Creative Evolution."[7]

Have we not heard of this sort of situation in *Back to Methuselah?*

In the fifth Fable we are alerted to another major change when we see on that significant building another new label, GENETIC INSTITUTE. We learn from a group of experts gathered outside the institute that the insemination of women by men is now a thing of the past and is regarded with repulsion. Seminal fluids are prepared in the laboratory to formulae prescribed by geneticists. But a problem that has haunted earlier pages of Shaw's works remains: "We are not yet agreed," says Rose, "as to the sort of mankind we ought to make."[8] An added advantage of the abandonment of coition is cited: the energy associated with the passions of the flesh can now be expended on a greater pursuit of knowledge and power.

The Fable ends with the statement, "The pursuit of knowledge and power will never end."[9]

So what happens in the sixth and last Fable? The ever-present building now bears the label, SIXTH FORM SCHOOL SCHEDULED HISTORIC MONUMENT and a group of students in uniform are greeted by a teacher in cap and gown. This hardly seems like a leap into the future. When the subject of the Disembodied Races is raised we soon learn that they did exist but are now extinct. The pupils have been forbidden by their teacher to ask the question "Why?" and the audience has no opportunity to do so.

Youth 2 has something to say on the subject. "My grandfather," he announces, "lectured about the theory of the Disembodied Races.... Of course the old man is now out-of-date: I dont take him seriously."[10] However, the boy is soon taken down a peg, for as the group talk about disembodied thought and related topics there enters "a youth, clothed in feathers like a bird" who claims to be a disembodied thought wishing to have experience of the flesh. His name is Raphael: "I am what you call the word made flesh," he tells them, quoting from the Bible. "Evolution can go backwards as well as forwards. If the body can become a vortex, the vortex can also become a body."[11] Wisely, he does not stay for much questioning.

Raphael's wish to have experience of the flesh stops short of the bodily functions of eating and drinking and sex. His passions are those which are dear to the heart of the author: "Intellectual passion, mathematical passion, passion for discovery and exploration: the mightiest of all the passions."[12]

It seems that others in the sixth and last Fable are not ready to learn from Raphael. After he has gone there is a dismissive comment: "We know how to make cyclotrons and hundred inch telescopes. We have harnessed atomic energy. He couldnt make a safety pin or a wheelbarrow to save his life."[13]

Thus does the author rebuke an over-proud post-atomic generation which prizes the flesh above the spirit.

Shakes versus Shav:
A Puppet Play (1949),
and a Conclusion

Shaw's Preface to his puppet play begins: "This in all actuarial probability is my last play and the climax of my eminence, such as it is."[1] And *Shakes versus Shav* was, in fact, the last play to be included in his published canon. It was written in response to a request from Waldo Lanchester of the Malvern Marionette Theatre, who, as Shaw recalls, sent him puppet figures of Shakespeare and himself with a note asking that he should write one of his "famous dramas," preferably lasting not longer than ten minutes or so.[2] Hence the puppet Shakes whose festival was held at Stratford-upon-Avon, was to meet the puppet Shav to whom the Malvern Festival was dedicated. The first performance was by the Waldo Lanchester Marionette Theatre at the Lyttleton Hall, Malvern, on August 9, 1949.

In the play the author shows no special deference to his immortal predecessor, and most of the brief text is unalloyed comedy. However, there is a deeply emotive conclusion when Shakes makes a serious challenge to Shav: "Couldst thou write King Lear?." Shav replies: "Couldst thou/ Have written Heartbreak House? Behold my Lear."[3] At this moment Captain Shotover appears on a transparency. He declares:

> I built a house for my daughters and opened the doors thereof
> That men might come for their choosing, and their betters spring
>   from their love;
> But one of them married a numskull: the other a liar wed;
> And now she must lie beside him even as she made her bed.[4]

Shav speaks the penultimate lines: "Peace, jealous Bard:/ We both are mortal. For a moment suffer/ My glimmering light to shine."

The last words go to Shakes: "Out, out, brief candle!"[5] He puffs the candle out.

Mortality and immortality coalesce.

Notes

The following abbreviations are used in these notes:

CL1, CL2, etc.   Dan H. Laurence, ed., *Bernard Shaw Collected Letters*, Volumes 1 to 4

CP1, CP2, etc.   *The Bodley Head Bernard Shaw Collected Plays with their Prefaces*, Volumes 1 to 7

Holroyd 1, Holroyd 2, etc. Michael Holroyd, *Bernard Shaw*: Volumes 1 to 3

Pease   Edward R. Pease, *History of the Fabian Society*

Chapter 1

1. Pease, p. 193.
2. Bernard Shaw, *Sixteen Self Sketches*, p. 39.
3. *Ibid.*, pp. 22, 25.
4. A.M. Gibbs, ed., *Shaw: Interviews and Recollections*, p. 42.
5. Bernard Shaw, *Sixteen Self Sketches*, p. 66.

Chapter 2

1. Pease, p. 37.
2. *Ibid.*, p. 269.
3. *Ibid.*, p. 40.
4. A.M. Gibbs, ed., *Shaw: Interviews and Recollections*, p. 41.
5. Beatrice Webb, *Our Partnership*, p. 91.
6. Bernard Shaw, *Sixteen Self Sketches*, p. 68.

Chapter 3

1. Ben Pimlott, ed., *Fabian Essays in Socialist Thought*, p. vii.

2. G. Bernard Shaw, ed., *Fabian Essays in Socialism*, p. 50.
3. *Ibid.*, p. 212.
4. *Ibid.*, p. 132.
5. *Ibid.*, p. iii.
6. *Ibid.*, p. 3.
7. *Ibid.*, p. 4.
8. *Ibid.*, p. 57.
9. *Ibid.*, p. 108.
10. *Ibid.*, p. 71.
11. *Ibid.*, p. 85.
12. *Ibid.*, p. 151.
13. *Ibid.*, p. 156.
14. *Ibid.*, p. 169.
15. *Ibid.*, p. 202.
16. *Ibid.*, p. 209.
17. *Ibid.*
18. *Ibid.*, p. 212.
19. *Ibid.*, p. 201.

Chapter 4

1. Pease, p. 42.
2. *Ibid.*, p. 43.
3. *Ibid.*, p. 117.

Chapter 5

1. CL1, p. 291.
2. *Ibid.*, p. 106.
3. Frank Harris, *Bernard Shaw*, p. 128.
4. *Ibid.*
5. Bernard Shaw, *Sixteen Self Sketches*, p. 40.
6. Frank Harris, *Bernard Shaw*, p. 133.
7. CL1, p. 754.
8. Frank Harris, *Bernard Shaw*, p. 134.
9. *Ibid.*, p. 153.
10. Hesketh Pearson, *Bernard Shaw*, p. 242.

Chapter 6

1. Bernard Shaw, *Major Critical Essays*, p. 163–164.
2. *Prefaces by Bernard Shaw*, p. 200.
3. *Ibid.*, p. 196.
4. Bernard Shaw, *Major Critical Essays*, p. 192.
5. *Ibid.*
6. *Ibid.*, p. 198.
7. *Ibid.*, p. 240.
8. *Ibid.*, p. 242.
9. *Ibid.*, p. 249.
10. *Ibid.*, p. 316.
11. *Ibid.*, p. 336.
12. *Ibid.*, p. 343.
13. *Ibid.*, p. 344.
14. *Ibid.*, pp. 343–44.

Chapter 7

1. CP1, p. 34.
2. *Ibid.*, p. 114.
3. *Ibid.*, p. 119.
4. *Ibid.*, p. 185.
5. *Ibid.*, p. 220.
6. *Ibid.*, p. 180.
7. Frank Harris, *Bernard Shaw*, pp. 223–24.
8. CP1, pp. 185–86.

9. CL1, p. 632.
10. *Ibid.*, p. 711.
11. Pease, p. 41.
12. CP1, p. 351.
13. *Ibid.*, p. 330.
14. *Ibid.*, p. 328.
15. *Ibid.*, p. 331.
16. *Ibid.*, p. 289.
17. *Ibid.*, p. 341.
18. *Ibid.*, pp. 343–44.

Chapter 8

1. CP1, pp. 453–54.
2. *Ibid.*, p. 454.
3. *Ibid.*, p. 458.
4. *Ibid.*, p. 375.
5. *Ibid.*, pp. 542–43.
6. *Ibid.*, p. 593.
7. *Ibid.*, p. 573.
8. Holroyd 1, p. 317.
9. CP1, p. 594.
10. *Ibid.*, p. 591.
11. CL1, p. 612.
12. CP1, p. 705.
13. *Ibid.*
14. *Ibid.*, p. 785.
15. *Ibid.*, p. 709.
16. Fabian Tract No. 2; see Pease, p. 42.
17. CP1, p. 751.

Chapter 9

1. Robert Rhodes James, *The British Revolution: British Politics 1880–1939*, p. 170.
2. *Ibid.*
3. *Ibid.*, p. 24.
4. CP2, p. 105.
5. *Ibid.*, p. 113.
6. *Ibid.*, p. 116.
7. *Ibid.*, p. 138.
8. *Ibid.*, p. 165.
9. *Ibid.*, p. 166.
10. *Ibid.*, p. 45.
11. *Ibid.*, p. 182.
12. *Ibid.*, p. 288.

13. *Ibid.*, p. 270.
14. *Ibid.*, p. 278.
15. A.M. Gibbs, ed., *Shaw: Interviews and Recollections*, p. 391.
16. CP2, p. 339.
17. *Ibid.*, p. 361.
18. *Ibid.*, p. 367.
19. *Ibid.*, p. 384.
20. *Ibid.*, p. 416.
21. *Ibid.*, p. 417.

Chapter 10

1. CL3, p. 601.
2. CL2, p. 553.
3. CP2, p. 798.
4. *Ibid.*, p. 512.
5. *Ibid.*, p. 501.
6. *Ibid.*, p. 512.
7. *Ibid.*, p. 729.
8. *Ibid.*, p. 733.
9. *Ibid.*, p. 547.
10. *Ibid.*, pp. 571–72.
11. *Ibid.*, p. 558.
12. *Ibid.*, p. 589.
13. *Ibid.*, p. 703.
14. *Ibid.*, p. 621.
15. *Ibid.*, p. 624.
16. *Ibid.*, p. 653.
17. *Ibid.*, p. 684.
18. *Ibid.*, p. 663.
19. *Ibid.*, p. 674.
20. *Ibid.*, p. 689.
21. *Ibid.*, p. 780.
22. *Ibid.*, p. 741.
23. *Ibid.*, p. 743.
24. *Ibid.*, p. 747.
25. *Ibid.*, p. 780.
26. Hesketh Pearson, *Bernard Shaw*, p. 249.

Chapter 11

1. CP2, p. 853.
2. Hesketh Pearson, *Bernard Shaw*, p. 248.
3. CP2, p. 1023.
4. *Ibid.*, p. 898.

5. *Ibid.*, p. 911.
6. *Ibid.*, p. 976.
7. *Ibid.*, p. 1014.
8. *Ibid.*, p. 1019.
9. *Ibid.*, p. 1022.
10. CP3, pp. 151–52.
11. *Ibid.*, p. 168.
12. *Ibid.*, p. 180–181.
13. *Ibid.*, p. 95.
14. *Ibid.*, p. 26.
15. *Ibid.*, p. 129.
16. *Ibid.*, p. 136.
17. *Ibid.*, p. 121.
18. *Ibid.*, p. 184.
19. *Ibid.*, p. 185.
20. *Ibid.*, pp. 442–43.
21. *Ibid.*, p. 351.
22. *Ibid.*, p. 378.
23. *Ibid.*, p. 419.
24. *Ibid.*, p. 580.
25. *Ibid.*, p. 562.
26. *Ibid.*, p. 661.
27. CP4, p. 143.
28. *Ibid.*, p. 244.
29. *Ibid.*, p. 249.
30. *Ibid.*, p. 241.
31. *Ibid.*, p. 165.

Chapter 12

1. CL3, p. 12.
2. C.E.M. Joad, ed., *Shaw and Society*, p. 250.
3. CP4, p. 395.
4. *Ibid.*, p. 396.
5. *Ibid.*, p. 397.
6. *Ibid.*, p. 380.
7. *Ibid.*, p. 428.
8. *Ibid.*, p. 440.

Chapter 13

1. CL1, p. 803.
2. *Ibid.*, p. 565, 572.
3. Hesketh Pearson, *Bernard Shaw*, p. 205.
4. CP1, pp. 650–51.
5. *Ibid.*, p. 651.

6. CP2, p. 1032.
7. *Ibid.*, p. 1033.
8. *Ibid.*, p. 1048.
9. *Ibid.*, p. 1051.
10. *Ibid.*, p. 1032.
11. CP3, p. 218.
12. *Ibid.*, p. 205.
13. *Ibid.*, p. 675.
14. *Ibid.*, p. 774.
15. *Ibid.*, p. 797.
16. Holroyd 2, p. 229–30.
17. CP3, p. 833.
18. *Ibid.*, p. 823.
19. *Ibid.*, p. 822.
20. *Ibid.*, p. 835.
21. *The Complete Plays of Bernard Shaw*, p. 1089, Odham's Press Ltd.
22. CP3, p. 877.
23. *Ibid.*, p. 852.
24. *Ibid.*, pp. 853–54.
25. *Ibid.*, p. 850.
26. *Ibid.*, p. 863.
27. *Ibid.*, p. 910.
28. CP4, p. 303.
29. *Ibid.*, p. 323.
30. *Ibid.*, pp. 324–25.

Chapter 15

1. Bernard Shaw, *What I Really Wrote About the War*, p. 4.
2. CL3, pp. 315–16.
3. *Ibid.*, p. 291.
4. *Ibid.*, p. 292.

Chapter 16

1. Bernard Shaw, *What I Really Wrote About the War*, p. 1.
2. Adrian Smith, *The New Statesman: Portrait of a Political Weekly 1913–31*, p. 85.
3. Bernard Shaw, *What I Really Wrote About the War*, p. 26.
4. *Ibid.*, p. 23.
5. *Ibid.*, p. 68.
6. *Ibid.*, p. 266.
7. *Ibid.*, p. 271.

8. *Ibid.*, p. 323.
9. *Ibid.*, p. 315.
10. *Ibid.*
11. *Ibid.*, p. 356.
12. *Ibid.*
13. *Ibid.*, p. 392.
14. *Ibid.*, p. 399.
15. *Ibid.*, p. 398.

Chapter 17

1. Hesketh Pearson, *Bernard Shaw*, p. 302.
2. CP4, pp. 633–34.
3. *Ibid.*, p. 637.
4. Bernard Shaw, *What I Really Wrote About the War*, p. 143.
5. CP4, p. 518.
6. *Ibid.*
7. CL3, p. 271.
8. CP4, p. 734.
9. *Ibid.*, p. 676.
10. *Ibid.*, p. 679.
11. *Ibid.*, p. 680.
12. *Ibid.*, p. 700.
13. *Ibid.*
14. *Ibid.*, p. 714.
15. *Ibid.*, p. 763.
16. *Ibid.*, p. 730.
17. *Ibid.*, p. 731.
18. *Ibid.*, p. 782.
19. *Ibid.*, p. 795.
20. CL3, p. 230.

Chapter 18

1. CP4, p. 827.
2. Holroyd 2, p. 275.
3. CP4, p. 878.
4. *Ibid.*, p. 881.
5. *Ibid.*, p. 893.
6. *Ibid.*
7. *Ibid.*
8. Holroyd 2, p. 273.
9. CL3, pp. 207–8.

Chapter 19

1. CP4, pp. 980–81.

2. *Ibid.*, p. 980.
3. Robert Rhodes James, *The British Revolution: British Politics 1880–1939*, p. 343.
4. *Ibid.*
5. CP4, p. 986.
6. CL3, p. 517.
7. CP4, p. 994.
8. *Ibid.*, p. 1000.
9. *Ibid.*, p. 996.
10. *Ibid.*, p. 1013.
11. *Ibid.*, p. 1009.
12. CL3, p. 451.
13. CP5, p. 215.
14. *Ibid.*
15. *Ibid.*, p. 222.
16. *Ibid.*, p. 231.
17. Robert Rhodes James, *The British Revolution: British Politics 1880–1939*, p. 375.
18. CP5, p. 245.
19. *Ibid.*, p. 249.
20. *Ibid.*, p. 231.

Chapter 20

1. CP5: see p. 10 for editorial comments on the date of composition.
2. *Ibid.*, p. 12.
3. *Ibid.*
4. *Ibid.*, p. 13.
5. Fabian Tract No. 151, "The Point of Honour. A Correspondence on Aristocracy and Socialism," by Ruth Cavendish Bentinck, p. 3.
6. CP5, p. 168.
7. Fabian Tract No. 108, "Twentieth Century Politics: A Policy of National Efficiency," by Sidney Webb, p. 7.
8. CP5, p. 147.
9. *Ibid.*, p. 176.
10. *Ibid.*, p. 177.
11. *Ibid.*, p. 146.
12. *Ibid.*, p. 124.
13. *Ibid.*, p. 99.
14. *Ibid.*, p. 95.

15. *Ibid.*, p. 100.
16. *Ibid.*, p. 105.
17. *Ibid.*, p. 144.
18. *Ibid.*, p. 181.
19. *Ibid.*, p. 160.
20. *Ibid.*, pp. 69–70.
21. *Ibid.*, p. 74.
22. *Ibid.*, p. 109.
23. *Ibid.*, p. 163.
24. *Ibid.*
25. *Ibid.*, p. 175.
26. *Ibid.*, p. 173.
27. *Ibid.*, p. 177.
28. *Ibid.*, p. 178.
29. *Ibid.*, p. 181.
30. *Ibid.*, p. 159.
31. *Ibid.*, p. 22.
32. *Ibid.*, p. 181.
33. *Ibid.*, p. 184.

Chapter 21

1. Warren Sylvester Smith, ed., *The Religious Speeches of Bernard Shaw*, "Modern Religion II," p. 79.
2. Bernard Shaw, *Everybody's Political What's What?*, p. 327.
3. Bernard Shaw, *Major Critical Essays*, pp. 173–74.
4. CP5, p. 698.
5. *Ibid.*, p. 478.
6. *Ibid.*, pp. 478–79.
7. *Ibid.*, p. 503.
8. *Ibid.*, p. 560.
9. *Ibid.*, p. 561.
10. *Ibid.*, p. 612.
11. *Ibid.*, p. 629.
12. *Ibid.*
13. *Ibid.*, p. 630.
14. T.C. Kemp, *The Birmingham Repertory Theatre*, p. 5.

Chapter 23

1. CL4, p. 6.
2. *Ibid.*, p. 4. The square brackets are as shown in CL4.
3. *Ibid.*, p. 3.

4. *Ibid.*
5. *Ibid.*, p. 258.
6. *Ibid.*, p. 257.
7. *Ibid.*, pp. 73 and 74.

Chapter 24

1. CL3, p. 900.
2. Robert Rhodes James, *The British Revolution: British Politics 1880–1939*, p. 496.
3. Frank Harris, *Bernard Shaw*, p. 139.
4. Bernard Shaw, *The Intelligent Woman's Guide to Socialism and Capitalism*, p. 126.
5. *Ibid.*, p. 154.
6. *Ibid.*, p. 330.
7. *Ibid.*, p. 466.
8. *Ibid.*, p. 477.
9. *Ibid.*, p. 483.
10. *Ibid.*, p. 484.
11. *Ibid.*, p. 485.
12. *Ibid.*, p. 486.
13. *Ibid.*, p. 492.
14. *Ibid.*, p. 500.

Chapter 25

1. Bernard Shaw, *What I Really Wrote About the War*, p. 403. ("The League of Nations" was published in 1929 as Fabian Tract No. 226. Subsequently it was published as the concluding chapter of *What I Really Wrote About the War*. Page numbers of quotations are from Chapter 16 of the latter work, as published in the standard edition, 1931.)
2. *Ibid.*, p. 402.
3. *Ibid.*, p. 400.
4. *Ibid.*, p. 402.
5. *Ibid.*, p. 404.
6. *Ibid.*, pp. 404–05.
7. *Ibid.*, p. 407.
8. *Ibid.*
9. *Ibid.*
10. *Ibid.*
11. *Ibid.*, p. 344.

Chapter 26

1. Fabian Tract No. 233, p. 3.
2. *Ibid.*, p. 9.
3. *Ibid.*
4. *Ibid.*
5. *Ibid.*, p. 10.
6. Bernard Shaw, *The Intelligent Woman's Guide to Socialism and Capitalism*, p. 28.
7. Fabian Tract No. 233, p. 11.
8. *Ibid.*
9. *Ibid.*
10. *Ibid.*
11. *Ibid.*
12. *Ibid.*, p. 12.
13. *Ibid.*
14. *Ibid.*, p. 16.
15. *Ibid.*
16. *Ibid.*, p. 20.
17. *Ibid.*, p. 19.
18. *Ibid.*, p. 16.

Chapter 28

1. CP6, p. 73.
2. *Ibid.*, p. 154.
3. *Ibid.*, pp. 183–84.
4. A.M. Gibbs, ed., *Shaw: Interviews and Recollections*, p. 310.
5. CP6, p. 160.
6. *Ibid.*, p. 190.
7. *Ibid.*, p. 208.

Chapter 29

1. This quotation is taken from editorial comment in *The Diary of Beatrice Webb: Volume Four, 1924–1943*, p. 197.
2. CP6, p. 381.
3. The Powermistress-General is said to be based on Margaret Bondfield, Minister of Labour, 1929–31, the first female minister in the British Government. See CL4, p. 45.
4. CP6, p. 344.
5. T.C. Kemp, *The Birmingham Repertory Theatre*, p. 32.

6. Hesketh Pearson, *Bernard Shaw*, pp. 411–12.

7. CP6, p. 531.

8. *Ibid.*, p. 481.

9. *Ibid.*, p. 482.

10. *Ibid.*

11. *Ibid.*, pp. 477–78.

12. *Ibid.*, p. 501.

13. *Ibid.*

14. *Ibid.*, p. 505.

15. *Ibid.*, p. 491.

16. *Ibid.*, p. 523.

17. *Ibid.*, p. 524.

18. *Ibid.*, p. 525.

19. *Ibid.*, pp. 525–26.

Chapter 30

1. CP6, p. 734.

2. *Ibid.*, p. 736.

3. *Ibid.*, p. 759.

4. Hesketh Pearson, *Bernard Shaw*, p. 445.

5. *Ibid.*

6. CP6, p. 844.

7. *Ibid.*, p. 832.

8. *Ibid.*, p. 831.

9. *Ibid.*, p. 763.

10. *Ibid.*, p. 839.

11. *Ibid.*, p. 834.

Chapter 31

1. Hesketh Pearson, *Bernard Shaw*, pp. 418–19.

2. CP6, p. 544.

3. *Ibid.*

4. *Ibid.*, pp. 555–56.

5. *Ibid.*, p. 566.

6. *Ibid.*, p. 568.

7. *Ibid.*, p. 570.

8. T.C. Kemp, *The Birmingham Repertory Theatre*, p. 34.

9. CP6, p. 922.

10. *Ibid.*, p. 919.

11. *Ibid.*, p. 938.

12. *Ibid.*, p. 946.

13. *Ibid.*, p. 959.

14. *Ibid.*, p. 965.

15. *Ibid.*, p. 967.

Chapter 32

1. CP6, p. 975.

2. CL4, p. 291.

3. *Ibid.*, pp. 504–5.

4. CP7, p. 66.

5. *Ibid.*, p. 71.

6. *Ibid.*, p. 83.

7. *Ibid.*, p. 99.

8. Bernard Shaw, *Everybody's Political What's What?*, p. 44.

9. CP7, p. 150.

10. *Ibid.*, p. 133.

11. *Ibid.*, p. 137.

12. *Ibid.*, p. 118.

13. *Ibid.*, p. 148.

14. *Ibid.*, p. 130.

15. *Ibid.*, p. 140.

16. *Ibid.*, pp. 154–55.

17. *Ibid.*, p. 155.

18. *Ibid.*, p. 165.

19. *Ibid.*, p. 236.

20. *Ibid.*, p. 237.

21. *Ibid.*, p. 234.

22. *Ibid.*, p. 206.

23. *Ibid.*, p. 221.

24. *Ibid.*

25. *Ibid.*, p. 247.

26. *Ibid.*, p. 253.

27. *Ibid.*, p. 204.

28. *Ibid.*, p. 292.

29. *Ibid.*, p. 295.

Chapter 34

1. CL4, p. 539.

2. *Ibid.*, p. 595.

3. *Ibid.*, p. 584.

4. *Ibid.*, p. 560.

5. *Ibid.*, p. 563.

6. *Ibid.*, p. 621. The letter is dated 14.11.1941.

7. *Ibid.*, p. 775.

8. *Ibid.*, p. 607. The theatre is

now known as the Royal Shakespeare Theatre, Stratford-upon-Avon.

9. *Ibid.*, p. 646.
10. *Ibid.*, p. 668.
11. *Ibid.*, p. 801.
12. *Ibid.*, p. 693.
13. *Ibid.*, p. 694.
14. *Ibid.*, p. 739.
15. *Ibid.*, p. 833.
16. Holroyd 4, p. 37.
17. CL4, p. 820.
18. *Ibid.*, p. 876.
19. Hesketh Pearson, *Bernard Shaw*, p. 500.

Chapter 35

1. Bernard Shaw, *Everybody's Political What's What?*, p. 356.
2. *Ibid.*, p. 350.
3. *Ibid.*
4. *Ibid.*
5. *Ibid.*, p. 295.
6. *Ibid.*, p. 335.
7. *Ibid.*
8. *Ibid.*, p. 366.

Chapter 36

1. CP7, p. 306.

2. CL4, pp. 691–92.
3. Holroyd 3, p. 374.
4. Hesketh Pearson, *Bernard Shaw*, p. 449.

Chapter 37

1. CP7, pp. 320–21.
2. *Ibid.*, p. 322.
3. *Ibid.*, p. 307, 308.
4. *Ibid.*, p. 431.
5. *Ibid.*, p. 432.
6. *Ibid.*, p. 433.
7. *Ibid.*, p. 448.
8. *Ibid.*, p. 452.
9. *Ibid.*, p. 454.
10. *Ibid.*, p. 460.
11. *Ibid.*, p. 464.
12. *Ibid.*, p. 465.
13. *Ibid.*, pp. 465–66.

Chapter 38

1. CP7, p. 469.
2. *Ibid.*
3. *Ibid.*, p. 475.
4. *Ibid.*, p. 476.
5. *Ibid.*, p. 477.

Bibliography

The place of publication is London unless otherwise stated. Most tracts were printed privately for members of the Fabian Society.

Fabian Tracts by Shaw

No. 2, A Manifesto, 1884.

No. 3, To Provident Landlords and Capitalists: A Suggestion and a Warning, 1885.

No. 6, The True Radical Programme (Fabian Parliamentary League), 1887.

No. 13, What Socialism Is, 1890.

No. 40, The Fabian Election Manifesto, 1892.

No. 41, The Fabian Society: What it has done and how it has done it."

No. 43, Vote! Vote! Vote! 1892.

No. 45, Impossibilities of Anarchism, 1893.

No. 49, A Plan of Campaign for Labour, 1894.

No. 70, Report on Fabian Policy, 1896.

No. 93, Women as Councillors, 1900.

No. 107, Socialism for Millionaires, 1901.

No. 116, Fabianism and the Fiscal Question: An Alternative Policy, 1904.

No. 146, Socialism and Superior Brains: A Reply to Mr Mallock, 1909.

No. 226, The League of Nations, 1929.

No. 233, "Socialism: Principles and Outlook" (reprinted by permission of the author [Shaw] from the *Encyclopædia Britannica*, 14th Edition, 1929) and "Fabianism" (reprinted from the new edition of Chamber's Encyclopædia by permission of the publishers, Messrs. W. & R. Chambers Ltd), 1930.

No. 493, A reprint of Tract No. 41, with a preface by Melvyn Bragg, 1984.

Note: A list of Fabian tracts from 1884 to 1915 is given in Appendix IV of Pease's *History of the Fabian Society*, 1916 edition. The titles in the above list up to and including No. 146 are taken from Pease.

Letters, Diaries and Autobiography

Laurence, Dan H., ed., *Bernard Shaw: Collected Letters*, 4 volumes. Vol. 1, 1874–1897 (1965), Vol. II, 1898–1910 (1972), Vol. III, 1911–1925 (1985), Vol. IV, 1926–1950 (1988).

Shaw: An Autobiography 1898–1950: The Playwright Years, selected from his writings by Stanley Weintraub, 1971.

Shaw: *Sixteen Self Sketches*, 1949.

Weintraub, Stanley, ed., *Bernard Shaw: The Diaries*, 1885–1897, 2 volumes, University Park, Pennsylvania, 1986.

Weiss, Samuel A., ed., *Bernard Shaw: Letters to Siegfried Trebitsch*, Palo Alto, California, 1986.

Essays, Criticism and Sociology

"Common Sense About the War," in *What I Really Wrote About the War*, 1930.

Essays in Fabian Socialism, 1932.

Everybody's Political What's What?, 1944.

Fabian Essays, edited by Bernard Shaw, Jubilee Edition, 1948.

Fabian Essays in Socialist Thought, edited by Ben Pimlott, 1984.

Major Critical Essays, Penguin, 1986.

"Modern Religion II," in *The Religious Speeches of Bernard Shaw*, edited by Warren Sylvester Smith, University Park, Pennsylvania, 1963.

Our Theatres in the Nineties, 3 volumes, 1932.

Prefaces by Bernard Shaw, 1934.

Shaw on Theatre, edited by E. J. West, New York, 1958.

Shaw's Dramatic Criticism (1895–98), A Selection by John F. Mathews, Westport, Connecticut, 1959.

"Sixty Years of Fabianism: A Postscript by Bernard Shaw," in *Fabian Essays*, Jubilee edition, 1948.

"The Basis of Socialism: Economics," in *Fabian Essays*, edited by Bernard Shaw, Jubilee edition 1948.

The Common Sense of Municipal Trading, 1904.

The Intelligent Woman's Guide to Socialism and Capitalism, 1928.

"The Quintessence of Ibsenism," in *Major Critical Essays*, Penguin, 1986.

"The Sanity of Art," in *Major Critical Essays*, Penguin, 1986.

What I Really Wrote About the War, 1930.

Plays

Bodley Head Edition: *The Bodley Head Bernard Shaw: Collected Plays with Their Prefaces*, 7 volumes, editorial supervisor, Dan H. Laurence. Definitive edition. Includes pertinent essays and program notes by Shaw, and self-drafted interviews. Vol. 1 (1970), Vol. II (1971), Vol. III (1971),

Vol. IV (1972), Vol. V, (1972), Vol. VI (1973), Vol. VII (1974). Titled in U.S.A., *Complete Plays with Their Prefaces*, 7 volumes, 1976.
Odham's Press. *The Complete Plays of Bernard Shaw.*
Penguin Edition: *Bernard Shaw Penguin Plays*. Definitive text under the editorial supervision of Dan H. Laurence.

Books About Shaw and Related Topics

Bentley, Eric, *Bernard Shaw: A Reconsideration*, New York, revised edition, 1957.

Broad, C. Lewis, and Violet M. Broad, *Dictionary to the Plays and Novels of Bernard Shaw with Bibliography of His Works and of the Literature Concerning Him with a Record of the Principal Shavian Play Productions*, 1919.

Cole, Margaret, *Beatrice Webb*, 1945.

_____, *The Story of Fabian Socialism*, 1961.

Dukore, Bernard F., *Shaw's Theatre*, 2000.

Ervine, St. John, *Bernard Shaw: His Life, Work and Friends*, 1956.

Gibbs, A. M., editor, *Shaw: Interviews and Recollections*, 1990.

Harris, Frank, *Bernard Shaw*, 1931.

Henderson, Archibald, *George Bernard Shaw: Man of the Century*, New York, 1956.

Holmes, Katherine, editor, *The Pictorial Stage: Twenty-Five Years of Vision and Design at the Shaw Festival*, Niagara-on-the-Lake, Canada, 1986.

Holroyd, Michael, *Bernard Shaw*—Volume 1 1856–1898: *The Search for Love* (1988); Volume II 1898–1918: *The Pursuit of Power* (1989).

James, Robert Rhodes, *The British Revolution: British Politics 1880–1939*.

Joad, C.E.M., ed., *Shaw and Society.*

Laurence, Dan H., *Bernard Shaw: A Bibliography*, 2 volumes, Oxford, 1983.

Lowenstein, F. E., *Bernard Shaw Through the Camera*, 1948.

Meisel, Martin, *Shaw and the Nineteenth Century Theatre*, Princeton, 1963.

Patch, Blanche, *Thirty Years with G.B.S.*, 1951.

Pearson, Hesketh, *Bernard Shaw: A Biography*, 1987.

Pease, Edward R., *The History of the Fabian Society*, 1925.

Pugh, Patricia, *Educate, Agitate, Organize: 100 Years of Fabian Socialism*, 1984.

Reynold, Jean, *Pygmalion's Wordplay: The Postmodern Shaw*, 1999.

Silver, Arnold, *Bernard Shaw: The Darker Side*, Palo Alto, California, 1982.

Vallency, Maurice, *The Cart and the Trumpet: The Plays of George Bernard Shaw*, New York, 1973.

Webb, Beatrice, *Our Partnership*, 1948.

Webb, Sidney, and Beatrice Webb, *A Constitution for the Socialist Commonwealth of Great Britain*, 1920.

Weintraub, Stanley, *Bernard Shaw 1914–1918: Journey to Heartbreak*, 1973.

Whitman, Robert F. *Shaw and the Play of Ideas*, 1977.

Wilson, Colin, *Bernard Shaw: A Reassessment*, 1981.

Index

213